Best Hikes Near
LOS ANGELES

HELP US KEEP THIS GUIDE UP TO DATE

Every effort has been made by the authors and editors to make this guide as accurate and useful as possible. However, many things can change after a guide is published—trails are rerouted, regulations change, techniques evolve, facilities come under new management, and so on.

We would appreciate hearing from you concerning your experiences with this guide and how you feel it could be improved and kept up to date. While we may not be able to respond to all comments and suggestions, we'll take them to heart, and we'll also make certain to share them with the authors. Please send your comments and suggestions to the following address:

GPP
Reader Response/Editorial Department
P.O. Box 480
Guilford, CT 06437

Or you may e-mail us at: editorial@globepequot.com

Thanks for your input, and happy trails!

Best Hikes Near
LOS ANGELES

ALLEN RIEDEL AND MONIQUE RIEDEL

FALCONGUIDES

GUILFORD, CONNECTICUT
HELENA, MONTANA

AN IMPRINT OF GLOBE PEQUOT PRESS

For Michael, Makaila, and Sierra

To buy books in quantity for corporate use
or incentives, call **(800) 962–0973**
or e-mail **premiums@GlobePequot.com**.

FALCONGUIDES®

FalconGuides is an imprint of Globe Pequot Press.
Falcon, FalconGuides, and Outfit Your Mind are registered trademarks of Morris Book Publishing, LLC.

Art on page iii © Shutterstock

TOPO! Explorer software and SuperQuad source maps courtesy of National Geographic Maps. For information about TOPO! Explorer, TOPO!, and Nat Geo Maps products, go to www.topo.com or www.natgeomaps.com.

Maps by Trailhead Graphics Inc. © Morris Book Publishing LLC
Text design: Sheryl P. Kober
Project editor: Julie Marsh
Layout artist: Melissa Evarts

Library of Congress Cataloging-in-Publication Data

Riedel, Allen.
 Best hikes near Los Angeles / Allen Riedel and Monique Riedel. — 1st ed.
 p. cm. — (Best hikes near series)
 Summary: "Featuring more than 40 of the best hikes in the greater Los Angeles metro area, this exciting new guidebook points locals and visitors alike to trailheads within an hour's drive of Los Angeles" — Provided by publisher.
 ISBN 978-0-7627-4641-5 (pbk.)
 1. Hiking—California—Los Angeles Metropolitan Area—Guidebooks. 2. Trails—California—Los Angeles Metropolitan Area—Guidebooks. 3. Los Angeles Metropolitan Area (Calif.)—Guidebooks. I. Riedel, Monique. II. Title.
 GV199.42.C22L6569 2011
 917.94'93—dc23
                                                                                          2011019084

Printed in the United States of America

10 9 8 7 6 5 4 3 2 1

Contents

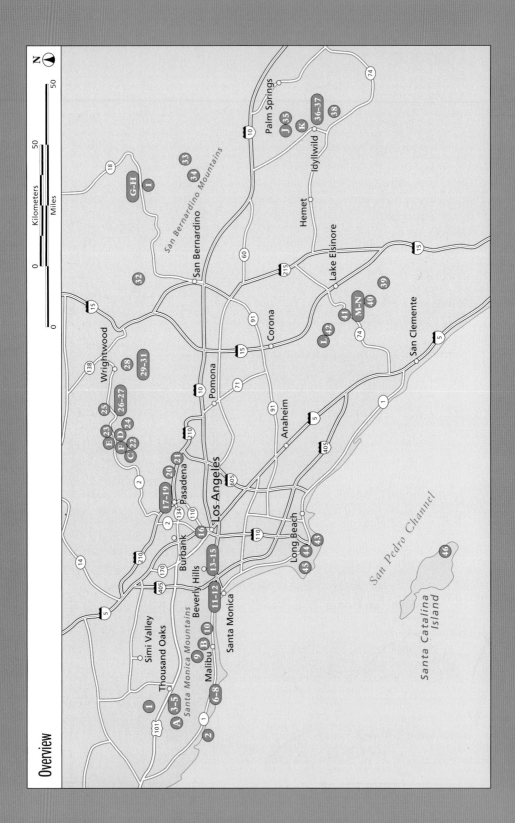

Overview

Acknowledgments

There are so many people who have supported my husband and me along the way. Some of our dear friends have struck out on the trails with us and some have given us encouragement and motivation from afar.

First, I would like to thank my parents, Anna and Richard Chavez, for being the best parents. The following people have in some way brought encouragement and light into our lives and I would like to acknowledge them for that: Donn Debaun, Dawn and Alex Wilson, "Fish" Nate Olmos, Leuren Arenberg, Tanya Esparza, Rebecca Bowen, Melanie and Aaron Swann, Julie Hupp, Julie Ellis, Jane Weal, Chris Chromiak, Elena Maria Lopez, Mark Martinez, Ryan Arne and his company Infinite Power Inc., Stephanie Franco, Sandra Samaniego, my uncle John Acevedo, Adam Mendelsohn, Esperanza Gonzalez and her wonderful family, along with many other fabulous people.

I would like to especially thank my son, Michael J. Millenheft III, for being patient with us and joining us on many of these adventures whether he wanted to or not. To my wonderful step-daughters, Sierra and Makaila Riedel, for loving me unconditionally and honoring me with the "Best Step-Mommy in the World" award. And finally to my husband, best friend, and twin flame, Allen Riedel, for inspiring me to do things I never thought possible.

—*Monique*

I would like to first and foremost thank all of the people who have spent time hiking with me in the mountains, deserts, hills, forests, jungles, and coastal beaches. Many of you, my friends, have inspired me in countless ways, and I can't thank you enough. I would like to mention some of you by name: Monique Riedel, Sean Coolican, Adam Mendelsohn, Michael Millenheft III, Sierra Riedel, Makaila Riedel, Tom Kashirsky, Cameron Alston, Matt Piazza, Bruno Lucidarme, Chrissy Ziburski, Eric Walther, Bob Romano, Jim Zuber, Danny Suarez, Dylan Riedel, Eric Romero, Donn DeBaun, Alex Wilson, Dawn Wilson, Shannon Parsons, Mike Besold, Paul Murphy, and Jane Weal.

I would also like to acknowledge my family: Monique, Michael, Sierra, and Makaila. All four of you have spent lots of time with me on trails that were great and some "not so much". . . I love you with all my heart.

I also owe a lot to my mom and dad, Barbara and Elmer Riedel, who raised me to believe in myself. Thanks! Thanks to my brother, Larry; my grandparents, Herbert and Vivian Ward, and Elmer and Lucille Riedel; and my in-laws, Anna and Richard Chavez. I am a better person because of all of you.

I am also grateful for the opportunities that I have been granted by writing for the most amazing website: www.localhikes.com. It seems Jim Zuber has been my biggest resource in the writing world, and I can never thank him enough for the awesome site and the amount of work he has sent my way. You rule, Jim!

Patricia Mays, Dave Ammenheuser, and Scott Ammons were great to work with and so helpful—thank you for your time and effort.

I would like to thank Scott Adams, John Burbidge, and the wonderful people at Globe Pequot Press.

Lastly, I would like to thank all of the students and teachers I have worked with over the past thirteen years. It has been a joy knowing all of you.

—*Allen*

Introduction

This book contains forty-six hikes situated near the metropolitan region of Los Angeles. The hikes are located in a variety of areas ranging from county, city, and/or local parks to the surrounding national forests. This book highlights some of the best hikes in the region and covers a vast range of scenery, historical interests, and natural beauty.

Some of the best hiking in Southern California exists within a sixty- to ninety-minute drive from the city center of Los Angeles. The book is intended to be a sampling of the region and an introduction to the incredible wonders that the area has to offer. The hikes are also varied enough to provide interest for many disparate groups of people. There are hikes for waterfall lovers, peak baggers, the young, the young at heart, and even for those looking to get some quick exercise in the great outdoors. The hikes have been selected for their variety and their proximity to Los Angeles. Some are farther away than others, but even without assigning definitive borders to the city or county of Los Angeles, the greater Los Angeles area is a massive region.

While it's known for Hollywood, movies, and stars, Los Angeles is a hikers' paradise with stunning natural beauty as well (hike 33). Sierra Riedel

Unbeknownst to many outside of the region, the Los Angeles area contains a great deal of austere and captivating pastoral beauty, from the chaparral-covered slopes of the Santa Monica Mountains to the lush alpine forests of the San Gabriel, San Bernardino, and San Jacinto ranges. Numerous nature preserves, reserves, and specially designated parks protect valuable ecosystems and wildlife around the southland.

Los Angeles is the second-largest city/urban area in the United States. When people outside of the state think of Los Angeles, hiking is hardly the first subject to come to mind. Hollywood, beaches, celebrities, music, and fashion all trump the idea of the outdoors, and many people who live within the region fail to realize that high-altitude mountains exist just a short drive away. Many people walk down Sunset Boulevard in shorts while others are skiing down Mount Baldy's slopes— merely a sixty-minute drive away. And the mountains aren't the only region ripe for hiking. The deserts, beaches, and local parks all have a uniquely Angelino feel to them. There are an infinite number of places to go when looking for a hike near Los Angeles, and there are no shortages on variety either.

Typically Southern Californian, the region is a semiarid Mediterranean ecosystem, ringed by the mountains uplifted by the tectonic forces of the San Andreas Fault. Seasonal arroyos dot the terrain and flow intermittently through steep rugged canyons. Varied species of mammals, reptiles, and amphibians inhabit the landscape. The flora of the region, mostly desert and coastal chaparral, can be magnificent in

Spotting desert big horn sheep is not very easy. Count yourself lucky if you see one. Allen Riedel

color, especially during certain times of the year and after a significant amount of rainfall. Oak, pine, and cedar forests grow into the upper elevations.

Mammals abound in the mountainous regions, with larger creatures such as black bear and mule deer inhabiting the higher reaches. Mountain lions and coyotes prowl throughout most of the foothill, park, and mountain areas, occasionally making their way into populated regions. Not really presenting much of a danger, attacks on humans are rare and the danger can be greatly reduced by traveling in groups of three or more. Smaller creatures and rodents such as squirrels, skunks, possums, and mice are also abundant.

Several dams and waterways exist in the Los Angeles area, and while there are no major regional stopping points along the Pacific Flyway, there are opportunities for bird watching. The region's mostly man-made lakes offer sanctuary, recreation, and fishing, and over 400 species of birds can be spotted throughout the year.

Hiking in the region is a popular activity, especially in the early morning and evening during summertime, and throughout the day during the fall, winter, and spring. Depending upon the location, summer days can be pleasant at higher elevations, and absolutely desiccating in lower climes. Winter temperatures are

The Los Angeles area contains some of the best hiking in the United States, encompassing deserts, waterfalls, tall mountains, and cultural wonders.

Garter snakes are harmless and can be found swimming in ponds and slinking along the trail. Allen Riedel

generally mild at lower elevations, but alpine conditions in the high mountains can lead to rapid hypothermia and death. Caution should be taken anytime you are hiking above 7,000 feet.

Typically, the only animal that is dangerous to humans is the rattlesnake, and during hotter months they can be prevalent on certain trails. Do not walk through tall grasses or place hands and feet into locations unseen. Snakes are afraid of humans, and they understand the world through sensing vibrations. Typically, snakes will be alerted and flee long before a human approaches on the trail. Rattlesnakes will only strike if threatened, so the best thing to do is back away or walk in a wide berth around them on the trail. Mountain lions and bears can present an uncommon but real danger. Making noise as you walk along the trail and hiking in groups can significantly lessen the chance of encounters with these creatures, even though such encounters are already very rare.

Insects are not normally a problem anywhere around Los Angeles, though after rains, ticks can present a small problem, as can mosquitoes and other pests. Flies and gnats can be slightly troublesome in wetter areas, but are not normally a common problem. A mild insect repellent should do the trick for most hikes, and dogs should be protected with proper vaccinations and pet medicines.

The grasslands on the La Jolla Valley Loop Trail (hike 2).
Makaila Riedel

WEATHER

The Los Angeles metro area is mostly semiarid and the lower elevations can be stifling during the months of June, July, August, and September. Heat can be a factor any time of the year, though late October through May is generally mild even in the hottest parts of the region.

Rain is not the normal state of affairs in Southern California, and the Los Angeles metro area is no exception, getting between 10 to 12 inches of rain annually. The rainy season is typically from November to February, though showers are more likely during December and January. Most rainstorms are over as quickly as they begin, though the region does see periods of continuing rainfall during the winter.

The mountains present an entirely different climate and create weather patterns that are separate from the rest of the region. Summer thunderstorms can be a common occurrence in the highest elevations, though rainfall does not typically occur elsewhere in the region during the summer.

Summer temperatures can reach triple digits, though the higher mountain ranges rarely reach above the 80s. The best times of year to hike in the Los Angeles metro area (outside of the mountains) are fall through spring, when the temperatures are mild during the day. Early morning, just before and after sunrise, and evening, just before and after sunset, are pleasant in the summer almost anywhere in the region.

PREPARING FOR YOUR HIKE

Before you go hiking, always be prepared. Let someone know where you are planning to go and leave an itinerary of your hiking destination with a reliable friend. Give them an expected return time and the name of the trailhead you are visiting, along with specific routes you are taking. Be sure that your friend will contact authorities should you not return as expected.

Water is essential in desert environments. Hydrate before you leave and during your hike, and leave extra water in the vehicle so that you may hydrate upon return. A good rule of thumb for hiking is one-half to one liter of water per hour of hiking. On hot days without shade you should drink as much as one gallon of water per hour of hiking. Salty snacks can help aid water retention. Hikers should avoid overexertion during the hottest part of the day. Make no mistake, the Los Angeles area is a dry one, and hikers should drink plenty of water even on cool days.

When you hike, you should always bring along the so-called "Ten Essentials" so that you can provide yourself with the basic necessities for survival should the unexpected occur. Hiking is a relatively safe activity, especially when care is taken, although it is always best to prepare for any eventuality. Minor mishaps like taking a wrong turn, getting back after dark, or being lost for a short while can be frightening, but as long as cool heads prevail, most outdoor mishaps can be easily rectified. The Ten Essentials are designed to keep people safe and provide a backup plan should something go wrong.

1. Navigation (map, compass, GPS)
2. Sun protection (hat, sunscreen)
3. Insulation (layered clothing)
4. Illumination (headlamp, flashlight)
5. First aid supplies (Band-Aids, bandages, gauze, tape, tweezers, etc.)
6. Repair kit and tools (knife, duct tape, etc.)
7. Nutrition (extra food)
8. Hydration (extra water)
9. Emergency shelter (tarp, tent, sleeping bag, or emergency blanket)
10. Fire starter (necessary for life-threatening emergencies only)

This is only a basic list, and of course other items may also be of use. The more time you spend on the trail, the more time you will have to modify and fine tune this basic list. Some items may be more important than others.

CLOTHING, SHOES, SOCKS, AND GEAR

Clothing should be made up of layers to protect your body from the elements, whether wind, heat, rain, or cold.

An insulating layer of water- and sweat-wicking fabric (polyester, neoprene, Capilene, or other synthetic fiber) is best for a base layer. These fabrics wick sweat away from your body and keep you warm. On hot days cotton can be a good

Many trails were once wagon roads such as the route that leads to Big Horn Mine (hike 27). Allen Riedel

choice only because the sweat will remain on the fabric, keeping you cooler than a synthetic material. Cotton is a bad choice for cold and rainy days, because the material retains water and loses its ability to insulate, which in even less than extreme circumstances can lead to hypothermia.

A fleece shell is good for an insulating layer, because the material is lightweight and dries quickly. On days without a hint of precipitation, a fleece jacket may be the only necessary outerwear to bring along.

Lastly, a lightweight rain shell should be brought along in case of emergencies. Rain and snow can be deadly in the mountains. A waterproof shell and pants offer protection from the elements.

Improvements in lightweight hiking boots and shoes over the past decade have revolutionized the sport. Boots no longer need to be bulky, heavy, cumbersome, Frankenstein-like appendages that cause blisters, chafing, and sore feet. Instead, many outdoor specialty shops can measure a hiker's feet and find a great-fitting shoe that can be worn immediately on the trail. These shoes are typically durable, sturdy, and excellent for short day hikes, though they may not be ideal for longer and more difficult trekking.

Socks made of wool or synthetic materials are best, because they take moisture away from the feet, reducing chafing and blisters.

Backpacks for day hiking should be small, fit comfortably, and carry ten to twenty pounds. Carrying more than twenty pounds on a day hike is actually kind of silly, and will probably only serve to make the experience less enjoyable. In today's ultralight market, weeklong backpacking trips can be made carrying only twenty to twenty-five pounds (water and food included). Find a backpack that is large enough to carry what is needed, but light enough to be comfortable. Hydration systems have become the norm, and drinking from a reservoir tube is pure bliss compared to the days of cumbersome canteens or stopping to retrieve water bottles from a pack when thirsty.

CAUTION

The Los Angeles metro area is an extremely arid region and wildfire is a constant danger and threat. Fires are not permitted in parks, forests, and hiking areas outside of designated campgrounds and "yellow post" campsites, which are specifically marked trailside campsites. If a life-threatening emergency requires building a fire, an area must be cleared 8 feet in diameter around the fire and a rock ring should be constructed to contain the fire itself. Lighting a fire is not recommended nor endorsed by this book. Do not build new fire rings as these are very destructive to a wilderness environment; use established rings.

Other items may be fun to have along as well. Cameras can be used to record an excursion for posterity. Binoculars can come in handy for wildlife viewing. Plant, bird, animal, and insect identification guides can prove to be informative and educational. Handheld global positioning satellite units are becoming more and more inexpensive and are a great tool to use on the trail. Maps should be taken, but most trails are well marked.

TRAIL REGULATIONS/RESTRICTIONS

Trails in this guide are located in national parks, national forests, preserves, and local and regional parks. Trails in the national forests require an Adventure Pass for parking. Daily or annual Adventure Passes can be purchased at sporting goods stores, specialty outdoor shops, and in the local mountains. Some city parks and natural areas are free, while others require day use fees. Fees for trailhead usage are not required anywhere, though camping permits may carry fees.

LEAVE NO TRACE

Trails in the Los Angeles area and neighboring foothills are heavily used year-round. We, as trail users and advocates, must be especially vigilant to make sure our passage leaves no lasting mark. Here are some basic guidelines for preserving trails in the region:

The trailhead from FR 3N06 (hike 28). Allen Riedel

Pack out all your own trash, including biodegradable items like orange peels and sunflower seeds. In the arid Southern California climate, items such as these take ten or more years to decompose. If everyone who hiked these trails left peels and shells behind, the trails would look more like a waste dump than a forest or wild landscape. You might also pack out garbage left by less considerate hikers. Take a plastic bag and make the place better for your having been there.

Don't approach or feed any wild creatures—the ground squirrel eyeing your snack food is best able to survive if it remains self-reliant.

Don't pick wildflowers or gather rocks, antlers, feathers, and other treasures along the trail. Removing these items will only take away from the next hiker's experience.

Avoid damaging trailside soils and plants by remaining on the established route. This is also a good rule of thumb for avoiding poison oak and stinging nettle, common regional trailside irritants.

Don't cut switchbacks, which can promote erosion. Be courteous by not making loud noises while hiking.

Small cascades dot Arroyo Sequit after winter and spring rains (hike 6). Allen Riedel

The Leave No Trace Principles

1. Plan ahead and prepare.
2. Travel and camp on durable surfaces.
3. Dispose of waste properly.
4. Leave what you find.
5. Minimize campfire impacts.
6. Respect wildlife.
7. Be considerate of other visitors.

For more information visit www.LNT.org.

Many of these trails are multiuse, which means you'll share them with other hikers, trail runners, mountain bikers, and equestrians. Familiarize yourself with the proper trail etiquette, yielding the trail when appropriate. If in doubt, be courteous and simply let other users pass.

Use outhouses at trailheads or along the trail.

As you take advantage of the spectacular scenery offered by the Los Angeles area, remember that our planet is very dear, very special, and very fragile. All of us should do everything we can to keep it clean, beautiful, and healthy, including following the Green Tips you will find throughout this book.

PLAY IT SAFE

Generally, hiking in and around the Los Angeles metro area is a safe and fun way to explore the outdoors. Hiking is not without its risks, but there are ways to lessen those risks. Following a few simple steps and guidelines will help to make the activity as benign as possible.

It is a good idea to know simple first aid, including how to treat bleeding, bites, stings, fractures, strains, and/or sprains. Make sure to take along at least a basic first aid kit. It won't help to have the skills without any supplies.

The Los Angeles metro area—and Southern California, for that matter—is known for its sunny skies and warm climate. The sun can be powerful, especially at higher elevations; use sunscreen and wear a wide-brimmed hat.

Weather patterns can change abruptly, especially in the mountains and during winter and spring months (November through April). Carry layered clothing items to protect you from temperature changes and rain. Remember, summer thunderstorms aren't uncommon in the mountains and may bring dangers such as freezing temperatures, lightning, hail, and high winds.

The hills and mountains are home to a variety of wildlife. Some can be host to disease, and others may attack if prompted by hunger or the smell of food. Rattlesnakes may be found on any of the hikes described, particularly from early spring to mid-fall. Be careful where you place your hands and feet.

Learn how to spot and identify poison oak. Its appearance will change throughout the year. During spring and summer, the distinctive three-pronged leaves are green, and then turn to red and brown as the seasons progress through fall and into winter. In winter, the leaves may completely fall off the plant, leaving a hard-to-identify stalk that still contains and spreads toxins that may cause an itchy rash when touched by human skin. The noxious plant grows abundantly near water, in the canyons, and along the hillsides below 6,000 feet.

Ticks are another pest to be avoided. They are more likely to be found near water or after rains. They hang in the brush waiting to drop on warm-blooded animals. It is a good idea to check for ticks whenever stopping 1along the trail. Ticks will generally hang onto clothing or hair and not bite until the host has stopped moving. Remove them before they have a chance to bite.

The Los Angeles metro area is almost a desert ecosystem and temperatures can soar. Bring more drinking water than you think you'll need. Any water you find on these hikes is generally considered unsafe to drink if untreated. Boil, filter, or treat before consumption.

The open space around Paramount Ranch is pastoral and idyllic (hike 9). Allen Riedel

How to Use This Guide

Start: This gives the general location of the trailhead and the parking area for the starting point or trailhead of each hike.

Distance: This is the total distance of the hike, whether out and back, around a loop, or one-way with a car shuttle. Distances were measured by uploading a GPS track, where available, to topo-mapping software, and then overlaying the track with a hand-drawn route line.

Hiking time: The approximate time for an average hiker to do the hike. These times err on the conservative side, estimating that the average hiker travels about 1 mile per thirty minutes. These estimations do not take into account rest stops, elevation gain, photography, and other non-hiking activities. Fast hikers will need less time, while slow or out-of-shape hikers may use more time. In instances of difficult hikes, novice hikers may need double the time to complete hikes.

Difficulty: All hikes are rated as easy, moderate, or strenuous, with multiple reasons for the rating. Although this is necessarily a highly subjective rating, nearly anyone who can walk should be able to do an easy hike in just a few hours. Moderate hikes are longer—up to a full day—and may involve 1,000 feet or more of elevation gain, and possibly cross-country hiking as well. Experienced

The Pacific Ocean is a beautiful backdrop for many hikes in Southern California (hike 43). Monique Riedel

hikers will have no problems; beginners should hike with someone more experienced and will have more fun if they are in reasonable shape. Strenuous hikes are very long, requiring a full day of hiking by fit hikers, and include possibly more than 2,000 feet of elevation gain. The hiking may involve cross-country hiking on faint, rough trails that require good map and compass skills, and some rock scrambling may be required on rough terrain. Only fit, experienced hikers should tackle these hikes.

Trail surface: Most trails in the Los Angeles region are dirt and rocks. Other trail surface conditions are described here, including hikes on old roads, paved trails, and cross-country.

Nearest town: This is the location of the nearest populated area from which to procure gas, supplies, and phone services. In populated areas, the nearest town may be redundant, but in the mountains, knowing where to stock up on a missing item may mean the difference between a twenty minute detour and a two-hour drive up and down the mountain.

County: This is the county where the hike is located.

Other trail users: You may encounter horses, mountain bikers, and endemic wildlife such as rattlesnakes or mountain lions on some of the trails.

Canine compatibility: Many people like to hike with their furry friends, so this section mentions whether dogs are allowed, and restrictions, if any. All areas that are open to dogs are subject to local and state statutes regarding leash laws. Some people are not amenable to interaction with dogs for personal reasons, therefore it is important not only as a matter of law but as a common courtesy to leash your dogs.

Trailhead facilities/amenities: Availability or lack of water, restrooms, picnic tables, and so on.

Land status: National forest, national recreation area, city or state park, etc.

Fees and permits: If any fees, including entry fees, are required, they are mentioned here. Any permits required are also listed.

Schedule: If access is limited to certain times of the day for administrative reasons such as road closures, you'll find that information here.

Maps: The National Geographic Topo! Map set covering the hike, the U.S. Geological Survey (USGS) 7.5-minute series quads, and any other useful maps are listed here .

Trail contacts: Look here for the name and contact information of the agency or organization responsible for managing the land crossed by the hike. It's a good idea to call or e-mail the land-management agency before your hike to check on road and trail conditions. Where possible, the contact information includes the mailing and street address, phone number, and website. E-mail addresses are not included because they change frequently; check the agency website for an e-mail address, generally found under a "Contact" link. Sometimes web addresses change as well, but you can usually find land-management units on the web with a search engine.

Finding the trailhead: This section gives driving directions for the Santa Monica hikes from the intersection of I-10 and CA 1; all other hikes originate from the intersection of I-10 and US 101. We've also provided the GPS coordinates in latitude and longitude for the trailheads.

The Hike: Here's the meat of the hike—a detailed description of the trail or route and the features and attractions along the way. We describe the route using landmarks as well as trail signs when possible, because trail signs can be missing. Refer to the next section, Miles and Directions, for a description with distances between key points.

Miles and Directions: This table lists the key points, such as trail intersections, or turning points on a cross-country hike, by miles and tenths. You should be able to find the route with this table alone. The mileages in this book do not necessarily agree with distances found on trails signs, agency mileages, and other descriptions, because trail miles are measured by a variety of methods and personnel. All mileages were carefully measured using digital topographic mapping software for accuracy and consistency within the book.

California horned lizards are threatened by a dwindling food supply. Nonnative ants and pesticides have caused a decline in their fodder of choice, the harvester ant. Allen Riedel

Trail Finder

Hike No.	Hike Name	Best Hikes for Backpackers	Best Hikes for Waterfalls	Best Hikes for Geology Lovers	Best Hikes for Children	Best Hikes for Dogs	Best Hikes for Peak Baggers	Best Hikes for Great Views	Best Hikes for Canyons	Best Hikes for Nature Lovers
1	Paradise Falls		●		●	●				
2	La Jolla Valley Loop	●					●		●	
3	Mishe Mokwa			●		●		●		
4	The Grotto		●	●				●	●	●
5	Backbone Trail–Malibu Springs									
6	Arroyo Sequit				●					●
7	Nicholas Flat							●		●
8	Charmlee Wilderness Park				●	●		●		●
9	Paramount Ranch				●					
10	Calabasas Peak			●			●	●		
11	Temescal Gateway Park		●					●		
12	Will Rogers State Historic Park				●			●		
13	Franklin Canyon				●				●	
14	Wilacre Park				●	●				
15	Runyon Canyon				●	●				

Trail Finder

Hike No.	Hike Name	Best Hikes for Backpackers	Best Hikes for Waterfalls	Best Hikes for Geology Lovers	Best Hikes for Children	Best Hikes for Dogs	Best Hikes for Peak Baggers	Best Hikes for Great Views	Best Hikes for Canyons	Best Hikes for Nature Lovers
16	Griffith Park				•	•		•		
17	Echo Mountain					•		•		
18	Rubio Canyon		•	•		•			•	
19	Eaton Canyon Falls		•						•	
20	Sturtevant Falls		•		•	•			•	•
21	Monrovia Canyon Falls		•		•	•			•	
22	Twin Peaks					•	•	•		
23	Devils Chair			•				•		
24	Mount Hawkins	•					•	•		
25	Mount Lewis						•	•		
26	Mount Baden-Powell						•	•		
27	Big Horn Mine				•	•				
28	Dawson Peak						•	•		
29	Mount Baldy						•	•		
30	Timber Mountain	•				•	•	•		

Trail Finder

Hike No.	Hike Name	Best Hikes for Backpackers	Best Hikes for Waterfalls	Best Hikes for Geology Lovers	Best Hikes for Children	Best Hikes for Dogs	Best Hikes for Peak Baggers	Best Hikes for Great Views	Best Hikes for Canyons	Best Hikes for Nature Lovers
31	Etiwanda Peak	●				●	●	●		
32	Heart Rock Falls		●	●		●			●	●
33	Aspen Grove to Fish Creek	●							●	●
34	Jepson Peak	●					●	●		
35	San Jacinto Peak	●					●	●		
36	Ernie Maxwell Scenic Trail				●					
37	Red Tahquitz	●		●				●		
38	Spitler Peak					●	●	●		
39	Santa Rosa Plateau Loop			●	●	●				●
40	Tenaja Falls		●		●					
41	Chiquito Trail	●			●	●			●	
42	Holy Jim Falls		●		●				●	
43	White Point				●			●		●
44	Portuguese Bend				●			●		●
45	Point Vicente			●	●	●		●		●
46	Avalon Canyon/Wrigley Gardens						●	●		●

Map Legend

Transportation

- Freeway/Interstate Highway
- U.S. Highway
- State Highway
- Forest/Other Paved Road
- Unpaved Road

Trails

- Selected Route
- Trail
- Direction of Route

Water Features

- Body of Water
- River or Creek
- Intermittent Stream
- Waterfall
- Spring

Symbols

- Bridge
- Building/Point of Interest
- Campground
- Gate
- Lighthouse
- Lookout Tower
- Mountain/Peak
- Parking
- Pass/Gap
- Picnic Area
- Ranger Station/Park Office
- Restroom
- Scenic View/Overlook
- Towns and Cities
- Trailhead
- Visitor Center/Information

Land Management

- National Forest
- Wilderness Area
- State/Local Park

Wildwood Park

The trails in Wildwood Canyon are very well marked and easy to follow (hike 1) Allen Riedel

Wildwood Regional Park is an exercise mecca for those in the Conejo Valley. It is a favorite of hikers, mountain bikers, schoolchildren, and anyone looking for a little bit of outdoor adventure with a spectacular payoff.

It is extensively marked and signed. There are many different trails and routes, and lots of interesting things to see in Wildwood Canyon, but nothing is as outstanding as the 50-foot waterfall that pours over limestone into a large pool lined by oaks, sycamores, and cattails. There isn't as remarkable a waterfall anywhere else in the Conejo Valley, and there are only a few that cascade so vigorously and this beautifully in all of Southern California. Paradise

For outdoor adventure with a spectacular payoff

Falls is a treasure that is unknown to most outside of the region, but is heavily visited by those in the know.

The park contains two waterfalls, nearly 1,800 acres of open space, sixty species of birds, thirty-seven different mammals, and twenty-two species of reptiles and amphibians. Consisting mostly of coastal chaparral and sage scrub, the park's ecology is decidedly Mediterranean. Wildflowers put on their best displays between February and May. The trails range from infrequently used, narrow, singletrack ridgeline traverses to well-traveled open dirt roads that lead most visitors to the popular Paradise Falls.

Several notable movie and television programs were filmed here, including *Spartacus*, *Wuthering Heights*, *Wagon Train*, *The Rifleman*, and *Gunsmoke*.

Local organizations: Allied Artists, Santa Monica Mountains, (310) 457-9130; The Children's Nature Institute, (310) 860-9484; California Native Plant Society, (818) 348-5910; Concerned Off-Road Bicyclists Association, (818) 206-8213; Coastwalk California, (310) 394-2799; Los Angeles Audubon Society, (323) 876-0202; Mountains Recreation and Conservation Authority, (310) 858-7272, ext.131; Mountains Restoration Trust, (818) 591-1701; The Nature of Wildworks, (310) 455-0550; National Park Service, (805) 370-2301; Sierra Club, (213) 387-4287; San Fernando Valley Audubon Society, (310) 457-5796; San Fernando Valley Gourd Patch, (818) 996-3606; Santa Monica Bay Audubon Society, (310) 395-6235; Santa Monica Mountains Conservancy, (310) 589-3200; Santa Monica Mountains Fund, (805) 370-2341; Santa Monica Mountains Natural History Association, (805) 488-1827; Santa Monica Mountains Trails Council, (818) 222-4531

Shooting Stars are fairly common at higher elevations. Allen Riedel

Paradise Falls

Wander through a huge swath of open space wedged in suburban sprawl to find one of Southern California's most spectacular waterfalls. Marvel at the wildlife and untamed feel of a place so close to human settlement.

Start: At the corner of Avenida De Los Arboles and Big Sky Drive

Distance: 3.7-mile loop

Hiking time: About 2 hours

Difficulty: Easy

Trail surface: Singletrack dirt trail and dirt road

Nearest town: Thousand Oaks

County: Ventura

Other trail users: Bicyclists, joggers, equestrians

Canine compatibility: Leashed dogs permitted

Trailhead facilities/amenities: Restrooms, water, picnic tables along trail

Land status: City and regional parkland

Fees and permits: None

Schedule: Open year-round, sunrise to sunset, except during inclement weather

Maps: USGS Newbury Park, CA; www.cosf.org/website/html/wildwood-map.html

Trail contacts: Conejo Open Space Foundation (COSF), P.O. Box 2113, Thousand Oaks, CA 91358; www.cosf.org; (805) 492-6000. Conejo Open Space Conservation Agency (COSCA), Administration: City Hall/Civic Arts Plaza, 2100 Thousand Oaks Boulevard, Thousand Oaks 91362; (805) 449-2505. Ranger Offices: 403 West Hillcrest Drive, Thousand Oaks 91360; http://conejo-openspace.org; (805) 381-2741

Finding the trailhead: From Los Angeles take US 101 north. Take exit 45 for Lynn Road, turn right onto Lynn Road, and drive for 2.5 miles. Turn left onto Avenida De Los Arboles and drive for 0.9 mile. Park in the lot on the left at the end of the road, at the intersection with Big Sky Drive. GPS: N 34 13.2' / W 118 54.1'

THE HIKE

Head to the southeast end of the parking area and descend the stairs to take the Moonridge Trail. This is definitely the less-traveled route through this portion of the park, though saying any trail is less traveled in Wildwood Canyon is like saying there aren't very many people in the city of Los Angeles. There will be fewer people here though, as this section is a bit tougher than (and not as straightforward as) the mostly fire road trails that traverse the Wildwood Park open space. It does meander up and down in some spots, losing and gaining elevation fairly rapidly. The trail wanders through mostly coastal chaparral and scrub sage.

Fewer people realize that a trail begins on the remote side of the parking lot, which also contributes to drawing fewer newcomers to this route. The Moonridge Trail crosses a public access road as it approaches 0.5 mile and continues on for another 0.4 mile before a T junction at North Tepee Trail.

Turn left and walk south and down for 0.1 mile along the North Tepee Trail, toward the giant replica of a modern man-made tepee, which will be of great interest to children, but probably not anyone else. Turn right onto Tepee Trail and walk for about 0.1 mile to the junction with the Paradise Falls Trail. Here, you will catch glimpses of the falls, the overlook, and possibly hear the falls if the water is flowing heavily. Everything is clearly marked, making it practically impossible to lose your way in the park. Turn left at the junction with the Wildwood Canyon Trail, although a short jaunt of 30 yards to the left provides an excellent vantage point and overlook of the falls. Turn right and follow the signs toward the waterfall.

The stream below the waterfall can be crossed during low and normal water runoff for a fantastic frontal vantage point of the 50-foot fall, but should not be attempted during times of high runoff. At such times when the water level is dangerous, the park is usually closed by officials. Use common sense and never cross deep or fast-moving water. In the previous decade, three deaths have been recorded below the falls. While this is not normally a cause for concern, it is a caveat for hiker safety and caution.

From the waterfall, continue west on the Wildwood Canyon Trail, following it for 0.5 mile to the junction with the Lizard Rock Trail. Here the trail becomes wilder and definitely less traveled. There are some great vantage points along the way and the canyon itself is especially lovely. It wraps around the Hill Canyon Water

Hiking Tip: If hiking out and back, look around, especially at trail junctions, to better remember the return trail.

Treatment Facility and climbs 600 feet to the top of Lizard Rock. From afar the rock looks strikingly like a giant lizard peeking its head over the Conejo Valley. From up close Lizard Rock provides an excellent view. The trail zigzags up the hillside for just over 0.8 mile.

From the rock follow the Stagecoach Bluff Trail for 0.2 mile to the connector to the Mesa Trail, which leads to the Mesa Trail in another 0.2 mile. Follow the Mesa Trail, which is an old dirt road, 0.6 mile back to the parking area.

While walking along these roads and trails, remember that some of your father's and grandfather's favorite Western movies and television shows were filmed right here. If you look hard enough, you might even recognize the landscape.

MILES AND DIRECTIONS

0.0 Start from the southeast corner of the parking lot on Avenida De Los Arboles on the Moonridge Trail.

0.5 Stay straight at the intersection with the road.

0.9 Turn left at the intersection with the road onto the North Tepee Trail.

1.0 Turn right onto the Tepee Trail at the tepee.

Paradise Falls is a hidden treasure not known to many outside of the Conejo Valley. Allen Riedel

Paradise Falls

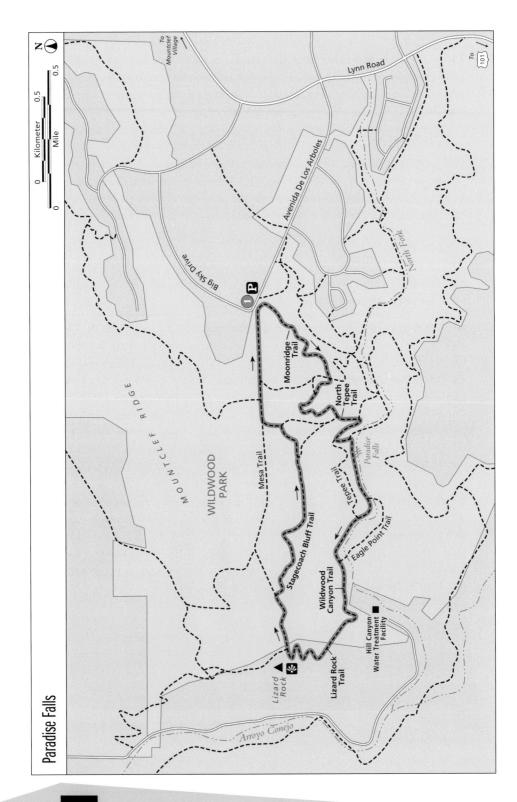

1.1   Turn left onto the Paradise Falls Trail.

1.2   Turn right onto the Paradise Falls Trail.

1.3   Arrive at Paradise Falls. Return via the same trail.

1.4   Turn left onto Wildwood Canyon Trail.

1.9   Turn right onto Lizard Rock Trail.

2.7   Arrive at Lizard Rock. Turn right onto Stagecoach Bluff Trail.

2.9   Turn left onto the connector trail that leads to the Mesa Trail.

3.1   Turn right onto Mesa Trail.

3.7   Arrive back at the parking area.

HIKE INFORMATION

Local information: Conejo Open Space Conservation Agency (COSCA), City Hall/Civic Arts Plaza, 2100 Thousand Oaks Blvd., Thousand Oaks, (805) 449-2505; Ranger Headquarters, Old Meadows Center, 1600 Marview Dr., Thousand Oaks, (805) 381-2741; Conejo Recreation and Park District, 403 W. Hillcrest Dr., Thousand Oaks, (805) 495-6471; California State Parks, (818) 880-0363

Camping: Circle X Ranch Group Campground, (805) 370-2300; Leo Carrillo State Park campgrounds, Malibu Creek State Park, Topanga State Park Campground, Point Mugu State Park Campground, McGrath State Beach, Emma Wood State Beach, California State Park campgrounds reservations (800) 444-7275, customer service (800) 695-2269; www.reserveamerica.com

Local retailers: A-16 (Adventure 16), www.adventure16.com; REI, www.rei.com

Restaurants: Jack's Deli, 966 S. Westlake Blvd., Suite 2, Westlake Village, (805) 495-8181; Neptune's Net, 42505 Pacific Coast Hwy., Malibu, (310) 457-3095; Moonshadows, 20356 Pacific Coast Hwy., Malibu, (310) 456-3010; Old Place Restaurant, 29983 Mulholland Hwy., Agoura Hills, (818) 706-9001; Inn of the Seventh Ray, 128 Old Topanga Canyon Rd., Topanga, (310) 455-1311

Buckwheat, lupine, and wallflower make for a fine canvas of wildflowers in the Santa Monica Mountains. Allen Riedel

Part of the Transverse Ranges of Southern California, the Santa Monica Mountains run west to east from Point Mugu to Griffith Park. They are rimmed on the north by the Conejo and San Fernando Valleys, and to the south, they are entirely bounded by the Pacific Ocean. Located in southeast Ventura County and western Los Angeles County, the mountains span 40 miles from end to end and are bisected by several roads and highways. The Santa Monica Mountains National Recreation Area (SMMNRA) is the world's largest urban national park. At nearly 240 square miles, the park encompasses a whopping twenty-six different zip codes and five separate area codes.

Established on November 10, 1978, the Santa Monica Mountains National Recreation Area has been a beneficiary of land donations, private and public acquisitions, concerned citizens, generous donors, activists, and celebrity bene-factors. To this day the Santa Monica Mountains Conservancy is working to buy back, preserve, protect, and restore land in the region for public access and wild-life habitat. The recreation area is made up of a conglomeration of nationally operated sites headquartered in Thousand Oaks, state parks, regional and local parks, and private lands, with over seventy different parks and open space properties included.

The Santa Monica Mountains are a conglomerate of private, local, city, and state parks administered by the National Park Service.

Historically, the Santa Monica Mountains were home to the Chumash, Tataviam, and Gabrieleno/Tongva peoples. The Santa Monicas formed an overlap in the three cultures' territory. The 1542 arrival of explorer Juan Rodriguez Cabrillo brought the Spanish, Catholicism, the mission culture, and nonnative plants, and forever changed the region, usher-ing in the modernization and urbanization of the region.

Despite being adjacent to the world's eleventh-largest metropolitan area, much of the Santa Monica range has been protected. There are places that feel so remote it is difficult to believe the park is located in Los Angeles. It is quite pos-sible that many of the canyons, ridgelines, and plateaus look nearly unchanged from the days of the Native Americans.

Local organizations: Allied Artists, Santa Monica Mountains, (310) 457-9130; The Children's Nature Institute, (310) 860-9484; California Native Plant Society, (818) 348-5910; Concerned Off-Road Bicyclists Association, (818) 206-8213; Coastwalk California, (310) 394-2799; Los Angeles Audubon Society, (323) 876-0202; Mountains Recreation and Conservation Authority, (310) 858-7272 ext. 131; Mountains Restoration Trust, (818) 591-1701; The Nature of Wildworks, (310) 455-0550; National Park Service, (805) 370-2301; Sierra Club, (213) 387-4287; San Fernando Valley Audubon Society, (310) 457-5796; San Fernando Valley Gourd Patch, (818) 996-3606; Santa Monica Bay Audubon Society, (310) 395-6235; Santa Monica Mountains Conservancy, (310) 589-3200; Santa Monica Mountains Fund, (805) 370-2341; Santa Monica Mountains Natural History Asso-ciation, (805) 488-1827; Santa Monica Mountains Trails Council, (818) 222-4531; TreePeople, (818) 753-4600

La Jolla Valley Loop

Hike up the oldest trail in Southern California, ascend to the top of a magnificent coastal peak with dynamite views, explore the beautiful flower-filled landscape, and walk through a historic valley where native Chumash thrived in the pre-Columbian era.

Start: Pacific Coast Highway 0.5 mile north of Mugu Rock across from the navy firing range
Distance: 6-mile lollipop
Hiking time: About 3 hours
Difficulty: Moderate
Trail surface: Singletrack dirt trail and dirt road
Nearest town: Malibu
County: Ventura
Other trail users: Equestrians
Canine compatibility: No dogs allowed

Trailhead facilities/amenities: None
Land status: California state park
Fees and permits: None
Schedule: Open year-round
Maps: USGS Point Mugu, CA; www.nps.gov/samo
Trail contact: Point Mugu State Park, 9000 W. Pacific Coast Hwy., Malibu 90265; www.parks.ca.gov/default.asp?page_id=630; (818) 880-0363

Finding the trailhead: From Los Angeles take the Pacific Coast Highway / CA 1 for 31.5 miles north and west of Sunset Boulevard. The parking lot is on the right-hand side of the freeway, 0.5 mile north of Mugu Rock, across from the navy firing range. GPS: N 34 5.5' / W 119 3.9166'

THE HIKE

The Chumash Trail begins rather ignominiously from an unsightly dirt parking pullout across from the Point Mugu Naval Base's shooting range. Visitors to the area may hear early morning gunfire while ascending the vertical, cardio-blasting slope that gains 900 feet in elevation in 0.5 mile. Get there before the sun does, because even on a cool day in the morning, this trail can be hot if the sun is bearing down, and the initial climb is up, up, up. Half a mile of steep elevation gain isn't so bad though, as it ends rather quickly and views of the mighty Pacific open up almost immediately. It does make for a heck of a workout. After the initial push, and the climb to the summit of Mugu Peak, the remainder of the trail is mostly an easy walk.

Perhaps the coolest thing about the Chumash Trail is its age. The trail is purported to be anywhere from 5,000 to 9,000 years old, making this a very old and a very established trail. One thing that is certain is that in October 1542, when the explorer Juan Rodriguez Cabrillo sailed through the region, he was greeted by local Chumash who called their village *muwu*, meaning "beach" or "seashore." The trail was then in use for bringing the bounty of the sea up to the teeming village that occupied a good portion of lush La Jolla Valley. Cabrillo's writings describe a bountiful population that thrived beneath the holy backdrop of Boney Mountain.

Hiking through the grasslands on the La Jolla Valley Loop Trail. Makaila Riedel

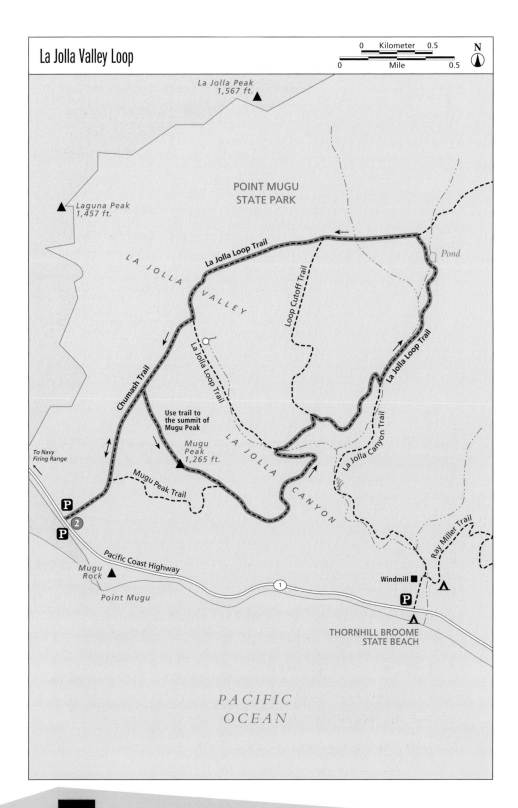

La Jolla Valley Loop

0 Kilometer 0.5
0 Mile 0.5

N

La Jolla Peak
1,567 ft.

POINT MUGU
STATE PARK

Laguna Peak
1,457 ft.

Pond

LA JOLLA

La Jolla Loop Trail

VALLEY

Loop Cutoff Trail

La Jolla Loop Trail

La Jolla Loop Trail

Chumash Trail

LA JOLLA

Use trail to
the summit of
Mugu Peak

La Jolla Canyon Trail

CANYON

To Navy
Firing Range

Mugu
Peak
1,265 ft.

Mugu Peak Trail

P

2

P

Pacific Coast Highway

Ray Miller Trail

Mugu
Rock

1

Windmill

P

Point Mugu

THORNHILL BROOME
STATE BEACH

PACIFIC
OCEAN

Pondering the Chumash life here and contemplating what their everyday existence must have been like is a great meditation for the hike.

After arriving on the plateau, a side trail/road takes off to the right; this is the Mugu Peak Trail. Ignore it; it leads around the base of the mountain, circumventing the summit. Instead, take the use trail that leads obviously upward just a short way ahead. At 0.8 mile, turn right onto the use trail that leads to the top of Mugu Peak. The trip up is pretty steep too, gaining 400 feet more of elevation in 0.4 mile. The plant life along the way is interesting and quite varied. Wildflowers are everywhere if timed right—spring can last here through late June. Atop the summit are an American flag and spectacular views of the Pacific Ocean and La Jolla Valley, as well as the ridgeline of Boney Mountain. From there, continue down the other side of the summit as the trail wanders through cacti and drops to the Y connector. Veer left and follow the trail down into the La Jolla Valley.

At 2.2 miles, the trail drops into a wooded canyon and connects with the La Jolla Loop. Turn right. The grasslands grow high here, so make sure to check for ticks whenever you stop. Follow the loop around the outside of the canyon. At 3.0 miles, the loop trail continues toward the pond on the northeast end of the loop; turn left to stay on the trail. Turning right heads out through La Jolla Canyon. The pond is quite lovely. The picturesque backdrop beneath Boney Mountain's spiny ridge is a photographer's and nature lover's dream.

Just after the pond, continue left at the trail junction. The route opens up here, and the views all look downward into the open valley grasslands. The navy's watchful communication dish sits atop Laguna Peak and moves every so often; those paying attention can even see it in action. For the remainder of the hike, stay straight and veer right at all junctions, enjoying the scenery and the serenity of this magical, peaceful, and historic place.

MILES AND DIRECTIONS

0.0   Start by heading northeast up the Chumash Trail.

0.8   Turn right onto the Mugu Peak use trail.

1.2   Arrive atop Mugu Peak. Continue southeast along the trail.

1.4   Veer left and straight at the Y junction.

2.2   Turn right onto La Jolla Loop Trail.

3.0   Turn left onto La Jolla Loop Trail.

3.6   Turn left to stay on La Jolla Loop Trail/Fire Road.

4.0   Continue straight on the La Jolla Loop Trail at the intersection with Loop Cutoff Trail.

4.9 Stay straight and to the right at the junction with La Jolla Loop Trail.

5.2 Stay right and continue down the Chumash Trail.

6.0 Arrive back at the trailhead and parking area.

HIKE INFORMATION

Local information: California State Parks, (818) 880-0363; Santa Monica Mountains National Recreation Area, (805) 370-2301

Camping: Circle X Ranch Group Campground, (805) 370-2300; Leo Carrillo State Park campgrounds, Malibu Creek State Park, Topanga State Park Campground, Point Mugu State Park Campground, McGrath State Beach, Emma Wood State Beach, California State Park campgrounds reservations (800) 444-7275; customer service (800) 695-2269; www.reserveamerica.com.

Local retailers: A-16, www.adventure16.com; REI, www.rei.com

Restaurants: Jack's Deli, 966 S. Westlake Blvd., Suite 2, Westlake Village, (805) 495-8181; Neptune's Net, 42505 Pacific Coast Hwy., Malibu, (310) 457-3095; Moonshadows, 20356 Pacific Coast Hwy., Malibu, (310) 456-3010; Old Place Restaurant, 29983 Mulholland Hwy., Agoura Hills, (818) 706-9001; Inn of the Seventh Ray, 128 Old Topanga Canyon Rd., Topanga, (310) 455-1311

Juan Rodriguez Cabrillo

Born in 1499, Cabrillo was a Portuguese explorer who led the first European expedition along the coast of California. He set sail from Mexico in June of 1542. His three ships traveled up the coast with two years' worth of supplies exploring what is now San Diego, Santa Monica, San Pedro, Anacapa, Catalina, San Miguel, Point Conception, Point Reyes, and the Russian River.

Cabrillo's expedition missed San Francisco Bay entirely. The armada returned south to spend the winter in the Channel Islands after vicious storms threatened. There, the native Chumash population clashed with the conquistadors, and Cabrillo was injured going ashore. He fell leaving his ship and broke a bone. The bone became gangrenous and he died on January 3, 1543.

The final resting place of Cabrillo is not known. It is reported that he was laid to rest on San Miguel, Santa Cruz, or Catalina Island.

Mishe Mokwa

The showcase hike of the Santa Monica Mountains, this route has it all: spectacular vistas, strange geology, wildflowers, varying plant communities, and multiple eco-systems. While not incredibly difficult, strenuous, or long, the hike is just about the perfect length for those looking to get a sample of what the Santa Monica Mountains National Recreation Area has to offer. Children and adults alike will enjoy the points of interest scattered remarkably evenly along the route.

Start: At the parking lot 6.3 miles north of CA 1 on Yerba Buena Road

Distance: 6-mile lollipop

Hiking time: About 3 hours

Difficulty: Moderate

Trail surface: Singletrack dirt trail and dirt road

Nearest town: Malibu

County: Ventura

Other trail users: Bicyclists and equestrian users allowed only on the Backbone Trail

Canine compatibility: Leashed dogs permitted

Trailhead facilities/amenities: Picnic areas at trailhead and Split Rock; no restrooms or water

Land status: National recreation area

Fees and permits: None

Schedule: Open year-round

Maps: USGS Newbury Park, CA and Triunfo Pass, CA; www.nps.gov/samo/planyourvisit/loader.cfm?csModule=security/getfile&PageID=376833

Trail contacts: Circle X Ranch, 12896 Yerba Buena Rd., Malibu 90265. Santa Monica Mountains National Recreation Area, 401 W. Hillcrest Dr., Thousand Oaks 91360; www.nps.gov/samo; (805) 370-2301

Finding the trailhead: From Los Angeles take the Pacific Coast Highway/CA 1 for 24.7 miles north and west of Sunset Boulevard. Turn right onto Yerba Buena Road and drive north for 6.3 miles. The parking lot is on the left-hand side of the road. GPS: N 34 6.7' / W 118 55.6'

The trail begins rather humbly, leading up and away from an unsightly dirt parking lot along a gated road toward what appears to be a set of barren summits. As unassuming as the intro to the hike is, the route quickly becomes breathtakingly beautiful. It climbs rather rapidly up the dirt road for the first 0.25 mile, gaining nearly 300 feet before the trail junction. At the junction, follow the branch to the right and walk along the more gentle Mishe Mokwa Trail. Here, the trail levels off and the rest of the route follows an incredibly gentle incline, gaining only 700 feet over a 3-mile stretch.

As soon as the trail becomes singletrack, the views begin to open up into the canyons that serve as a drainage for Lake Sherwood. From Triunfo Pass to the various outcroppings of Boney Mountain, the views are spectacular. As close to civilization as this hike is proximity-wise, it certainly does not feel that way. It is difficult to believe the machinations of downtown Los Angeles are a mere 20 miles away, yet they are . . . and the beauty of this natural area is left to the hiker to enjoy.

Since most people follow this loop trail in the same direction, it feels less traveled than it really is and you won't see many fellow hikers. On weekends, the parking lot can be full to overflowing, although on weekdays, one or two cars is the norm. This is a well-used trail, though, and many count it as an all-time favorite. It

The andesite breccia volcanic formations of the Boney Mountain region along the Mishe Mokwa Trail are eerily awesome. Allen Riedel

is easy to understand why. Time this trip for the spring and a fantastic wildflower display is sure to be in the works, though the lupine, wallflower, and buckwheat put on a pretty good show for much of the year.

The narrow trail hugs the side of the canyon and offers jaw-dropping views. Just before the trail hits the 1-mile mark and rounds a bend, the first point of interest comes into view. Across the canyon sits an enormous triangular rock reminiscent of Easter Island's giant Moai statues, and it just happens to be precariously balanced atop a smaller outcropping of stone. This natural acrobatic feat has earned the stone the painfully obvious appellation of "Balanced Rock." While not very creative in the naming department, the mammoth boulder is certain to garner everyone's favor and attention.

As the trail wanders away from Balanced Rock, it begins to enter a riparian canyon along an unnamed creek bed. The trees and bushes grow onto the trail and overhead, giving the route a "jungle" feel, quite a bit different from the open cliff-side section that begins the hike.

At 1.75 miles, the trail opens into a small clearing near the creek, and a giant boulder that has cracked in half can be walked through, scrambled upon, and photographed. This is the second point of high interest along the hike, especially for children, who will marvel at being able to maneuver through the crack. The split in the middle of the rock has also helped to generate another awe-inspiring name . . . wait for it . . . "Split Rock." Yes, the names leave a lot to be desired, but hikers will find lots of joy in these simple pleasures. From Split Rock the hike continues along some more jungle-esque trail for about another mile, at which point the trail opens up into a dirt road and leaves the canyon and its shady confines.

On the road, the views and geology become the main attraction. Andesite breccia is the name for the volcanic rock that appears very similar to sandstone, hence one of the names given to a peak in the area. The region has a very prehistoric feel to it, something akin to *Jurassic Park* or *The Land Before Time*. Pointed conical outcroppings are everywhere and the scenery is just fantastic. Here, the route becomes convoluted with many road crossings; stay left at the first three, and follow the signs for Inspiration Point/Sandstone Peak when there are signs. The widest road is the main route.

Stay left again at the junction with the Tri-Peaks Trail and follow the route as it curves around toward some water towers and back toward Inspiration Point and Sandstone Peak. At 3.5 miles, stay left again at the junction with the water tower road. At 3.7 miles take the small spur trail on the right and hike 0.1 mile to Inspiration Point. The views are incredible on clear days. The Pacific Ocean glimmers like a gem, and faraway peaks can be seen and even identified with the handy disc plaque affixed by the Boy Scouts.

Head back to the main trail and at 4.2 miles take the spur use trail to the top of Sandstone Peak. Alternately called Mount Allen, in honor of a local Boy Scout

Mishe Mokwa

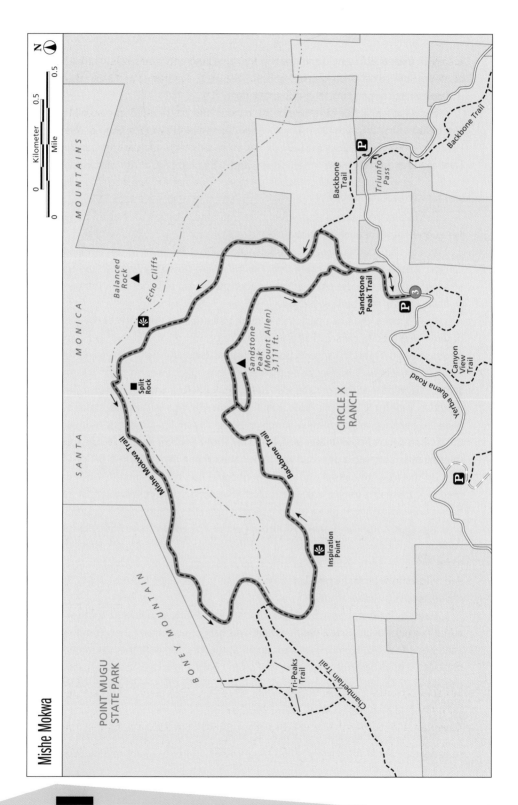

Santa Monica Mountains National Recreation Area

leader and SMMNRA benefactor (there is a plaque dedicated to his honor atop the summit), the naming request was denied by the USGS due to the fact that Mr. Allen was still living at the time of the application.

Enjoy the magnificent views and then head down the trail back toward the dirt road leading into the parking area. The way is all downhill and steeply so. Those looking for invigorating uphill cardio workouts can turn the trip around and start backwards around the loop.

MILES AND DIRECTIONS

0.0   Start north up the Sandstone Peak Trail.

0.4   Turn right onto the Mishe Mokwa Trail.

0.5   Stay left at the junction with the Backbone Trail.

1.0   Enjoy views of Balanced Rock.

1.75 Arrive at Split Rock and a picnic area.

2.9   Stay straight/left at the road junction.

3.0   Stay left at the junction with Tri-Peaks Trail onto the Backbone Trail.

3.5   Turn left at the junction, heading away from the water tanks.

3.7   Turn right to Inspiration Point. Check out the views, then return to the main trail.

3.9   Turn right onto the Backbone Trail.

4.2   Turn right onto the Sandstone Peak use trail.

4.4   Arrive atop Sandstone Peak (Mount Allen) at 3,111 feet. Return to the main trail.

4.6   Turn right onto the Backbone Trail.

5.6   Stay right onto the roadway, Sandstone Peak Trail, back to the parking area.

6.0   Arrive back at the trailhead and parking lot.

HIKE INFORMATION

Local information: California State Parks, (818) 880-0363; Santa Monica Mountains National Recreation Area, (805) 370-2301

Camping: Circle X Ranch Group Campground, (805) 370-2300; Leo Carrillo State Park campgrounds, Malibu Creek State Park, Topanga State Park Campground,

Point Mugu State Park Campground, McGrath State Beach, Emma Wood State Beach, California State Park campgrounds reservations (800) 444-7275; customer service (800) 695-2269; www.reserveamerica.com

Local retailers: A-16, www.adventure16.com; REI, www.rei.com

Restaurants: Jack's Deli, 966 S. Westlake Blvd., Suite 2, Westlake Village, (805) 495-8181; Neptune's Net, 42505 Pacific Coast Hwy., Malibu, (310) 457-3095; Moonshadows, 20356 Pacific Coast Hwy., Malibu, (310) 456-3010; Old Place Restaurant, 29983 Mulholland Hwy., Agoura Hills, (818) 706-9001; Inn of the Seventh Ray, 128 Old Topanga Canyon Rd., Topanga, (310) 455-1311

Chumash/Tongva

The Native American peoples of Southern California once thrived on the bounty of the land and the sea. With no immunological resistance to European diseases, entire populations were nearly wiped out by influenza and smallpox in the 1700s and 1800s.

The Chumash and Tongva tribes both navigated the Pacific Ocean in boats called *tomols*. When the Portuguese explorer Juan Rodriguez Cabrillo sailed up the California coast, Tongva and Chumash people sailed out to meet the ships. While the Chumash settled more to the north, and the Tongva inhabited the region that is now Los Angeles County, the two peoples interacted and traded with one another and shared boundaries in what is now the Santa Monica Mountains.

The Spanish brought Christianity, missions, and diseases in the 1770s, and the native peoples, their languages, and traditions have mostly been left to history, but traces remain. In many parks, there are exhibits and even cultural centers where visitors can learn about the ways of the past and the people who once inhabited these regions.

The Grotto

Amble along shady trails, across creeks, and through meadows while enjoying scenic vistas of sandstone formations in a seemingly uninhabited portion of Southern California. This trail offers something for everyone: Verdant foliage, waterfalls, abundant wildlife, and boulder-hopping are a few of the perks associated with this trail. The most coveted aspect of this hike is The Grotto, a subterranean cave only attainable by scrambling down capacious boulders. Personal skill is not going to be the only deciding factor in this endeavor, because water levels and seasonal changes in the creek will likely be the preeminent element in your venture.

Start: At the parking lot for Circle X Ranch

Distance: 3 miles out and back

Hiking time: About 2 hours

Difficulty: Easy

Trail surface: Singletrack dirt trail and dirt road

Nearest town: Westlake Village

County: Ventura

Other trail users: Joggers

Canine compatibility: Dogs not allowed in the streambed or grotto area

Trailhead facilities/amenities: Restrooms, water, picnic area at trailhead and ranger station

Land status: National recreation area

Fees and permits: None

Schedule: Open year-round, sunrise to sunset, except during inclement weather

Maps: USGS Triunfo Pass, CA; www.nps.gov/samo/planyourvisit/loader.cfm?csModule=security/getfile&PageID=376833

Trail contacts: Circle X Ranch, 12896 Yerba Buena Rd., Malibu 90265. Santa Monica Mountains National Recreation Area, 401 W. Hillcrest Dr., Thousand Oaks 91360; www.nps.gov/samo; (805) 370-2301

Finding the trailhead: From Los Angeles take the Pacific Coast Highway / CA 1 for 24.7 miles north and west of Sunset Boulevard. Turn right onto Yerba Buena Road and drive north for 5.3 miles. The parking lot and visitor center are on the right-hand side of the road. GPS: N 34 6.55' / W 118 56.2333'

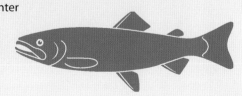

The first part of the hike is primarily downhill, into what seems like a tunnel of trees heading into the unknown. Shortly after this canopied downhill stretch, the trail opens up and offers very little if any shade for some time. The trail itself is a bit worn and, depending on the time of year, it may be a bit washed out and muddy since water naturally runs the course of the downhill trail. There is a series of curves and bends, which adds to the feeling of anticipation to see what is "just around the corner."

One of the first rewards you will come to around a significant bend is a stream (or brook, depending on the water level) to cross and a grand vista of a 30-foot waterfall. The trees become more abundant and the foliage more verdant. Moss-covered rock walls provide for a unique ambience, feeling as if somehow the trail has taken you far away from the hustle and bustle of Los Angeles.

Spectacular seasonal falls dot the landscape just after rains.
Allen Riedel

Continuing up and down the winding trail, be prepared for more creek crossings. Again, depending on the season and water level, these may be a muddy hop over a trickle of water or a rock-balancing feat over a bubbling brook. Make sure to take a good look into the creek water because salamanders are endemic to these streams. You can see these mysterious creatures lounging in the cool water by rocks and sunken logs.

After having crossed creeks, viewed waterfalls, and ventured into canopied forests, the trail opens up into a meadow teeming with wildflowers and winged creatures of all varieties, such as butterflies, dragonflies, and birds.

After crossing the meadow, the trail really begins to give you a flavor of its namesake, The Grotto, as it leads into a tree-lined stream peppered with large and small boulders. The trail becomes a little more difficult to discern at this point, so keep in mind that this is natural for this part of the hike. Follow the trail over the creek bed, and you will see the trail continue on the other side. This part of the hike is where the jackpot lies. For some, the challenge of scrambling over 6- to 8-foot boulders presents a welcome thrill, while other, less-adventuresome souls may wish to sit and enjoy the mysterious beauty of the shady creek, perched safely on a boulder. Those who decide to boulder-hop down the creek bed a bit will be generously rewarded with a great watering hole and an underground grotto with a waterfall.

Keep in mind that this option is only ideal dependent on the season and the water level. Sometimes the water level is too high to scramble the boulders, and The Grotto may be out of reach while maintaining personal safety. At other times, the water level is too low and the creek bed may be too dry to enjoy the pool or absent waterfall.

This is definitely a hike that requires perfect timing to enjoy this part of the adventure. But no matter what season, it is certain that this hike will not disappoint. The otherworldly ambience and verdant scenery provides enough variety for everyone with or without a glimpse of The Grotto.

> *Fitness Tip: Use two trekking poles and the strength of your arms to help propel you along the trail for a better workout.*

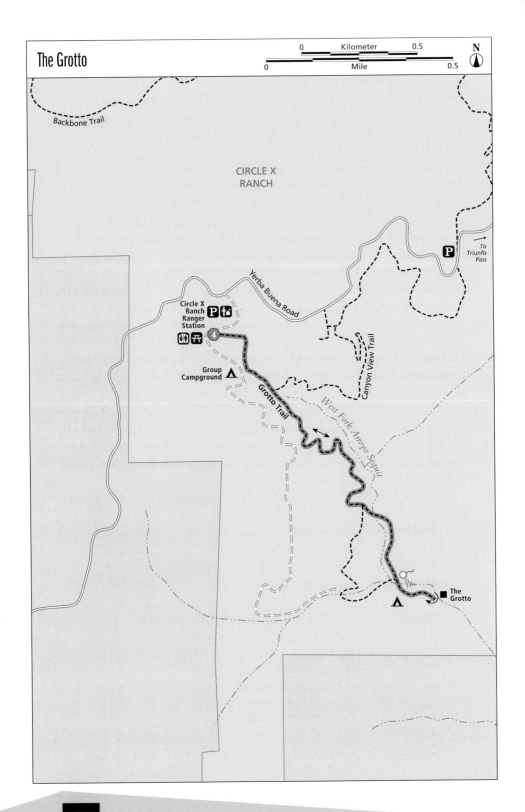

Kilometer
0   0.5

Mile
0   0.5

N

Backbone Trail

CIRCLE X
RANCH

P

To
Triunfo
Pass

Yerba Buena Road

Circle X
Ranch
Ranger
Station

P

Canyon View Trail

Group
Campground

Grotto Trail

West Fork Arroyo Sequit

The
Grotto

MILES AND DIRECTIONS

0.0 Start from the parking area and head south along the trail.

0.5 Continue straight at the junction with the Canyon View Trail.

1.5 Arrive at The Grotto. Return via same route.

3.0 Arrive back at the trailhead.

HIKE INFORMATION

Local information: California State Parks, (818) 880-0363; Santa Monica Mountains National Recreation Area, (805) 370-2301

Camping: Circle X Ranch Group Campground, (805) 370-2300; Leo Carrillo State Park campgrounds, Malibu Creek State Park, Topanga State Park Campground, Point Mugu State Park Campground, McGrath State Beach, Emma Wood State Beach, California State Park campgrounds reservations (800) 444-7275; customer service (800) 695-2269; www.reserveamerica.com

Local retailers: A-16 (Adventure 16), www.adventure16.com; REI, www.rei.com

Restaurants: Jack's Deli, 966 S. Westlake Blvd., Suite 2, Westlake Village, (805) 495-8181; Neptune's Net, 42505 Pacific Coast Hwy., Malibu, (310) 457-3095; Moonshadows, 20356 Pacific Coast Hwy., Malibu, (310) 456-3010; Old Place Restaurant, 29983 Mulholland Hwy., Agoura Hills, (818) 706-9001; Inn of the Seventh Ray, 128 Old Topanga Canyon Rd., Topanga, (310) 455-1311

Bumblebees are effective pollinators of wildflowers like this snapdragon variety. Allen Riedel

Backbone Trail–Malibu Springs

Hike along the Santa Monica Mountains National Recreation Area's wondrous Backbone Trail, traversing a ridgeline with tremendous unimpeded views of the Pacific coastline. On clear days the vantage is unparalleled. This point-to-point hike requires a car shuttle and provides a fine workout.

Start: Triunfo Pass at the Backbone Trailhead on Yerba Buena Road

Distance: 4.25 miles point to point

Hiking time: About 2 hours

Difficulty: Moderate

Trail surface: Singletrack dirt trail and dirt road

Nearest town: Westlake Village

County: Ventura

Other trail users: Bicyclists, joggers, equestrians

Canine compatibility: Leashed dogs permitted

Trailhead facilities/amenities: None

Land status: National recreation area

Fees and permits: None

Schedule: Open year-round

Maps: USGS Triunfo Pass, CA; www.nps.gov/samo/planyourvisit/upload/BBTMap.pdf

Trail contact: Santa Monica Mountains National Recreation Area, 401 W. Hillcrest Dr., Thousand Oaks 91360; www.nps.gov/samo; (805) 370-2301

Finding the trailhead: From Los Angeles take the Pacific Coast Highway / CA 1 north for 24.7 miles, then turn right onto Yerba Buena Road. Drive north for 6.9 miles. Park in the lot on the right-hand side of the road. Drive a shuttle car 2.1 miles farther along Yerba Buena and park in the right-side turnout area. GPS: N 34 6.85' / W 118 55.1'

The Backbone Trail system extends nearly 70 miles across the Santa Monica Mountains, from Point Mugu State Park in the west to Will Rogers State Historic Park in the east.

THE HIKE

This hike is solely for people looking to enjoy a Southern California coastal view. It is best taken on clear winter days when the wind is sharp, the breeze is cool, and the visibility is perfect. It can be splendid to hike here in the fog as well, when the hazy quality gives off an effect similar to Bronte's *Wuthering Heights*, and eternal callings for Heathcliff out on the moors. The ecosystem of the region is undoubtedly coastal chaparral, and only in the fog could one remotely consider it to be similar to English countryside. Wildflowers are common from February to May. During years of high rainfall, the period of full bloom transforms the hike into a marvelous jaunt, with golds and purples dominating the mountainsides.

From the parking area at Triunfo Pass, take the Backbone Trail south. The trail loses elevation for the first 0.25 mile and stays fairly close to Yerba Buena Road, dropping just beneath the roadway. From the beginning, the views are nice, but rather pedestrian compared to what will be coming later in the hike.

The trail meanders up and down for a bit before reaching a steep section that climbs a few hundred feet at the 0.5-mile mark. Here the trail bends westward

Purple sage can be found on almost any trail in the Southern California lowlands. Allen Riedel

Backbone Trail–Malibu Springs

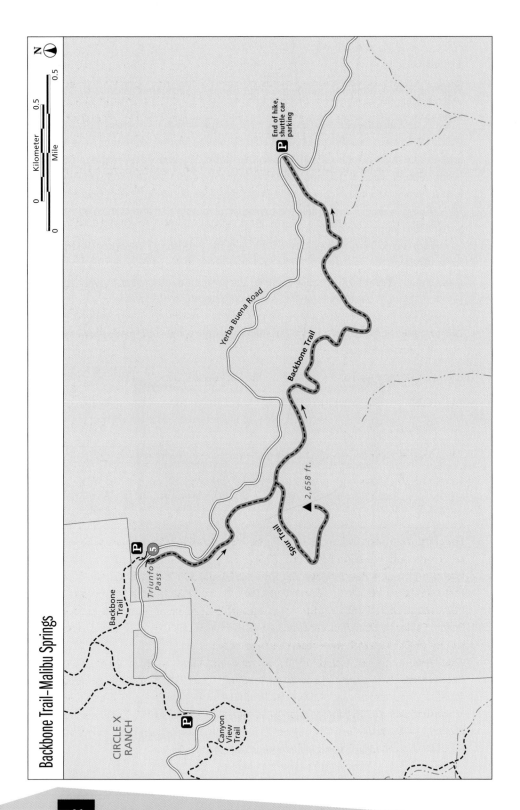

N

Kilometer
0   0.5   0.5

Mile
0   0.5

Yerba Buena Road

End of hike,
shuttle car
parking
P

Backbone Trail

▲ 2,658 ft.

Spur Trail

P
5
Triunfo Pass

Backbone
Trail

CIRCLE X
RANCH

P

Canyon
View
Trail

and follows a long finger toward the end of the ridgeline and the ocean. As the route wraps around and turns southeastward, the views truly open up. To catch that unmatched 360-degree view, turn right (southwest) at 1.25 miles and take the short spur to the top of the mountain at 2,658 feet. The coastline sparkles in crystal blue where wave upon wave crashes on the beach. The spur trail is about 0.4 mile long and gains 300 feet of elevation very rapidly.

Return to the Backbone Trail. It curves northward once more around 2.5 miles, and nears the roadway once again at 3 miles, before heading east and south for more otherworldly vantage points.

At 3.5 miles the trail turns northward again, heading back toward Yerba Buena Road and the drop-off point for the car shuttle.

MILES AND DIRECTIONS

0.0 Start by heading east and south along the Backbone Trail.

1.25 Reach the spur trail to the summit. Turn right and climb to the summit. Return via the same route.

2.0 Turn right (east) and continue on the Backbone Trail.

2.5 Curve toward the north.

3.0 Approach Yerba Buena Road.

3.5 Veer left (north), heading again to Yerba Buena.

4.25 Arrive at the end of the route and the drop-off point for your car.

HIKE INFORMATION

Local information: California State Parks, (818) 880-0363; Santa Monica Mountains National Recreation Area, (805) 370-2301
Camping: Circle X Ranch Group Campground, (805) 370-2300; Leo Carrillo State Park campgrounds, Malibu Creek State Park, Topanga State Park Campground, Point Mugu State Park Campground, McGrath State Beach, Emma Wood State Beach, California State Park campgrounds reservations (800) 444-7275; customer service (800) 695-2269; www.reserveamerica.com
Local retailers: A-16 (Adventure 16), www.adventure16.com; REI, www.rei.com
Restaurants: Jack's Deli, 966 S. Westlake Blvd., Suite 2, Westlake Village, (805) 495-8181; Neptune's Net, 42505 Pacific Coast Hwy., Malibu, (310) 457-3095; Moonshadows, 20356 Pacific Coast Hwy., Malibu, (310) 456-3010; Old Place Restaurant, 29983 Mulholland Hwy., Agoura Hills, (818) 706-9001; Inn of the Seventh Ray, 128 Old Topanga Canyon Rd., Topanga, (310) 455-1311

Arroyo Sequit

A short jaunt through verdant meadows peppered with streams and seasonal waterfalls is enticingly close to the extravagance and luxury of prestigious Malibu estates. This trail is ideal for nature lovers seeking solace and a quick getaway in an idyllic setting.

Start: At the Arroyo Sequit parking area at Mason Road and Mulholland Highway

Distance: 1.9-mile lollipop

Hiking time: About 1 hour

Difficulty: Easy

Trail surface: Singletrack dirt trail and dirt road

Nearest town: Malibu

County: Los Angeles

Other trail users: Joggers

Canine compatibility: Leashed dogs permitted

Trailhead facilities/amenities: Restroom and picnic facilities near the ranger residence

Land status: National recreation area

Fees and permits: None

Schedule: Open year-round, sunrise to sunset

Maps: USGS Triunfo Pass, CA; www.nps.gov/samo/planyourvisit/arroyosequit.htm

Trail contacts: Arroyo Sequit Park, 34138 Mulholland Hwy., Malibu. Santa Monica Mountains National Recreation Area, 401 W. Hillcrest Dr., Thousand Oaks 91360; www.nps.gov/samo; (805) 370-2301

Finding the trailhead: From Los Angeles take the Pacific Coast Highway/CA 1 north for 22.9 miles. Turn right onto Mulholland Highway and drive for 5.6 miles. Turn right onto Mason Road (unsigned if you are traveling from the south), and park in the parking lot. GPS: N 34 5.3166'/W 118 53.45'

THE HIKE

A rroyo Sequit is undeniably one of the most glorious havens in the Santa Monica Mountains. Ideal for those seeking tranquility and solitude, this easy loop trail embraces a titillating variety of meadows carpeted with wildflowers, perennial streams, rocks, and breathtaking views of the inland mountain range.

This trail is probably one of Malibu's best-kept secrets. It is not uncommon to complete this entire hike without encountering another soul. Because of this rare opportunity to enjoy the serenity and beauty of this unscathed landscape, this is one destination not to be missed.

At the trailhead, there is an informational kiosk with a posted map of the trail loop. From the parking lot follow the clearly marked trail past a quaint park ranger residence, a white clapboard house reminiscent of a distant era, on the right-hand side. At 0.3 mile you will enter a small oak grove that commences the 1.5-mile nature trail loop.

The trail is lush with flora and fauna most anytime of year, so look out for wildflowers and endemic wildlife such as a variety of bird species and coyotes. While the distance of this trail is short, there are some steep areas to traverse, creek crossings to negotiate, and little or no shade from the sun for a large part of the trail. Therefore, it is advised to be prepared for these circumstances and bring plenty of water.

Arroyo Sequit is small but rugged and ringed by mountains. Allen Riedel

Arroyo Sequit

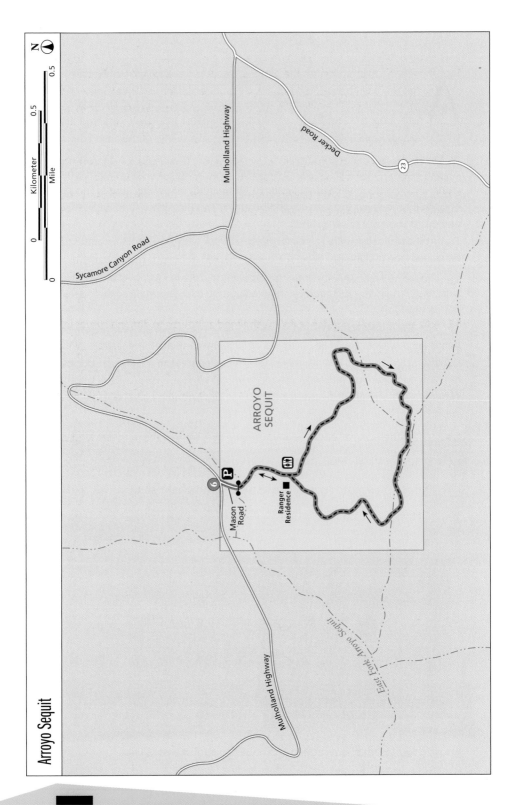

At 0.6 mile, beyond the oak grove, you will reach the East Fork of the Arroyo Sequit drainage. Depending on the season, the water level may be high and portions of the trail may be washed out. It may be necessary to do some inspecting and use common sense in following the intended trail. Be prepared to cross the stream and trek through muddy patches. Since the vegetation is lush, be wary of ticks, especially if you have your dog along. Stay on the trail.

At 1.3 miles, after descending into the creek bed and trailing up onto a meadowland plateau, you will find yourself back in the same area as the beginning of the trail but at the opposite side, having made a complete loop. Follow the trail back toward the rangers' house and down toward the parking area.

MILES AND DIRECTIONS

0.0 Start by heading south along paved Mason Road and walk through the opening in the locked gate.

0.2 Near the ranger residence, follow the road as it turns to dirt and curves left.

0.3 After passing through a grove of woodland oaks, the 1.5-mile nature trail begins.

0.6 The trail enters the drainage of the East Fork of the Arroyo Sequit and turns westward.

1.3 Cross the Arroyo Sequit; begin climbing back toward the ranger residence.

1.4 Stay straight at the trail intersection.

1.7 Turn left onto Mason Road and return to the parking area.

1.9 Arrive back at the trailhead and the Arroyo Sequit parking area.

🍃 **Green Tip:**
Bring a bag along to help pack out trash;
leave the trail cleaner than you found it.

Local information: California State Parks, (818) 880-0363; Santa Monica Mountains National Recreation Area, (805) 370-2301

Camping: Circle X Ranch Group Campground, (805) 370-2300; Leo Carrillo State Park campgrounds, Malibu Creek State Park, Topanga State Park Campground, Point Mugu State Park Campground, McGrath State Beach, Emma Wood State Beach, California State Park campgrounds reservations (800) 444-7275; customer service (800) 695-2269; www.reserveamerica.com

Local retailers: A-16, www.adventure16.com; REI, www.rei.com

Restaurants: Jack's Deli, 966 S. Westlake Blvd., Suite 2, Westlake Village, (805) 495-8181; Neptune's Net, 42505 Pacific Coast Hwy., Malibu, (310) 457-3095; Moonshadows, 20356 Pacific Coast Hwy., Malibu, (310) 456-3010; Old Place Restaurant, 29983 Mulholland Hwy., Agoura Hills, (818) 706-9001; Inn of the Seventh Ray, 128 Old Topanga Canyon Rd., Topanga, (310) 455-1311

It is obvious how the white shooting star got its name. Allen Riedel

Nicholas Flat

The beauty of Nicholas Flat is understated and the region is surprisingly undervisited. The old ranch area is rustic and loaded with scenic splendor. The ridgeline views are phenomenal, as is the tranquility. Nicholas Flat feels like an escape from the hustle and bustle of modern life—and it is.

Start: At the end of Decker School Road

Distance: 3.6-mile loop

Hiking time: About 2 hours

Difficulty: Easy

Trail surface: Singletrack dirt trail and dirt road

Nearest town: Malibu

County: Los Angeles

Other trail users: Joggers

Canine compatibility: No dogs allowed

Trailhead facilities/amenities: None

Land status: California state park

Fees and permits: None

Schedule: Open year-round

Maps: USGS Triunfo Pass, CA; www.parks.ca.gov/pages/616/files/LeoCarrilloPDF.pdf

Trail contact: Leo Carrillo State Park, 35000 W. Pacific Coast Hwy., Malibu 90265; www.parks.ca.gov/default.asp?page_id=616; (310) 457-8143

Finding the trailhead: From Los Angeles take the Pacific Coast Highway/CA 1 north for 20.6 miles. Turn right onto Decker Road/Decker Canyon Road/CA 23 and drive for 2.4 miles. Turn left onto Decker School Road and drive for 0.2 mile. Veer right and stay on Decker School Road, and drive 1.4 miles to the parking area at the end of the road. Do not block the gate. GPS: N 34 4.2333'/W 118 54.4'

From the parking area at the end of Decker School Road, continue south through the closed gate along the dirt road. Trails here aren't very well marked and there are too many side and use trails to mention. Those with a poorly defined sense of direction and without a GPS device may want to stick solely to the roadways, but the route should be easy enough to follow with the simple directions below.

The trail starts down a lovely wooded oak path with a canopy flowing overhead and poison oak below. An intermittent arroyo flows beside the roadway and the region is very quaint and contemplative. Some old farm equipment and foundations still exist along the hike giving it a rustic feeling, but for views, this seldom-traveled little section of Leo Carrillo State Park is quite the hidden gem.

At the signed roadway for Nicholas Flat, continue straight toward lovely Nicholas Pond, follow its western contour, and turn right, continuing along the trail to the west. Turn right almost immediately at the fork and follow the route along the more open pathway and not into the arroyo.

The route skirts a hill around a meadow and joins back up with the roadway. Stay to the left at each Y intersection. The route heads south toward a smaller and usually dry pond, following a path sparsely lined with oaks. Turn left just before the

The views from the ridgeline around Nicholas Flat are glorious. Monique Riedel

pond to take a small detour to the top of a very nice vista point. From the top return to the main path and continue left past the depression/pond. The trail meanders and curves north again. At the next Y intersection, turn left and continue upward. The next vista point is the best one on the hike for taking in views of the Pacific Ocean. Turn left again at the T junction and continue uphill. Topping out at 1,737 feet, this is the tallest peak this far south, so the views are unparalleled. Take them in and return to the T junction, continuing straight ahead.

At times, the trail can be quite a bit overgrown and messy. Eventually it meets back up with Nicholas Flat Road; turn right and then take an immediate left along the ridgeline. At this point the route begins to climb to the top of a tremendous ridge with some ocean views, but this time the vistas are mostly of the surrounding Santa Monica Mountains. Near sunset, this can be quite the magical place. Hikers will understand the true meaning of "purple mountains majesty" for certain.

At 2.8 miles, the Malibu Springs Trail descends into the Arroyo Sequit very sharply as it turns inward back toward Decker School Road. Turn sharply right here and return to the roadway, enjoying the views from this open field. Turn right again at the road and return to the parking area.

MILES AND DIRECTIONS

0.0 Start by heading south beyond the gate, continuing along Decker School Road.

0.3 Continue straight at the junction for Nicholas Flat Road.

0.4 Arrive at Nicholas Pond. Follow the western contour.

0.5 Turn right with the bend in the trail. Then turn right at the Y junction, following the open trail.

0.8 Continue straight and then veer left at the next two junctions. Follow the trail as it turns south.

1.0 Turn left and take a short spur trail to the top of a vista point.

1.2 Arrive at the top of a magnificent unnamed summit. Return to the main trail.

1.4 Turn left back onto the main route.

1.5 Reach a smaller (often dry) pond.

1.7 At the Y junction, veer left and up.

1.8 At the T junction, turn left and up. A bit farther on, continue straight at the main trail junction to the vista point above.

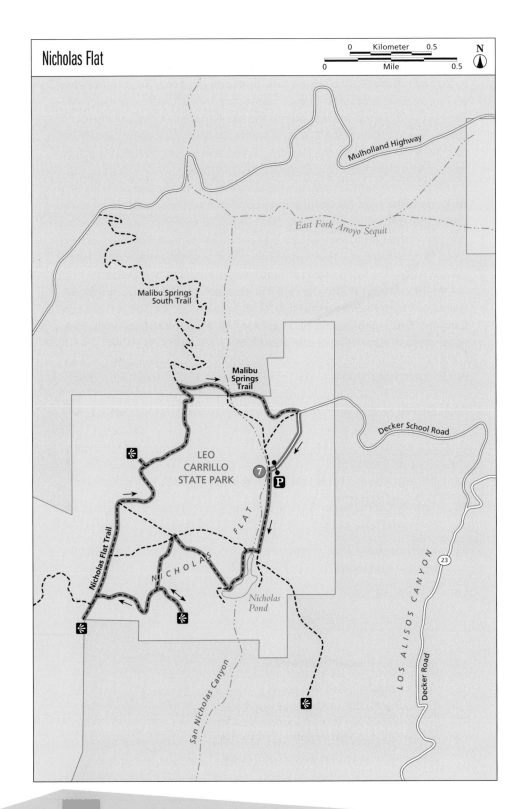

Nicholas Flat

1.9 Arrive atop a spectacular 360-degree vista point with wide-ranging views of the Pacific Ocean. Return to the T junction.

2.0 Continue straight and avoid all turns until the elbow junction with Nicholas Flat Road.

2.2 Turn right onto Nicholas Flat Road. Then turn left onto Malibu Springs Trail.

2.8 Turn sharply right at the T junction for the Malibu Springs Trail. Head east.

3.3 Turn right onto Decker School Road.

3.6 Arrive back at the trailhead and parking area.

HIKE INFORMATION

Local information: California State Parks, (818) 880-0363; Santa Monica Mountains National Recreation Area, (805) 370-2301

Camping: Circle X Ranch Group Campground, (805) 370-2300; Leo Carrillo State Park campgrounds, Malibu Creek State Park, Topanga State Park Campground, Point Mugu State Park Campground, McGrath State Beach, Emma Wood State Beach, California State Park campgrounds reservations (800) 444-7275; customer service (800) 695-2269; www.reserveamerica.com

Local retailers: A-16 (Adventure 16), www.adventure16.com; REI, www.rei.com

Restaurants: Jack's Deli, 966 S. Westlake Blvd., Suite 2, Westlake Village, (805) 495-8181; Neptune's Net, 42505 Pacific Coast Hwy., Malibu, (310) 457-3095; Moonshadows, 20356 Pacific Coast Hwy., Malibu, (310) 456-3010; Old Place Restaurant, 29983 Mulholland Hwy., Agoura Hills, (818) 706-9001; Inn of the Seventh Ray, 128 Old Topanga Canyon Rd., Topanga, (310) 455-1311

Hiking Tip: Use a GPS to mark waypoints before hiking, making it easier to find difficult trail crossings and take the correct path.

Charmlee Wilderness Park

It isn't a coincidence that the name Charmlee evokes visions of a charming and magical place. Nestled on a meadowland bluff above the Pacific Coast Highway, Charmlee Wilderness Park is an idyllic setting for hikers of all ages.

Start: At the parking area for Charmlee Wilderness Park off Encinal Canyon Road

Distance: 2.1-mile loop

Hiking time: About 1.5 hours

Difficulty: Easy

Trail surface: Singletrack dirt trail and dirt road

Nearest town: Malibu

County: Los Angeles

Other trail users: Joggers, bicyclists, equestrians

Canine compatibility: Leashed dogs permitted

Trailhead facilities/amenities: All facilities available at trailhead

Land status: Malibu city park

Fees and permits: Parking fee is charged

Schedule: Open year-round, 8 a.m. to sunset daily

Maps: USGS Triunfo Pass, CA and Point Dume, CA; www.ci.malibu.ca.us/download/index.cfm/fuseaction/download/cid/9197/

Trail contact: Charmlee Wilderness Park, 2577 Encinal Canyon Rd., Malibu, 90265; www.ci.malibu.ca.us/index.cfm/fuseaction/DetailGroup/CID/3801/NavID/174/; (310) 457-7247

Finding the trailhead: From Los Angeles take the Pacific Coast Highway / CA 1 north for 20 miles. Turn right onto Encinal Canyon Road and drive for 3.8 miles. Turn left at the large stone sign onto Carmichael Road and drive for 0.2 mile to the parking area for Charmlee Wilderness Park. GPS: N 34 3.5166' / W 118 52.7333'

THE HIKE

The Charmlee Wilderness Area comprises about 530 acres of meadowlands, oak woodlands, wildflower grasslands, and chaparral located conveniently on the coastal bluffs overlooking the Pacific Ocean. There are 9 miles of trails that meander throughout the park, providing an opportunity to stroll among an array of verdant wildflowers, view the remnants of a long-lost ranch house and water tower used during the days of cattle ranching, and revel in breathtaking ocean views.

It is said that when Leon and Charmian Schwartz purchased the land in the 1950s, they combined their first names to create the name "Charmlee" for their ranch. The two brothers built an A-frame ranch house, which to date is claimed to be the only residence ever built on the property. The ranch house was eventually destroyed by a wildfire in 1978, but the foundation remains as a relic from a not-so-

Beach views from the Old Reservoir at Charmlee Wilderness Park.
Allen Riedel

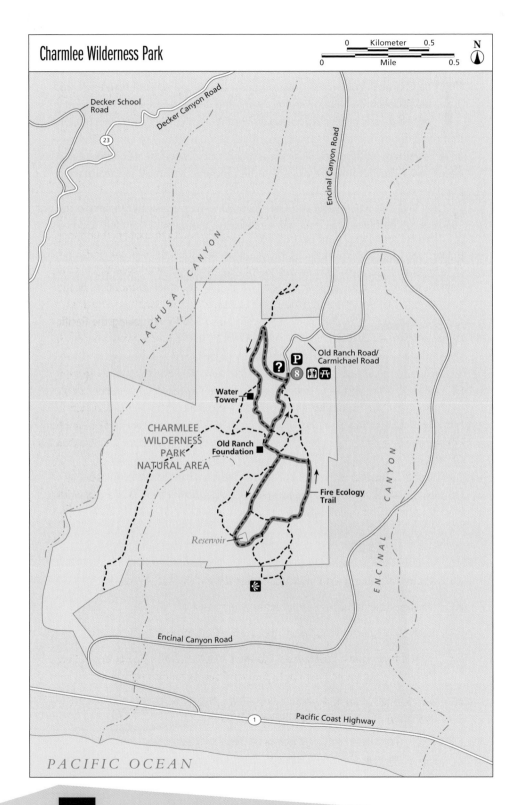

Charmlee Wilderness Park

0 Kilometer 0.5
0 Mile 0.5

N

Decker School Road

Decker Canyon Road

23

Encinal Canyon Road

L A C H U S A   C A N Y O N

Old Ranch Road/ Carmichael Road

? P 8

Water Tower

CHARMLEE WILDERNESS PARK NATURAL AREA

Old Ranch Foundation

Fire Ecology Trail

E N C I N A L   C A N Y O N

Reservoir

Encinal Canyon Road

1 Pacific Coast Highway

PACIFIC OCEAN

distant past. In June 2003, the City of Malibu obtained ownership of the property and dedicated it as Charmlee Wilderness Park.

The beauty of Charmlee lies not only in its name but in the variety of choices offered to the casual hiker. This hike is perfect for small children, people with dogs on leashes, and those seeking a serene and relaxing experience. The hike described is only one of the multitude of variations to choose from. Depending on the time of year and climate, any of the trail options will offer an incredible treat.

After a visit to the nature center, where you may pick up a map and guide, follow the trail northwest about 0.1 mile toward the old water tower that is made up of a concrete cistern used to provide irrigation and water for the old cattle ranch. The trail up to the old water tower presents an opportunity to spot an abundance of wildflowers. The water tower is perched above the park and offers an overview of the park grounds and the bluffs overlooking the ocean. From this vantage point, follow the main trail to Old Ranch Road and to the Old Ranch foundation. At the foundation, turn left at the junction and continue on Old Ranch Road across a grassy meadowland toward the Old Reservoir on a bluff overlooking the Pacific Ocean. The view from this bluff on a clear day bestows stunning ocean views. From the Old Reservoir, follow the trail east to the oak woodland area.

When you reach the shady woodland area, you will feel as if you have stepped into a different time and place. The oak grove provides a dark and mysterious backdrop in contrast to the openness of the rest of the park. This is a great chance to repose before heading onto the Fire Ecology Trail, which leads back to Old Ranch Road. Returning to the parking area, you can conclude your outing in the Oak Grove picnic area or the picnic area near the entrance of the park.

Due to the verdant nature of the flora and fauna on the trails, take special precautions to watch for ticks and rattlesnakes, as this wonderland is teeming with wildlife that call Charmlee Wilderness their home.

MILES AND DIRECTIONS

0.0 From the parking area, walk northwest toward the nature center.

0.1 Arrive at the nature center. Continue northwest.

0.2 Turn south along the fire road toward the water tower.

0.3 At the fork, veer left below and to the east of the water tower and follow the main route (unsigned) to Old Ranch Road (also unsigned).

0.5 Arrive at Old Ranch Road and turn right toward the ocean, staying on the trail to reach the Old Ranch foundation.

0.6 Turn left at the T junction and stay on Old Ranch Road, following it south across an open meadow toward the Pacific Ocean.

1.1 Reach the Old Reservoir. Turn east and follow the loop trail through the oak woodland.

1.4 Reach the oak woodland and turn north along the Fire Ecology Trail.

1.6 Turn left to get back onto Old Ranch Road and follow it back to the parking area.

2.1 Arrive back at the trailhead and parking area.

HIKE INFORMATION

Local information: California State Parks, (818) 880-0363; Santa Monica Mountains National Recreation Area, (805) 370-2301

Camping: Circle X Ranch Group Campground, (805) 370-2300; Leo Carrillo State Park campgrounds, Malibu Creek State Park, Topanga State Park Campground, Point Mugu State Park Campground, McGrath State Beach, Emma Wood State Beach, California State Park campgrounds reservations (800) 444-7275; customer service (800) 695-2269, www.reserveamerica.com

Local retailers: A-16 (Adventure 16), www.adventure16.com; REI, www.rei.com

Restaurants: Jack's Deli, 966 S. Westlake Blvd., Suite 2, Westlake Village, (805) 495-8181; Neptune's Net, 42505 Pacific Coast Hwy., Malibu, (310) 457-3095; Moonshadows, 20356 Pacific Coast Hwy., Malibu, (310) 456-3010; Old Place Restaurant, 29983 Mulholland Hwy., Agoura Hills, (818) 706-9001; Inn of the Seventh Ray, 128 Old Topanga Canyon Rd., Topanga, (310) 455-1311

> *Hiking Tip: Learn to identify poison oak during all seasons. Check for ticks regularly, especially when walking through tall grasses.*

Paramount Ranch

A stroll down Hollywood Boulevard is not your only option to walk in the footsteps of the stars—a visit to this "movie ranch" will conjure up visions of old Westerns and even more modern films. Whether you are an old-time movie buff or a more contemporary enthusiast, you will feel as if you have stepped into familiar surroundings with some of your favorite stars. Paramount Ranch has been the site of a variety of films, from television to the big screen. Who says you can't have it all—the bright lights of Hollywood in an agrarian surrounding? Here at Paramount Ranch, you can.

Start: At the parking area for Paramount Ranch State Park
Distance: 1-mile lollipop
Hiking time: About 1 hour
Difficulty: Easy
Trail surface: Singletrack dirt trail and dirt road
Nearest town: Malibu
County: Los Angeles
Other trail users: Joggers, bicyclists, equestrians
Canine compatibility: Leashed dogs permitted
Trailhead facilities/amenities: All facilities available
Land status: National recreation area

Fees and permits: None
Schedule: Open year-round, 8 a.m. to sunset
Maps: USGS Point Dume, CA; www.nps.gov/samo/planyourvisit/loader.cfm?csModule=security/getfile&PageID=376834
Trail contacts: Paramount Ranch, 2903 Cornell Rd., Agoura Hills 91301. Santa Monica Mountains National Recreation Area, 401 West Hillcrest Dr., Thousand Oaks 91360; www.nps.gov/samo/planyourvisit/paramountranch.htm; (805) 370-2301

Finding the trailhead: From the intersection of CA 134, US 101, and CA 170 in Los Angeles, take US 101 north and west for 21.6 miles. Take exit 36 for Kanan Road. Turn left onto Kanan Road and drive for 0.2 mile. Turn left onto Sideway/Cornell Road and drive for 2.1 miles. Turn right at Paramount Ranch Drive and go 0.1 mile. Turn left onto Paramount Ranch Road and follow it 0.1 mile to the visitor center and parking area. GPS: N 34 6.9666'/W 118 45.2666'

THE HIKE

Paramount Ranch was purchased from the Rancho Las Virgenes land grant governed by the Treaty of Guadalupe Hidalgo in 1927 for use as a "movie ranch," a place developed by Hollywood filmmakers to create a variety of distant locations right in their own backyard. With the ability to fabricate locations such as San Francisco, Montana, Africa, a South Seas island, and even colonial Massachusetts, combined with the convenience and economic advantage of not having to pack up and travel to distant locales, filmmaking boomed at Paramount Ranch.

Despite the fact that the property changed ownership several times from 1957 to 1980, moviemaking continued. The National Park Service gained ownership of part of the original ranch in the 1980s and restored the old movie set. The list of stars that have graced the set is a genuine who's who of Hollywood's elite. Movie legends such as Cary Grant, John Wayne, and Gary Cooper, along with Lucille Ball, Marlene Dietrich, Diane Keaton, and Jane Seymour are among the hundreds of Hollywood A-listers who have walked the streets of Paramount Ranch. Even music legend Ringo Starr filmed his music video, "Act Naturally," on location at the ranch. This is the only national park site that doubles as a movie set. More contemporary films and TV series, such as HBO's *Carnivale* and Showtime's *Weeds,* have been filmed on location at Paramount Ranch.

The Western Town at Paramount Ranch is a must-see for film fans. Allen Riedel

The park offers several trails, many aptly named for the set for which it was built or for other activities that took place along the trail. Some of the most popular trails are the Hacienda Trail, the Backdrop Trail, and the Coyote Canyon Trail. Along the Hacienda Trail, fans of *Dr. Quinn Medicine Woman* will recognize the homestead of Dr. Michaela Quinn. The Backdrop Trail is famous for its ability to accommodate most any kind of shot because it lacks modern telephone poles and is famously generic in nature. The Coyote Canyon Trail is a relatively easy stroll that travels through the heart of Western Town and onto the hillside above the town to a picnic overlook tucked away between the shrubs.

The visitor center located at the parking area provides brochures and maps of the park that document its eclectic history. From the visitor center, follow the road toward the old Western Town, visible on the other side of a wooden bridge crossing a creek. Once you have taken your first step on the other side of the wooden bridge you will feel as if you have traveled back in time to the days of the Old West. The town is well maintained and is very realistic, but keep in mind that the structures are mostly facades and were constructed as a set. While it is permitted to explore the exterior of the buildings, use caution when doing so.

Once you have reveled in the awe of Hollywood's craftsmanship in the Old West town, turn left at the Coyote Canyon Trail sign. The trail follows along a tributary of Medea Creek.

At about 0.4 mile veer to the right at the unmaintained trail junction; here the public trail ends at a private property border. The trail is lined with shrubbery and chaparral; depending on the time of year, be aware that wildlife abounds, especially ticks, wasps, and bees. At about 0.5 mile take a left turn where the trail ascends to the overlook that boasts an intimate picnic area.

From the overlook, continue down the Coyote Canyon Trail, turning left to follow the main trail loop. The trail gradually descends back toward the Western Town set and into the parking lot by the visitor center. A short optional excursion along the Medea Creek Trail, up to the Western Town Overlook, displays the Old West set from a different vantage point and is a great photo opportunity to capture the entire set from a distance.

MILES AND DIRECTIONS

0.0   Start by heading south on the road from the visitor center, and walk west toward the creek.

0.1   Walk across the bridge to the Western Town film set.

0.25 Turn left down Coyote Canyon Trail. Follow along the creek bed.

0.4   Stay right at the unmaintained trail junction.

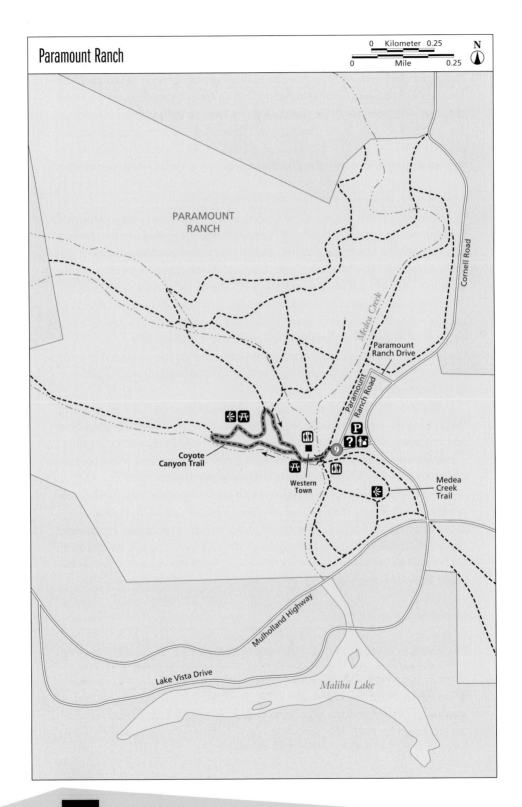

Paramount Ranch

PARAMOUNT RANCH

Coyote Canyon Trail

Western Town

Medea Creek Trail

Medea Creek

Paramount Ranch Drive

Paramount Ranch Road

Cornell Road

Mulholland Highway

Lake Vista Drive

Malibu Lake

0   Kilometer   0.25

0   Mile   0.25

N

0.5 Turn left for the picnic overlook. Head back to the Coyote Canyon Trail.

0.6 Turn left to continue along the main trail loop.

0.75 Continue south on the road back to the Western Town set.

0.9 Walk across the bridge and back to the visitor center.

1.0 Return to the trailhead and parking area.

Movies in the Mountains

The Santa Monica Mountains are no stranger to the city to the south. The Hollywood film industry has used the mountains to represent nearly every continent of the world, from Africa to South America. Many of the more prominent locations have been used so many times that hiking within park boundaries creates a sense of nostalgia and déjà vu.

A list of some of the movies and TV shows filmed in the SMMNRA:

The Rifleman	Spartacus
Van Helsing	Planet of the Apes
The Love Bug	Lassie
Reds	Dynasty
Herbie Rides Again	Murder She Wrote
Geronimo	True Blood
Wells Fargo	ER
The Adventures of Tom Sawyer	How I Met Your Mother
The Andy Griffith Show	Will and Grace
Platoon	Star Trek
The Creature From the Black Lagoon	On Golden Pond
M.A.S.H.	Kindergarten Cop
Beau Geste	Minority Report
Bonanza	Rambo II

HIKE INFORMATION

Local information: California State Parks, (818) 880-0363; Santa Monica Mountains National Recreation Area, (805) 370-2301

Camping: Circle X Ranch Group Campground, (805) 370-2300; Leo Carrillo State Park campgrounds, Malibu Creek State Park, Topanga State Park Campground,

Point Mugu State Park Campground, McGrath State Beach, Emma Wood State Beach, California State Park campgrounds reservations (800) 444-7275; customer service (800) 695-2269; www.reserveamerica.com

Local retailers: A-16 (Adventure 16), www.adventure16.com; REI, www.rei.com

Restaurants: Jack's Deli, 966 S. Westlake Blvd., Suite 2, Westlake Village, (805) 495-8181; Neptune's Net, 42505 Pacific Coast Hwy., Malibu, (310) 457-3095; Versailles, 17410 Ventura Blvd., Encino, (818) 906-0756; Moonshadows, 20356 Pacific Coast Hwy., Malibu, (301) 456-3010; Old Place Restaurant, 29983 Mulholland Hwy., Agoura Hills, (818) 706-9001; Inn of the Seventh Ray, 128 Old Topanga Canyon Rd., Topanga, (310) 455-1311

Western wallflower is common in mountain regions throughout Southern California. Allen Riedel

Calabasas Peak

Hike through the strange formations of Red Rock Canyon Park up to the high valley viewpoints of Calabasas Peak.

Start: At the end of Red Rock Road in the parking area for Red Rock Canyon Park

Distance: 5 miles out and back

Hiking time: About 2.5 hours

Difficulty: Moderate

Trail surface: Dirt road

Nearest town: Woodland Hills

County: Los Angeles

Other trail users: Joggers, bicyclists, equestrians

Canine compatibility: Leashed dogs permitted

Trailhead facilities/amenities: Water, restrooms

Land status: Regional park

Fees and permits: Parking fee is charged

Schedule: Open year-round, 8 a.m. to sunset daily

Maps: USGS Malibu Beach, CA; www.lamountains.com/maps/redRock.pdf

Trail contacts: Red Rock Canyon Park, 23601 W. Red Rock Rd., Topanga 90290. Mountains Recreation & Conservation Authority, 570 West Avenue 26, Suite 100, Los Angeles 90065; (323) 221-9944. Santa Monica Mountains National Recreation Area, 401 W. Hillcrest Dr., Thousand Oaks 91360; www.lamountains.com/parks.asp?parkid=47; (805) 370-2301

Finding the trailhead: From the intersection of CA 134, US 101, and CA 170 in Los Angeles, take US 101 north and west for 13.4 miles. Take exit 27B for CA 27/ South Topanga Boulevard; turn right and drive for 1.6 miles. Turn right onto Mulholland Drive and drive for 0.5 mile. Turn left onto Mulholland Highway and drive for 1.7 miles. Turn left onto Old Topanga Canyon Road and drive for 1.6 miles. Turn right and stay on Old Topanga Canyon Road for another 1.8 miles. Turn right onto Red Rock Road. Stay on Red Rock Road for 0.8 mile and park in the parking area. GPS: N 34 6.3833'/W 118 38.1166'

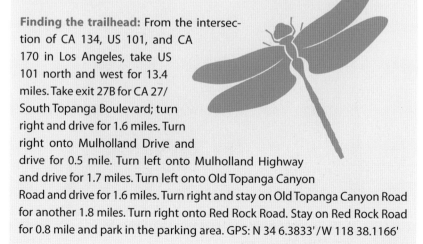

THE HIKE

ed Rock Canyon as a namesake is about as common as park appellations come. The park isn't even the only Red Rock Canyon in California, let alone the dozen or so that share the title in the western United States. Regardless, this is quite a nice little park with some colorful sandstone outcroppings. There are side trails that lead to more exploration within the park, but this route follows Red Rock Road to a T junction with the Calabasas Peak Motorway and climbs to the summit of Calabasas Peak.

At 2,165 feet, the peak is one of the tallest along the eastern end of the Santa Monica mountain chain. As such, the views are fairly spectacular. One can make out a teeny portion of the Pacific Ocean. On clear days, the San Fernando Valley is almost entirely within view, along with parts of Los Angeles. The tall peaks of

Some of the rock formations in Red Rock Canyon are quite stunning—and a little scary! Monique Riedel

Saddle and Temescal are nearby, so the summit of Calabasas isn't prominently situated to view the entire southland, but the views from on high are quite worthwhile, especially for the relative easiness of the hike itself.

From the parking area in Red Rock Canyon, follow the road past the restrooms and ranger residence into the canyon itself. After about 0.3 mile, a large, cave-filled, red rock formation appears on the left. This is a good place for a short side exploration, and a climb to the top reveals the entire canyon system and some good views to boot.

The route continues along the fire road, and the biggest problem with the hike is the unsightly aboveground wires that follow the roadway through the canyon. The road begins to climb and gains around 400 feet before reaching a bench high above the canyon. Here, an actual resting bench is placed at the overlook where the views aren't too bad.

Turn right and continue walking up Calabasas Peak Motorway toward the summit. The road travels through similar uplifted rocks that seem to jut from the earth as the route nears the peak. Once on top, the views of the surrounding countryside are fairly spectacular. Since this hike takes place in the valley, it is wise to go when temperatures are cooler; at those times the skies are clearer as well.

Enjoy the views and return via the same route.

MILES AND DIRECTIONS

0.0 From the parking area, head west down Red Rock Road.

1.2 Turn right at the T junction toward the summit of Calabasas Peak.

2.5 Arrive on the summit of Calabasas Peak. Return via the same route.

5.0 Arrive back at the trailhead and parking area.

HIKE INFORMATION

Local information: Conejo Open Space Conservation Agency (COSCA), City Hall / Civic Arts Plaza, 2100 Thousand Oaks Blvd., Thousand Oaks, (805) 449-2505; Ranger Headquarters, Old Meadows Center, 1600 Marview Dr., Thousand Oaks, (805) 381-2741; Conejo Recreation and Park District, 403 W. Hillcrest Dr., Thousand Oaks, (805) 495-6471; California State Parks, (818) 880-0363

Camping: Circle X Ranch Group Campground, (805) 370-2300; Leo Carrillo State Park campgrounds, Malibu Creek State Park, Topanga State Park Campground, Point Mugu State Park Campground, California State Park campgrounds reservations (800) 444-7275; customer service (800) 695-2269; www.reserveamerica.com

Local retailers: A-16 (Adventure 16), www.adventure16.com; REI, www.rei.com

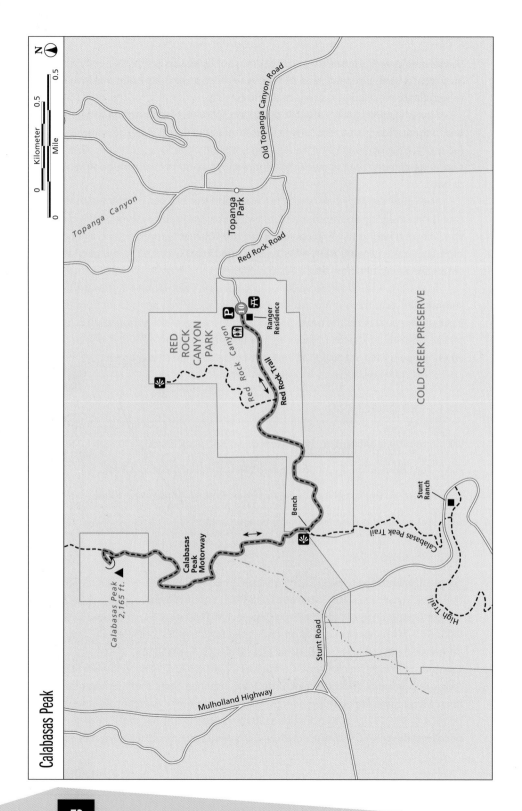

Calabasas Peak

Restaurants: Jack's Deli, 966 S. Westlake Blvd., Suite 2, Westlake Village, (805) 495-8181; Neptune's Net, 42505 Pacific Coast Hwy., Malibu, (310) 457-3095; Versailles, 17410 Ventura Blvd., Encino, (818) 906-0756; Moonshadows, 20356 Pacific Coast Hwy., Malibu, (310) 456-3010; Old Place Restaurant, 29983 Mulholland Hwy., Agoura Hills, (818) 706-9001; Inn of the Seventh Ray, 128 Old Topanga Canyon Rd., Topanga, (310) 455-1311

> *Much of the parkland in the Santa Monica Mountains National Recreation Area was donated by private individuals and movie stars.*

Volcanic rock at Red Rock Canyon Park. Monique Riedel

Temescal Gateway Park

Located in the heart of Pacific Palisades, a prestigious community also known as "Where the Mountains Meet the Sea," Temescal Gateway Park presents a prodigious opportunity to escape to what seems like a million miles from civilization—while remaining only minutes from the hustle and bustle of Los Angeles, Santa Monica, and Malibu.

Start: At the large parking area at the park entrance on Temescal Canyon Road

Distance: 3.25-mile lollipop

Hiking time: About 2 hours

Difficulty: Moderate

Trail surface: Dirt road, single-track dirt trail, and pavement

Nearest town: Pacific Palisades

County: Los Angeles

Other trail users: Joggers

Canine compatibility: Leashed dogs permitted (dogs not permitted in Topanga Canyon State Park)

Trailhead facilities/amenities: All facilities available

Land status: Regional park, California state park

Fees and permits: Parking fee is charged

Schedule: Open year-round, 7 a.m. to sunset

Maps: USGS Malibu Beach, CA; www.lamountains.com/maps/temescal.pdf

Trail contacts: Temescal Gateway Park, 15601 Sunset Blvd., Pacific Palisades 90272; (310) 454-1395. Mountains Recreation & Conservation Authority, 570 West Avenue 26, Suite 100, Los Angeles 90065; (323) 221-9944. Santa Monica Mountains National Recreation Area, 401 W. Hillcrest Dr., Thousand Oaks 91360; www.lamountains.com/parks.asp?parkid=58

Finding the trailhead: From the intersection of I-10 and the Pacific Coast Highway/CA 1, drive 3.2 miles north on Pacific Coast Highway. Turn right onto Temescal Canyon Road and drive for 1.1 miles to the parking area on the left. GPS: N 34 2.9833'/W 118 31.7333'

THE HIKE

What began as an enclave for intellectuals and luminaries, founded by Reverend Charles Scott in 1922 as part of the Chautauqua movement, has been transformed into one of the most popular destinations in the Santa Monica Mountains. The Chautauqua movement originated at Chautauqua Lake, New York, as a means to establish assemblies for families with stimulating topics concerning public issues, literature, art, science, and entertainment. This movement was highly popular in the early 1900s. In his desire to create one such community, Reverend Scott developed the area bounded by the Santa Monica Mountains and the Pacific coastline, which became known as Pacific Palisades.

Despite the fact that you may feel as if you are miles from civilization, there are a few reminders that you are still within the confines of the city. Be aware, while you are in the parking area, which has plenty of space to park, that there are traffic cameras at each stop sign. The self-parking iron ranger is conspicuously placed in the parking area and requires a fee that must be placed in an envelope

Enjoy this charming waterfall before finishing your hike. Monique Riedel

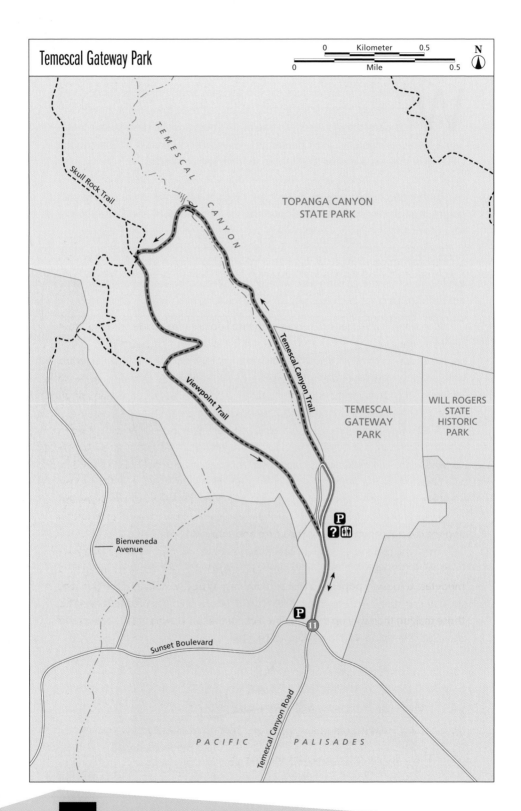

Temescal Gateway Park

0   Kilometer   0.5

0   Mile   0.5

N

TEMESCAL CANYON

Skull Rock Trail

TOPANGA CANYON
STATE PARK

Temescal Canyon Trail

Viewpoint Trail

TEMESCAL
GATEWAY
PARK

WILL ROGERS
STATE
HISTORIC
PARK

Bienveneda
Avenue

P
? ♿

P
11

Sunset Boulevard

Temescal Canyon Road

PACIFIC   PALISADES

and dropped into the receptacle. Make sure to display your receipt properly in your vehicle, as instructed on the envelope, to avoid any costly parking violations. Since this is a popular trail the parking regulations are strictly enforced by patrolling park rangers.

At the trailhead there are informational placards with historical information and photos of the original Methodist settlement founded by the Reverend Charles Scott. There is also a visitor center and a public restroom conveniently located at the onset of your journey. Aside from hiking, Temescal Gateway Park is host to a variety of activities, as well as home to several guest cabins and areas that may be reserved for private use.

The initial part of this trail is paved for a short bit, but don't be fooled: It quickly takes on the form of a traditional dirt road at 0.3 mile. Veer right at the intersection. Continue up the trail to the north, winding up a somewhat steep ridge along Temescal Canyon. Poison oak is abundant along this trail, so be cautious of your step and do not stray off the path.

Keep in mind that long stretches of the trail do not offer shade or respite from the heat. Bring plenty of water for hydration because the moderate ascent may seem extreme in hot weather. Once you have traversed the canyon ridge, through patches of dense foliage and open spaces, you will arrive at a charming waterfall and wooden footbridge. Boulders and strategically placed rocks are convenient for a tranquil interlude before forging on toward the next part of the trail.

After crossing the footbridge, the trail continues to ascend the other side of the canyon ridge, into a more dense area of vegetation lined with coastal chaparral, wildflowers, and, of course, poison oak. The trail continues to wind upward; at 1.7 miles veer left at the junction toward a windy plateau carpeted with profuse shrubbery. Here, you have reached the pinnacle of the trail. On a clear day you will be rewarded with magnificent 360-degree unimpeded views of the Pacific Ocean and the coastal communities to the north and south of Pacific Palisades.

From the plateau, the trail descends once again into dense foliage along the ridge of the canyon. Be mindful of trail etiquette during your descent as this is a moderate to heavily populated trail and others may be ascending. At this juncture the trail is, at times, narrow enough to require descending hikers to step aside for those making their way up the ridgeline. Follow the trail down past the cabins and the visitor center back to the parking area.

MILES AND DIRECTIONS

0.0 From the parking area, walk north up the paved road.

0.3 Turn right at the Y intersection to start the loop section of the hike.

0.5 The road meets the trail; continue north.

1.0 Enter Topanga Canyon State Park.

1.4 Arrive at the waterfall and footbridge.

1.6 Stay left at the trail junction.

1.7 Turn left at the trail junction.

2.7 Rejoin the paved road and walk south to the parking area.

3.25 Arrive back at the trailhead and parking area.

HIKE INFORMATION

Local information: California State Parks, (818) 880-0363; Santa Monica Mountains National Recreation Area, (805) 370-2301

Camping: Circle X Ranch Group Campground, (805) 370-2300; Leo Carrillo State Park campgrounds, Malibu Creek State Park, Topanga State Park Campground, Point Mugu State Park Campground, California State Park campgrounds reservations, (800) 444-7275/customer service (800) 695-2269; www.reserveamerica.com

Local retailers: A-16, www.adventure16.com; REI, www.rei.com

Restaurants: Neptune's Net, 42505 Pacific Coast Hwy., Malibu, (310) 457-3095; Bossa Nova, 10982 W. Pico Blvd., Los Angeles, (310) 441-0404; Moonshadows, 20356 Pacific Coast Hwy., Malibu, (310) 456-3010; Versailles, 10319 Venice Blvd., Los Angeles, (310) 558-3168; Old Place Restaurant, 29983 Mulholland Hwy., Agoura Hills, (818) 706-9001; Inn of the Seventh Ray, 128 Old Topanga Canyon Rd., Topanga, (310) 455-1311

Fitness Tip: Set realistic goals for trip times and try to maintain them.

Will Rogers State Historic Park

Will Rogers State Historic Park is the 186-acre ranch where the renowned Hollywood personality lived and pursued his passions. Visitors to the park can visit his ranch, a small museum, and take a hike around the property to the majestic sweeping view at Inspiration Point.

Start: At the large parking area on Will Rogers State Park Road
Distance: 2.25-mile lollipop
Hiking time: About 2 hours
Difficulty: Easy
Trail surface: Dirt road and single-track dirt trail
Nearest town: Pacific Palisades
County: Los Angeles
Other trail users: Joggers
Canine compatibility: Leashed dogs permitted
Trailhead facilities/amenities: All facilities available

Land status: California state park
Fees and permits: A parking fee is charged.
Schedule: Open year-round, 8 a.m. to sunset
Maps: USGS Topanga, CA; www.parks.ca.gov/pages/626/files/WillRogersPDF.pdf
Trail contact: Will Rogers State Historic Park, 1501 Will Rogers State Park Rd., Pacific Palisades 90272; www.parks.ca.gov/?page_id=626; (310) 454-8212

Finding the trailhead: From the intersection of I-10 and the Pacific Coast Highway / CA 1, drive 2.1 miles north on Pacific Coast Highway. Turn right onto Chautauqua Boulevard and drive for 0.9 mile. Turn right onto Sunset Boulevard and drive for 0.6 mile. Turn left onto Will Rogers State Park Road and drive for 0.6 mile to the large parking area. GPS: N 34 3.25' / W 118 30.7666'

From the parking lot follow the signs behind the visitor center or the old ranch house to the Inspiration Loop Trail. Turn left and begin hiking on the fire road/ trail that surrounds the property. The trail follows the dirt road through eucalyptus trees, and gently climbs as it begins to circle the property. Old photos describe the route from 1929, as it was designed for riding horses around the property.

The route climbs to a plateau and the views only get wider with each step. The trail meanders on its way toward Inspiration Point. At 1.1 miles take the short spur to the right that leads to the overlook. Here, visitors can survey the Los Angeles Basin from Long Beach and the entire Palos Verdes peninsula to blue Santa Monica Bay. Certainly, the view on a clear day is one of the more fetching in all of the Los Angeles area, especially for such a simple walk. The payoff is well worth the price of admission. Those new to hiking and children will undoubtedly enjoy the view and the mild trail.

From Inspiration Point, head back to the main trail and turn right, following the dirt road around and down and back to the visitor center and ranch house.

There are several exhibits in the park, and visitors can take a guided tour Tuesday through Sunday at 11 a.m., 1 p.m., and 2 p.m. On weekends, visitors can also watch the Will Rogers Polo Club on the only regulation-size polo field in Southern California.

Rabbits are ubiquitous along Southern California trails. Monique Riedel

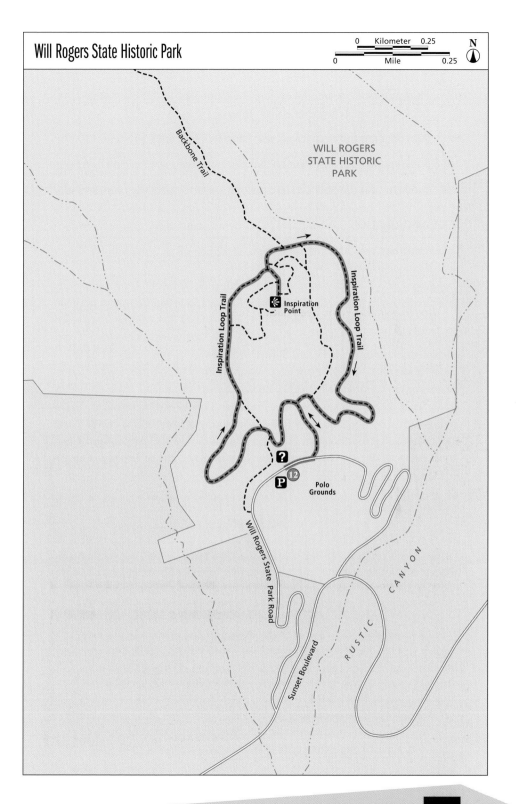

Will Rogers State Historic Park

MILES AND DIRECTIONS

0.0 From the parking area follow the trailhead sign to the Inspiration Loop behind the ranch house or visitor center.

0.1 Turn left onto the main Inspiration Loop Trail / fire road.

1.1 Turn right to reach Inspiration Point. Return to the main trail and turn right.

2.25 Arrive back at the trailhead and parking area in front of the polo grounds.

HIKE INFORMATION

Local information: California State Parks, (818) 880-0363; Santa Monica Mountains National Recreation Area, (805) 370-2301

Camping: Circle X Ranch Group Campground, (805) 370-2300; Leo Carrillo State Park campgrounds, Malibu Creek State Park, Topanga State Park Campground; Point Mugu State Park Campground, McGrath, California State Park campgrounds reservations (800) 444-7275; customer service (800) 695-2269; www.reserveamerica.com

Local organizations: Will Rogers State Historic Park Docents, (310)454-8212

Local retailers: A-16 (Adventure 16), www.adventure16.com; REI, www.rei.com

Restaurants: Neptune's Net, 42505 Pacific Coast Hwy., Malibu, (310) 457-3095; Bossa Nova, 10982 W. Pico Blvd., Los Angeles; (310) 441-0404; Versailles, 10319 Venice Blvd., Los Angeles, (310) 558-3168; Moonshadows, 20356 Pacific Coast Hwy., Malibu, (310) 456-3010; Old Place Restaurant, 29983 Mulholland Hwy., Agoura Hills, (818) 706-9001; Inn of the Seventh Ray, 128 Old Topanga Canyon Rd., Topanga, (310) 455-1311

Will Rogers

Will Rogers was born in 1879 in what is now Oklahoma on the Cherokee Nation. Rogers was a man of many talents, first gaining fame for his roping and cowboy skills. He became the most successful actor of his day, starring in seventy-one movies, some silent and some talking. He wrote books and more than 4,000 syndicated newspaper columns, and was known for his humor and wit.

He had the ability to connect with the common person, and his political humor was regarded fair to all sides of the political spectrum. People admired his philosophy, his morals and ethics, and his simple down-home wisdom. Rogers's quote, "I have never yet met a man that I didn't like," seemed to be the key to his success. He had the grand ability to make people feel uplifted. Will Rogers died in an airplane crash in 1935.

The property he owned with his wife, Betty, was donated to the State of California and became a state park when she passed away in 1944.

Franklin Canyon

Hike through the lovely shaded splendor of Franklin Canyon, the quieter and more peaceful alternative to Runyon Canyon. Franklin Canyon is one of the most popular filming parks in Los Angeles; movie and television buffs will undoubtedly recognize some of the more prominent spots.

Start: At the parking area on Franklin Canyon Drive
Distance: 3.5-mile double lollipop
Hiking time: About 2 hours
Difficulty: Easy
Trail surface: Dirt road and single-track dirt trail
Nearest town: Studio City
County: Los Angeles
Other trail users: Joggers
Canine compatibility: Leashed dogs permitted
Trailhead facilities/amenities: All facilities available

Land status: Regional park
Fees and permits: None
Schedule: Open year-round, sunrise to sunset
Maps: USGS Beverly Hills, CA; www.lamountains.com/maps/franklinCanyon.pdf
Trail contact: Franklin Canyon Park, 2600 Franklin Canyon Dr., Beverly Hills 90210; www.lamountains.com/parks.asp?parkid=14; (310) 858-7272

Finding the trailhead: From the intersection of CA 134, US 101, and CA 170 in Los Angeles, take US 101 north and west for 1.8 miles. Take exit 15 for Coldwater Canyon Avenue, turn left (south), and drive for 2.5 miles. At the intersection with Mulholland Drive, make a 90-degree right turn onto Franklin Canyon Drive (to the southwest). There is no sign for Franklin Canyon Drive; the sign says Road Closed 800 Feet. Park in the parking area. GPS: N 34 7.4833/W 118 24.5833

The reservoir at Franklin Canyon has famously been featured in many movies and television shows.

Franklin Canyon is the kind of park that families take their little ones to. Native Angelenos will want to bring out-of-state visitors here too, so that they can point out the famous pond from the opening of *The Andy Griffith Show* or the lagoon from *The Creature From the Black Lagoon*. It is a place for picnics, enjoying the scenery, taking in a few of the grand vistas down into Century City and over the Pacific Ocean (if the day is clear). Franklin Canyon isn't necessarily the place to get away from it all, but it is a huge swath of open land right next to Los Angeles and a pretty quick drive for most people living in the region.

The duck pond and reservoir are both fairly picturesque, and birders also flock to Franklin Canyon. The watering holes are both stops on the Pacific Flyway, so many migrating birds have layovers in Franklin Canyon. It is entirely possible to just laze around the pond and visitor center, which has some wonderful attractions and exhibits for children, but people who really want a hike can take one as well. The following loop is designed to get the maximum out of Franklin Canyon, taking in views, exploring the park, and getting some cardio in while doing it.

From the parking area, walk down Franklin Canyon Drive between Upper Franklin Reservoir and the Heavenly Pond. Follow the road as it continues down canyon, losing 250 feet in elevation toward the lower section of the park. The route is wooded and shaded for the most part, making this a peaceful stroll.

Franklin Canyon Drive splits at a Y intersection at 0.75 mile. Take the left fork and continue down Lake Drive. At around 1 mile, the Hastain Trail branches to the

Springtime brings wildflowers and bees. Allen Riedel

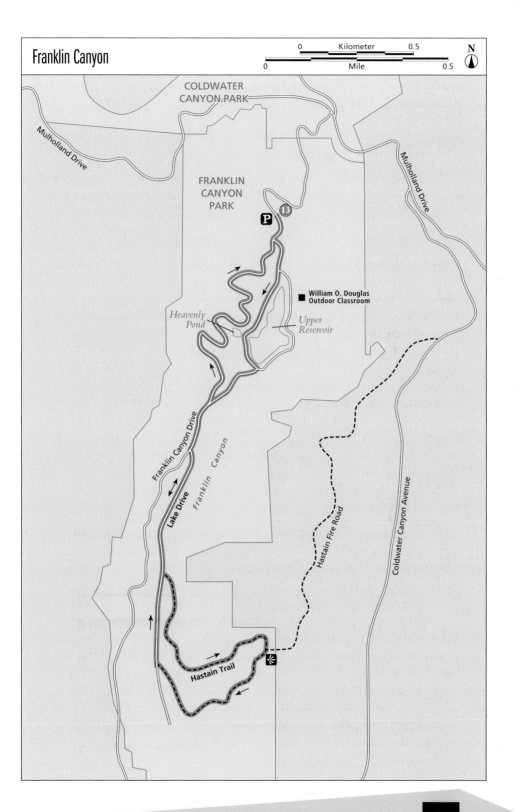

Franklin Canyon

left; take it and follow it as it loops around to a pretty viewpoint at 1.75 miles, looking down into Beverly Hills. The viewpoint sits right at the junction with the Hastain Fire Road, which climbs steeply to the left. Continue along the Hastain Trail to the right, and rejoin Lake Drive at 2.1 miles. Follow the road back to the intersection with Franklin Canyon Drive and take the trail on the left at 2.8 miles, which leads above the Heavenly Pond. Follow this trail for 0.7 mile back to Franklin Canyon Drive and the parking area.

MILES AND DIRECTIONS

0.0 Start by heading south down Franklin Canyon Drive.

0.75 Turn left down Lake Drive.

1.0 Turn left onto the Hastain Trail.

1.75 Intersect with the Hastain Fire Road at the viewpoint. Continue right along the Hastain Trail.

2.1 Turn right and rejoin Lake Drive.

2.35 Complete the southern loop. Continue north on Lake Drive, then Franklin Canyon Drive.

2.8 Take the trail branch on the left above Heavenly Pond.

3.5 Return to Franklin Canyon Drive, and arrive back at the trailhead and the parking area.

HIKE INFORMATION

Local information: California State Parks, (818) 880-0363; Santa Monica Mountains National Recreation Area, (805) 370-2301

Camping: Circle X Ranch Group Campground, (805) 370-2300; Leo Carrillo State Park campgrounds, Malibu Creek State Park, Topanga State Park Campground, Point Mugu State Park Campground, California State Park campgrounds reservations (800) 444-7275; customer service (800) 695-2269; www.reserveamerica.com

Local retailers: A-16 (Adventure 16), www.adventure16.com; REI, www.rei.com

Restaurants: Bossa Nova, 685 N. Robertson Blvd., West Hollywood, (310) 657-5070, or 7181 Sunset Blvd., Los Angeles, (323) 436-7999; Versailles, 1415 S. La Cienaga, Los Angeles, (310) 289-0392; Swingers, 8020 Beverly Blvd., Los Angeles, (323) 653-5858; Kings Road Cafe, 8361 Beverly Blvd., Los Angeles, (323) 655-9044; Toi, 7505½ W. Sunset Blvd., Los Angeles, (323) 874-8062; Canter's Deli, 419 N. Fairfax Ave., Los Angeles, (323) 651-2030

Wilacre Park

Wilacre Park is a wonderful slice of nature with open air views of the San Fernando Valley. It is a great place to get out into the outdoors with family or just to get a bit of exercise.

Start: At the parking area on Fryman Road
Distance: 1.8-mile lollipop
Hiking time: About 1.5 hours
Difficulty: Easy
Trail surface: Dirt road, paved road, and singletrack dirt trail
Nearest town: Studio City
County: Los Angeles
Other trail users: Joggers and equestrians
Canine compatibility: Leashed dogs permitted
Trailhead facilities/amenities: All facilities available

Land status: Regional park
Fees and permits: Parking fee is charged
Schedule: Open year-round, sunrise to sunset
Maps: USGS Van Nuys, CA; www.lamountains.com/maps/wilacre.pdf
Trail contacts: Santa Monica Mountains Conservancy, (310) 589-3200. Franklin Canyon Park, 2600 Franklin Canyon Dr., Beverly Hills 90210; www.lamountains .com/parks.asp?parkid=66

Finding the trailhead: From the intersection of CA 134, US 101, and CA 170 in Los Angeles, take US 101 north and west for 0.7 mile. Take exit 14 for Laurel Canyon Boulevard. Turn left (south) onto Laurel Canyon and drive for 1.5 miles. Turn right (west) onto Fryman Road. The parking lot is on the right. GPS: N 34 8.0166' / W 118 23.5'

Wilacre Park is fairly popular despite the recently raised parking fees, and it's just a great place to get out, stretch your legs, and take an urban hike. The best time to hike in Wilacre Park is during the winter months when views are clear and the air is crisp. Summer is not such a good time, due to smog and heat, but mornings and evenings are generally pleasant even during the hotter months.

The trail is composed of asphalt and dirt, and like the four other parks connected by Mulholland Drive, it is a simple yet powerful example of conservation within an urban area sorely in need of open space and outdoor recreation. It is possible to connect to all four parks (Wilacre, Coldwater Canyon, Fryman Canyon, and Franklin Canyon) along trails without being mindful of borders. This trail, however, takes the popular route up the Betty B. Dearing Trail and returns to the parking area along the U-Vanu Trail.

There will be lots of people along the trail; they will have their dogs and cell phones. Some people will be running and jogging, but overall, the park does not feel crowded. Surprisingly, it is quite peaceful and free from the noise of the city. Hikers can take a variety of trails and string together a long exercise routine or a

This wild phlox is one of the many fine examples of lovely wildflowers and photographic opportunities in the Santa Monica Mountains. **Allen Riedel**

simple short jaunt. The best reasons to hike here are because the park is close, it is good for families, and it is good for exercise.

From the parking area, walk through the gated entrance to the Betty B. Dearing Trail. Follow it up the hill to a viewpoint 0.75 mile from the entrance. The trail climbs 300 feet for wonderful clear-air views of the surrounding cityscape. At 1 mile turn left and take the dirt path of the U-Vanu Trail, following it back down to the junction with the Betty B. Dearing Trail. Turn right and continue back to the parking area.

MILES AND DIRECTIONS

0.0   Start by heading west through the gated entrance to the Betty B. Dearing Trail.

0.15 At a Y intersection take the right fork to walk the north side of a small loop around a picnic area.

0.2   At a four-way intersection stay to the right.

0.3   At a four-way intersection continue straight west on the Betty B. Dearing Trail.

0.45 Pass the U-Vanu Trail on the right.

0.75 Reach a viewpoint of the San Fernando Valley.

1.0   Make a sharp hairpin turn to the left and return on the U-Vanu Trail. 1.4 Turn right (south).

1.5   At the next three intersections, stay to the right.

1.65 Complete the loop and stay to the right.

1.8   Arrive back at the trailhead and parking area.

HIKE INFORMATION

Local information: Conejo Open Space Conservation Agency (COSCA), City Hall/Civic Arts Plaza, 2100 Thousand Oaks Blvd., Thousand Oaks, (805) 449-2505; Ranger Headquarters, Old Meadows Center, 1600 Marview Dr., Thousand Oaks, (805) 381-2741; Conejo Recreation and Park District, 403 W. Hillcrest Dr., Thousand Oaks, (805) 495-6471; California State Parks, (818) 880-0363

Camping: Circle X Ranch Group Campground, (805) 370-2300; Leo Carrillo State Park campgrounds, Malibu Creek State Park, Topanga State Park Campground, Point Mugu State Park Campground, California State Park campgrounds reserva-

Wilacre Park

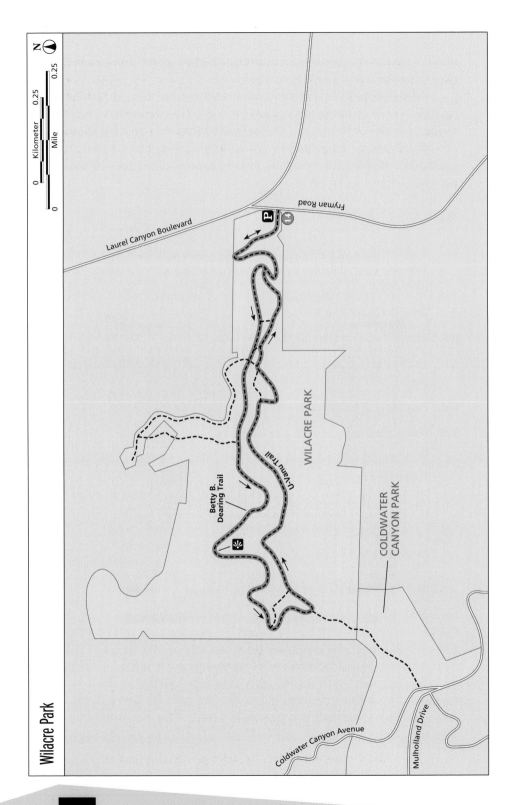

Betty B.
Dearing Trail

U-Vanu Trail

WILACRE PARK

COLDWATER
CANYON PARK

Laurel Canyon Boulevard

Fryman Road

Coldwater Canyon Avenue

Mulholland Drive

N

Kilometer
0   0.25

Mile
0   0.25

tions (800) 444-7275; customer service (800) 695-2269; www.reserveamerica.com

Local retailers: A-16 (Adventure 16), www.adventure16.com; REI, www.rei.com

Restaurants: Bossa Nova, 685 N. Robertson Blvd., West Hollywood, (310) 657-5070, or 7181 Sunset Blvd., Los Angeles, (323) 436-7999; Versailles, 1415 S. La Cienaga, Los Angeles, (310) 289-0392; Swingers, 8020 Beverly Blvd., Los Angeles, (323) 653-5858; Kings Road Cafe, 8361 Beverly Blvd., Los Angeles, (323) 655-9044; Toi, 7505½ W. Sunset Blvd., Los Angeles, (323) 874-8062; Canter's Deli, 419 N. Fairfax Ave., Los Angeles, (323) 651-2030

Hiking Tip: Getting out on shorter trails more often builds stamina for longer, more difficult trails.

Snow plants are not really plants at all, but fungi— they are red because they lack chlorophyll. Allen Riedel

Runyon Canyon

Though not very wilderness-like and full of people and dogs, this is the quintessential Los Angeles urban hike, and there are no two ways about it. Hike here for networking, fitness, to walk a dog, just to get outside, to take in some pretty darned good views, or to simply witness the freak show if you are so inclined.

Start: At the parking area just off Mulholland Drive

Distance: 2.5-mile loop

Hiking time: About 1.5 hours

Difficulty: Easy

Trail surface: Dirt road, paved road, and singletrack dirt trail

Nearest town: Hollywood

County: Los Angeles

Other trail users: Joggers, equestrians, bicyclists

Canine compatibility: Dogs permitted off-leash

Trailhead facilities/amenities: None

Land status: Los Angeles city park

Fees and Permits: None

Schedule: Open year-round, sunrise to sunset

Maps: USGS Hollywood, CA; www.ci.la.ca.us/rap/dos/parks/facility/runyonCanyonPk.htm

Trail contacts: Runyon Canyon Park, 2000 N. Fuller Ave., Los Angeles 90046; www.laparks.org/dos/parks/facility/runyonCanyonPk.htm; (323) 666-5046. Santa Monica Mountains Conservancy, www.lamountains.com/parks.asp?parkid=122, (213) 485-5572

Finding the trailhead: From the intersection of I-10, I-5, and US 101, take the 101 freeway north for 8.6 miles. Take exit 11A toward Barham Boulevard. Merge onto Cahuenga Boulevard east, drive 0.1 mile, and turn right onto Lakeridge Place. Turn right onto the overpass toward Mulholland Drive and drive over the 101 freeway. Turn left onto Mulholland Drive and drive for 1.5 miles to the parking area for Runyon Canyon Park.
GPS: N 34 7.1666' / W 118 21.1833'

THE HIKE

Without a doubt, Runyon Canyon is not the greatest hiking destination in Los Angeles—not even close. Runyon Canyon is the place where it seems nearly everyone who wanted to go for a walk in Los Angeles decided to go, and they brought their dog along too. Now, if you are a dog or have a dog, Runyon Canyon is the place to be—there are a multitude of off-leash areas, and even those areas that aren't so designated are effectively nonleash zones as well. There are dogs everywhere; this place is a great bet for dog owners, for sure. Hikers might even run into a famous dog or two . . . or three or four. Yes, the reason to go to Runyon Canyon is to see what Los Angeles is all about.

People who are working on their resumes and/or their acting chops are walking here. People who are writing their first, second, and third blockbusters all spend some time on the trail. The cast of *Friends,* before they were the cast of *Friends,* probably spent time walking up and down Runyon Canyon. When waiters and bus boys get a break from the action, they all seem to head to Runyon Canyon.

Now, with that said and all Hollywood jokes aside, the canyon is a pretty decent place to hike. A fantastic cardio workout can be had for sure, there are some really nice vista points, especially on clear days, and there are a lot of people. People-watching in the park is second nature—or maybe first nature. The trail is really close to the city and it is fairly easy to get to for a whole lot of people, which

Views from Runyon Canyon include the Hollywood landscape. Michael Millenheft III

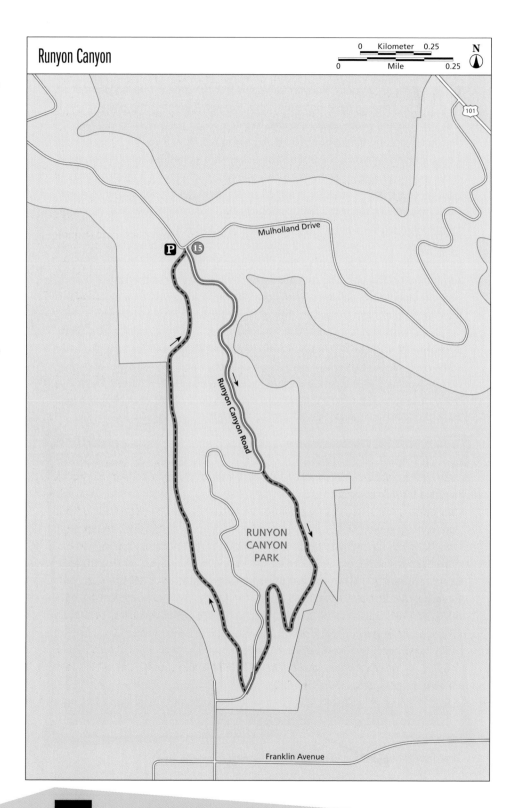

Runyon Canyon

Mulholland Drive

P 15

Runyon Canyon Road

RUNYON
CANYON
PARK

Franklin Avenue

is another reason for the crowds. There are also some very cool Hollywood homes, some right on the trail. While a multitude of routes can be taken in the park, this path showcases the best.

From Mulholland Drive, take the path on the left that heads down into Runyon Canyon. Follow the road for 0.6 mile to a high promontory. The road continues down on the right, and the trail continues straight, veering left ahead. Follow the trail. The route passes above some old ruins and a tennis court, and then leads right by them. The way gets a little confusing at the bottom, and there are a multitude of trails and roads. Turn left at the bottom of the hill to get back onto Runyon Canyon Road, and head for the ridgeline to the west. When the road intersects a dirt trail leading upward, take it. This path has the best views and leads back up to Mulholland Drive.

MILES AND DIRECTIONS

0.0 Start down Runyon Canyon Road toward the city.

0.6 Take the dirt path that continues straight and to the left.

1.3 Turn left onto Runyon Canyon Road and head for the ridgeline. Turn right onto a dirt trail.

2.5 Arrive back at the trailhead and parking area.

HIKE INFORMATION

Local information: California State Parks, (818) 880-0363; Santa Monica Mountains National Recreation Area, (805) 370-2301

Camping: Circle X Ranch Group Campground, (805) 370-2300; Leo Carrillo State Park campgrounds, Malibu Creek State Park, Topanga State Park Campground, Point Mugu State Park Campground, California State Park campgrounds reservations (800) 444-7275; customer service (800) 695-2269; www.reserveamerica.com

Local retailers: A-16 (Adventure 16), www.adventure16.com; REI, www.rei.com

Restaurants: Bossa Nova, 685 N. Robertson Blvd., West Hollywood, (310) 657-5070, or 7181 Sunset Blvd., Los Angeles, (323) 436-7999; Versailles, 1415 S. La Cienaga, Los Angeles, (310) 289-0392; Swingers, 8020 Beverly Blvd., Los Angeles; (323) 653-5858; Kings Road Cafe, 8361 Beverly Blvd., Los Angeles, (323) 655-9044; Toi, 7505½ W. Sunset Blvd., Los Angeles, (323) 874-8062; Canter's Deli, 419 N. Fairfax Ave., Los Angeles, (323) 651-2030

This hike highlights some magical Hollywood hotspots, from the Griffith Observatory to the views from Mount Hollywood to an overlook that takes hikers to the back of the Hollywood sign atop Mount Lee. There is something for everyone on this trip.

Start: Griffith Observatory
Distance: 8-mile lollipop
Hiking time: About 3.5 hours
Difficulty: Moderate
Trail surface: Dirt road, paved road, and singletrack dirt trail
Nearest town: Hollywood
County: Los Angeles
Other trail users: Joggers, equestrians, and bicyclists
Canine compatibility: Leashed dogs permitted
Trailhead facilities/amenities: All facilities available

Land status: Los Angeles city park
Fees and Permits: None
Schedule: Open year-round, sunrise to sunset
Maps: USGS Hollywood, CA; www.latrails.com/hike/gp.html
Trail contact: Griffith Park; 4730 Crystal Springs Dr., Los Angeles 90027; www.laparks.org/dos/parks/griffithPK/gp_location.htm; (323) 913-4688

Finding the trailhead: From the intersection of I-10, I-5, and US 101, take I-5 north for 5.8 miles. Take exit 141A for Los Feliz Boulevard and turn left (west). Drive for 1.3 miles on Los Feliz Boulevard. Turn right onto Hillhurst Avenue and drive for 0.2 mile. Turn right onto Vermont Canyon Road and drive for 1.1 miles. Stay to the right (straight) onto Mount Hollywood Drive and drive through the tunnel. The road becomes Observatory Avenue. Follow it 0.3 mile to the parking lot for the Griffith Observatory. GPS: N 34 7.1333' / W 118 18.0333'

THE HIKE

Hiking within Griffith Park is not as easy as it seems. There are trails galore, and some of them are incredibly steep and hot. The finest seasons to hike here are from fall to spring. It is best to avoid the summertime for two reasons: The heat can be oppressive and the smog makes visibility very poor. With that said, visitors should realize that the sun is present year-round, and anyone attempting this hike should be duly prepared with sunblock and water. This isn't an easy leg stretcher to take the kids on. This hike gains 1,400 feet of elevation on three separate uphill climbs, and hiking 8 miles round-trip is nothing to shake a stick at. Part of the trip is on pavement, making it a little bit tougher on the feet and knees than dirt roads or trails alone.

Visitors with children wishing only to climb Mount Hollywood (not the trip to the Hollywood sign) north of the observatory can do so, and children will more than likely enjoy the trip up and back. The observatory has been redesigned and

The iconic Hollywood Sign can be seen up close, but not touched.
Monique Riedel

Griffith Park

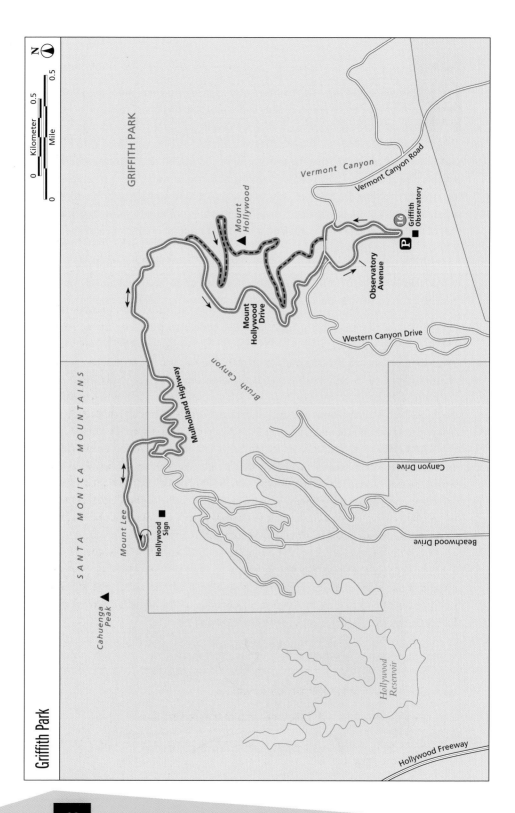

the revamped features are intriguing to both young and old. Take a visit to the observatory first, then start hiking north along the road.

Where the main parking lot ends, there is a curb with an obvious wide trail heading straight north as it parallels Observatory Avenue. Head north, and after about 0.3 mile the trail crosses a concrete overpass. Continue along the main path and ignore all of the smaller side routes. These trails will get to the summit faster, but are steep in spots and lead to erosion.

The trail winds westward, and views of Mount Lee and the Hollywood sign open up. It hairpins back to the east and begins working its way steeply up the slope. At 1.1 miles the path splits in three directions; take the far left fork and wrap around the backside of Mount Hollywood, following the graded road/trail beyond a water tower. Turn right, ascend the final push to the summit, and take in a grand vista of the Los Angeles Basin, the San Gabriel Mountains and valley, and the Hollywood sign.

At this point, the route gets a little convoluted. Head back down the main trail, which is the farthest road on the right. Pass an intersection and come immediately to a four-way intersection where trails lead off in the cardinal directions. Turn west along the roadway/trail. Follow the road as it turns and hairpins and meets up with Mount Hollywood Drive. Turn right at the Y intersection at 2.25 miles. At 2.5 miles, the trail meets another Y intersection; veer left off the pavement and onto the dirt road/trail. This is Mulholland Highway. In 0.25 mile there is another Y intersection; head right and continue upward toward the antennae atop Mount Lee.

At 3.25 miles, the trail meets yet another Y intersection. This time veer right and continue along Mulholland Highway. The last intersection is at 3.7 miles, where the dirt road reaches a T junction with Mount Lee Drive. Turn right and follow the roadway up steeply behind the Hollywood sign. The famous letters cannot be touched or even walked up to, but visitors can catch a glimpse from behind a chain-link fence protected by electronic security and cameras.

Enjoy the views of the sign, the Los Angeles Basin, and the Hollywood Reservoir, and then turn around and follow the road back to Mount Hollywood Drive. Instead of taking more ups and downs by returning along the same route, stay on the road until it intersects with Observatory Avenue at the tunnel. Turn right and follow Observatory Avenue back to the observatory.

MILES AND DIRECTIONS

0.0   Start north from the Griffith Observatory.

0.2   Head up the trail at the northern end of the parking area.

0.3   Cross over Mount Hollywood Drive on a concrete overpass. Stay on the main road/trail.

1.1   Take the far left fork around the back of Mount Hollywood.

1.2   Turn right and ascend the summit of Mount Hollywood. Head back down the large road on the right.

1.3   At the four-way intersection, head west along a fire road.

2.25   Turn right onto Mount Hollywood Drive.

2.5   Turn left onto the dirt road/trail (Mulholland Highway).

2.75   Stay right at the Y intersection to continue on Mulholland Highway.

3.25   Veer right at the Y intersection to continue on Mulholland Highway.

3.7   Turn right onto paved Mount Lee Drive.

4.5   Arrive behind the Hollywood sign atop Mount Lee. Return via Mulholland Highway.

6.5   Turn right onto Mount Hollywood Drive. Follow it to Observatory Avenue.

7.5   Turn right and follow Observatory Avenue back to the observatory and parking area.

8.0   Arrive back at the observatory trailhead and parking area.

HIKE INFORMATION

Local information: City of Los Angeles Department of Parks and Recreation, 221 N. Figueroa St., Suite 1550, Los Angeles, (213) 202-2633; Griffith Observatory, 2800 East Observatory Rd., Los Angeles, (213) 473-0800

Camping: Malibu Creek State Park, Topanga State Park Campground, California State Park campgrounds reservations, (800) 444-7275 / customer service (800) 695-2269; www.reserveamerica.com.

Local retailers: A-16 (Adventure 16), www.adventure16.com; REI, www.rei.com

Restaurants: Bossa Nova, 685 N. Robertson Blvd., West Hollywood, (310) 657-5070, or 7181 Sunset Blvd., Los Angeles, (323) 436-7999; Versailles, 1415 S. La Cienaga, Los Angeles, (310) 289-0392; Swingers, 8020 Beverly Blvd., Los Angeles; (323) 653-5858; Kings Road Cafe, 8361 Beverly Blvd., Los Angeles, (323) 655-9044; Toi, 7505½ W. Sunset Blvd., Los Angeles, (323) 874-8062; Canter's Deli, 419 N. Fairfax Ave., Los Angeles, (323) 651-2030

Griffith J. Griffith

Industrialist, philanthropist, city father, and convicted felon, Griffith J. Griffith was born in Wales in 1850. He immigrated to the United States at the age of fifteen. In the 1870s he worked for the California newspaper, *Alta California,* as a mining correspondent. From this job he learned the ins and outs of mining and succeeded in making a fortune with mines in Mexico.

He moved to Los Angeles in 1882 as a very wealthy man. He used some of his fortune to acquire the good majority of the Rancho Los Feliz Mexican land grant, purchasing two-thirds of the original land, and then donating over 3,000 acres to the City of Los Angeles so that an urban park could be built in the same vein as New York's Central Park. When Griffith donated the original 3,015 acres to the city in 1896, it was the largest city park in the world. His plans included building an observatory and science center. He called the donation a "Christmas present" and wanted it to be a place of serenity where the people of Los Angeles could relax and enjoy the outdoors.

The city passed an ordinance to name the park after its donor. Further plans for Griffith Park were placed on hold when he was convicted of shooting his wife in the face at the Arcadia Hotel. As the story goes, he handed her a prayer book and pulled out a revolver. Christina Griffith then threw herself out of a window, landed on an awning, and reentered the hotel through a window. She was disfigured and blind from the incident.

The sensational trial that followed found Griffith's defense being insanity by reason of alcohol. He was found guilty of assault with a deadly weapon and sent to San Quentin for two years, where his behavior was said to be exemplary. He returned to Los Angeles and lived out his remaining years trying desperately to remake his image in the mind of Angelenos. He was unable to do so. The city would not take his money, due to his notoriety, to improve the park that bore his name. In death, however, he bequeathed most of his wealth to the city, which funded the construction of the Griffith Observatory and the Greek Theater.

Drink plenty of water while hiking—
take a drink every fifteen minutes.

Honorable Mentions

A. Satwiwa/Rancho Sierra Vista

Satwiwa/Rancho Sierra Vista is a lovely parcel of land on the western end of the Santa Monica Mountains at the border of the national park lands, situated on the eastern escarpment of the range. The land had been used by the native Chumash peoples for as long as 10,000 years. With the arrival of the Spanish, their missions, and land grants, this portion of Southern California became the sprawling Rancho El Conejo. The surrounding area is still rather pastoral, though subdivisions and strip malls have cropped up nearby over the past forty years. The park contains a couple of waterfalls and a natural center complete with a Native American demonstration area where a Native American docent/park ranger is available for presentations and questions on Saturday and Sunday from 9 a.m. to 5 p.m. Art shows and interactive exhibits will fascinate the historically curious and children of all ages. Several hikes can be taken through the lovely little park. Wildlife seems to abound here, especially early in the morning. The park can literally feel like the land that was forgotten by time. Enjoy the loop trail or take a walk to the waterfall. Bring the family, all are certain to enjoy Satwiwa/Rancho Sierra Vista. Satwiwa/Rancho Sierra Vista is located off Lynn Road between Thousand Oaks and Malibu. Many hikes from very short to epically long can be taken on the parks' multitude of trails or connect with the larger Point Mugu State Park.

B. Solstice Canyon

Solstice Canyon is a very popular coastal park right in the middle of the Santa Monica Mountains. Multitudes of visitors come to the canyon to hike, exercise, and get out into nature with friends. There certainly is splendor here, even though the canyon has been repeatedly stricken by fire, evidence of which can be seen all around. There are some easy trails, like the one leading up to the ruins of the Roberts' Ranch House, built in 1952. Paul Williams, the famous African-American architect, designed the ranch house, which was burnt to the ground in the Dayton Canyon Fire of 1982. The Roberts family called their dream house Tropical Terrace, and even from the ruins, it is easy to see how lovely a structure this was. Behind the house sits a charming little waterfall, and despite its diminutive stature, it is absolutely one of the most beautiful falls in all of Southern California. The park also has its share of harder trails that can be used for trail running and exercise, such as the Rising Sun Trail. Getting off of the main path will, without a doubt, decrease the number of people that you will see, but it will also greatly increase exposure to the midday sun. The canyon itself is lovely and lush, filled with a beautiful riparian habitat and a wonderful trickling stream. Solstice Canyon is located just east of Point Dume in central Malibu up Corral Canyon Road; the hike to Roberts' Ranch is an easy 3-mile out-and-back trip.

Angeles National Forest

The Angeles National Forest is a beautiful and rugged range filled with fantastic vistas and lush forests.
Allen Riedel

The Angeles National Forest stretches from the Newhall Pass in the west to San Bernardino County in the east, covering over 650,000 acres with over 800 miles of hiking trails. The San Gabriel Mountains continue into the Cajon Pass and to I-15. The mountain range comprises two sets of mountains, a taller northern range and the front range, which looms high above the Los Angeles metro area. Since 1956, the 66-mile-long Angeles Crest Highway / CA 2 has bisected a path nearly straight through the mountains from west to east, from La Canada Flintridge to Wrightwood. Construction began in 1929, and from that date, travelers and

> Absolute treasures, especially the preponderance of waterfalls along the front range...

visitors were able to more easily flock to the higher regions of the forest. Due to its proximity to Los Angeles, the forest is one of the most heavily visited in the nation.

Historically, the front range was quite the hiking destination for those living in Los Angeles and in the Los Angeles metro area. Resorts flourished in the front range from the late 1800s to the 1930s, the remains of which can still be explored. Cabins cropped up along popular streams and rivers. Even naturalist and conservation hero John Muir tried his hand at hiking in the San Gabriels, calling the spiky chaparral and steep slopes " . . . Most ruggedly, thornily savage. Not even in the Sierra have I ever made the acquaintance of mountains more rigidly inaccessible." After the construction of the Angeles Crest Highway, the lower reaches lost their favor and their trappings of remoteness, though many of these areas are absolute treasures today, especially the preponderance of waterfalls along the front range.

The back range is known for its lofty heights and peaks above 9,000 feet, including Mount Baldy (also known as Mount San Antonio—the highest peak in the forest at 10,046 feet), Mount Dawson, Pine Mountain, Mount Baden-Powell, and Throop Peak. The views of the Los Angeles Basin and the high deserts are unmatched, and hiking in the high mountains can be a mystical and religious experience. There are numerous peaks above 8,000 feet, and most of the summits require little more than walking skills during the spring, summer, and fall months. However, the range can be very dangerous in winter, and the foolhardy and unprepared often underestimate the high country's potential for disaster. Unprepared hikers go missing in the winter almost every year. Higher elevations are not to be trifled with in bad weather conditions, and the inexperienced should descend at the slightest hint of severe weather and danger. Caution should always remain the better part of safety when hiking in these parts.

The San Gabriel Mountains were named for the river of the same name that flows out of the mountains 75 miles to the Pacific Ocean. The Angeles Crest Highway enters the mountains in La Canada Flintridge just north and west of Pasadena and divides the mountains in half, exiting onto CA 138 near I-15 in the high desert. Ample opportunity for outdoor activity exists along the highway. The hikes in this book only sample the lower country close to Pasadena, but no matter the destination, wild adventure awaits.

Local organizations: San Gabriel Mountains Trailbuilders, (626) 792-4573; San Gabriel Mountains Regional Conservancy, (626) 335-1771; Jet Propulsion Laboratory Hiking Club, (818) 354-2816; The Children's Nature Institute, (310) 860-9484; California Native Plant Society, (818) 348-5910; Concerned Off-Road Bicyclists Association, (818) 206-8213; Los Angeles Audubon Society, (323) 876-0202; The Nature of Wildworks, (310) 455-0550; Sierra Club, (213) 387-4287; Pasadena Audubon Society, (626) 355-9412

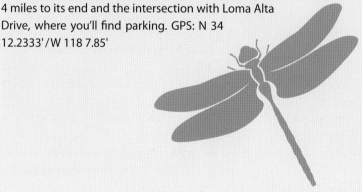

Echo Mountain

Experience vistas of the Los Angeles metro area while ascending to the ruins of a historic Victorian chalet, and follow the trail of the only scenic mountain electric traction railroad ever built in the United States.

Start: At the corner of Lake Avenue and Loma Alta Drive

Distance: 5 miles out and back

Hiking time: About 3 hours

Difficulty: Moderate

Trail surface: Dirt road and single-track dirt trail

Nearest town: Altadena

County: Los Angeles

Other trail users: Joggers, equestrians, bicyclists

Canine compatibility: Leashed dogs permitted

Trailhead facilities/amenities: Picnic tables atop Echo Mountain

Land status: National forest

Fees and Permits: None

Schedule: Open year-round

Maps: USGS Mount Wilson, CA; www.mtlowe.net/MtLowe Trail.htm

Trail contact: Angeles National Forest, 701 N. Santa Anita Ave., Arcadia 91006; www.fs.fed.us/r5/angeles; (626) 574-5200

Finding the trailhead: From the intersection of I-10, I-5, and US 101, take I-5 north for 1.1 miles. Take exit 137B to merge onto CA 110/Pasadena Freeway north. Drive for 6.6 miles to the end of the Pasadena Freeway. Continue north on Arroyo Parkway for 1.3 miles. Turn right onto Colorado Boulevard and drive for 0.9 mile. Turn left onto Lake Avenue and drive 4 miles to its end and the intersection with Loma Alta Drive, where you'll find parking. GPS: N 34 12.2333'/W 118 7.85'

THE HIKE

You will begin your expedition through a stone gateway at the top of Lake Avenue. It seems apropos to begin the journey through this seemingly otherworldly gateway of ancient stones. Follow the trail east about 0.2 mi toward the Sam Merrill Trail. Follow the Sam Merrill Trail, which descends into a creek bed. After this short descent, the trail quickly begins the ascent up the eastern ridge of the Los Flores Canyon. The trail is well maintained and relatively wide at most points early in the hike. As you make your ascent, you will be rewarded with breathtaking views of the Los Angeles metro area.

This is a relatively popular trail so prepare to come upon other visitors making the trek. This pet-friendly trail hosts many travelers with leashed dogs. The trail is lined with various local foliage and chaparral, and it's home to an array of fauna.

As you reach the summit, the trail begins to narrow and become rockier for a short length of time. About 0.5 mile after you passed the 2-mile marker, you will see the rail bed of the Mount Lowe Railway. This was the historic rail line established by Professor Thaddeus S. C. Lowe on July 4, 1893, the third scenic railroad of its kind to be established in the United States.

Variable checkerspot. Allen Riedel

Whether you believe in ghosts or not, you will feel the awe of the grand panoramic view at the remaining concrete stairs and slab of the Echo Mountain House, or White City ruins. The resort at the summit was aptly referred to as the "White City" because all of the buildings and even the railcars were referred to as the "white chariots." This provided a stark contrast to the hillside, such that any passerby could see the tiny white railcars climbing the mountainside from miles away.

The summit provides various opportunities to appreciate grand vistas of the Los Angeles metro area, the ruins, and the landscape of Echo Mountain. During its heyday, the Echo Mountain House provided its visitors with "echo phones," with which to bellow through toward the "sweet spot" in the canyon that can resonate a sound up to nine times. Take time to wander through the ruins of the old resort, which included a zoo, an observatory, and a tavern. Scattered throughout the site are placards and informational postings about the historic site, which is on the National Register of Historic Places.

Echo Mountain—the White City and the Mount Lowe Railway

The Mount Lowe Railway was created as a tourist attraction by Thaddeus Lowe, a man of some fame and fortune in the Pasadena area, and David MacPherson, a civil engineer. The two spoke of Lowe's vision of a railcar leading up to the crest of the San Gabriel Mountains, and began making plans for the railway. They hiked and fished in the region, enjoyed the spectacular waterfalls, and finally developed Southern California's most visited landmark, opening the railway on July 4, 1893.

The railway led a half mile up through the "Great Incline" of Rubio Canyon to Echo Mountain, where two hotels, a zoo, an observatory, and a casino awaited passengers. Riders could go farther, to the top of Mount Lowe and on to Inspiration Point, where travelers were dazzled by the lights of the city and the mountain views from on high. Here, visitors could stay at the Alpine Tavern and enjoy the majesty of the Mount Lowe Railway.

While Lowe's vision sounds fantastic, the reality is that he went broke funding it. He couldn't pay back the debt that he owed on the railway's construction, and despite its popularity he lost the railroad in just under seven years. Other owners came and went, and so did the buildings and eventually the railway itself. All were lost to fire, winds, rains, storms, and general calamity. The Mount Lowe Railway made its last run on December 5, 1937. What remains now is simply a magnificent relic of the past.

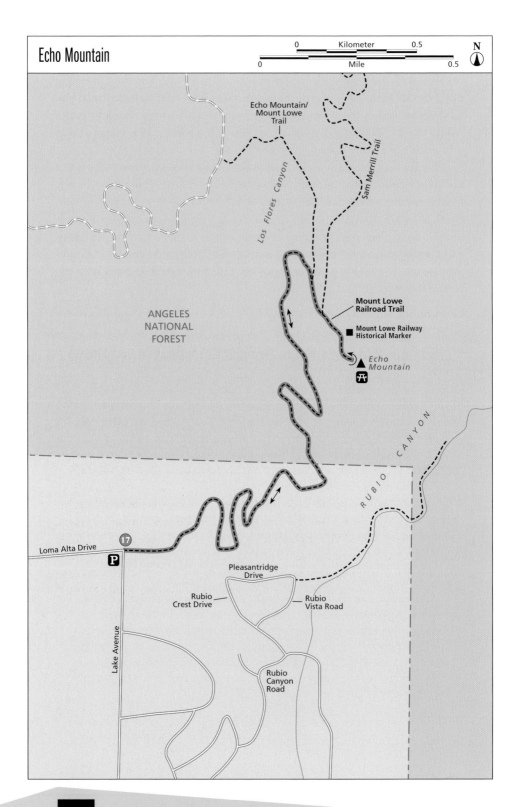

Echo Mountain

0   Kilometer   0.5
0   Mile   0.5

N

Echo Mountain/
Mount Lowe
Trail

Sam Merrill Trail

Los Flores Canyon

Mount Lowe
Railroad Trail

■ Mount Lowe Railway
Historical Marker

▲ Echo
Mountain

ANGELES
NATIONAL
FOREST

RUBIO CANYON

Loma Alta Drive

17

P

Pleasantridge
Drive

Rubio
Crest Drive

Rubio
Vista Road

Lake Avenue

Rubio
Canyon
Road

MILES AND DIRECTIONS

0.0 From Lake Avenue, walk east beyond the stone gateway along a chain-link fence.

0.1 Ignore the fire road and stay straight to enter the Sam Merrill Trail. Continue toward the top.

2.2 Turn right and follow the Echo Mountain/Mount Lowe Railroad Trail to the ruined foundations of the "White City."

2.5 Arrive at the summit of Echo Mountain. Return via the same route.

5.0 Arrive back at the trailhead and the Lake Avenue parking area.

HIKE INFORMATION

Local information: Angeles National Forest, 701 N. Santa Anita Ave., Arcadia 91006, (626) 574-1613

Camping: Angeles National Forest campgrounds (first come, first served / 14-day stay maximum): Appletree, Bear, Big Rock, Blue Ridge, Cabin Flat Trail Camp, Chilao, Cooper Canyon Trail Camp, Cottonwood, Devore Trail Camp, Guffy, Horse Flats, Idlehour Trail Camp, Little Jimmy Trail Camp, Lupine, Manker Flats, Millard Trail Camp, Monte Cristo, Mountain Oak, Oak Flats, Peavine, Sawmill, South; www .fs.fed.us/r5/angeles

Local retailers: A-16 (Adventure 16), www.adventure16.com; REI, www.rei.com

Restaurants: Green Street Restaurant, 146 Shoppers Lane, Pasadena, (626) 577-7170; Matt Denny's Ale House, 145 E. Huntington Dr., Arcadia, (626) 462-0250; Din Tai Fung, 1108 S. Baldwin Ave., Arcadia, (626) 574-7068; Shogun, 470 N. Halsted St., Pasadena, (626) 351-8945; Robin's Woodfire BBQ, 395 N. Rosemead Blvd., Pasadena, (626) 351-8885; Big Mama's Rib Shack, 1453 N. Lake Ave., Pasadena, (626) 797-1792; Domenico's Italian Restaurant, 2411 E. Washington Blvd., Pasadena, (626) 797-6459; Mediterranean Garden Grill, 335 W. Foothill Blvd., Monrovia, (626) 301-0555; Peach Cafe, 141 E. Colorado Blvd., Monrovia, (626) 599-9092

Rubio Canyon

Scramble across boulders and traverse narrow footpaths to historic Rubio Pavilion and majestic Ribbon Rock Falls. With unprecedented scenery and panoramic vistas of the Los Angeles metro area, Rubio Canyon is a worthwhile endeavor for hiking enthusiasts of all skill levels.

Start: Between two houses on Pleasantridge Drive
Distance: 1.5 miles out and back
Hiking time: About 2 hours
Difficulty: Moderate for steep and loose footing as well as creek crossings
Trail surface: Packed dirt and rock
Nearest town: Altadena
County: Los Angeles
Other trail users: None
Canine compatibility: Leashed dogs permitted

Trailhead facilities/amenities: None
Land status: National forest
Fees and permits: None
Schedule: Open year-round
Maps: USGS Mount Wilson, CA; www.altadenatrails.org/multi media/rubiotrailsmap.jpg
Trail contact: Angeles National Forest, 701 N. Santa Anita Ave., Arcadia 91006; www.fs.fed.us/r5/angeles; (626) 574-5200

Finding the trailhead: From the intersection of I-10, I-5, and US 101, take I-5 north for 1.1 miles. Take exit 137B to merge onto CA 110/Pasadena Freeway north. Drive for 6.6 miles to the end of the Pasadena Freeway. Continue north on Arroyo Parkway for 1.3 miles. Turn right onto Colorado Boulevard and drive for 0.9 mile. Turn left onto Lake Avenue and drive 3.4 miles. Turn right onto East Palm Street and drive for 0.2 mile. Continue straight as Palm becomes Maiden Lane for 0.3 mile.
Make a slight right onto Rubio Canyon Road. Drive for 0.1 mile and veer left to stay on Rubio Canyon Road. Continue for 0.2 mile. Turn left onto Rubio Crest Drive. Drive for 0.3 mile. At the sharp right, Rubio Crest Drive becomes Pleasantridge Drive. Continue for 0.2 mile to the corner. Park on the street. The signed trailhead is between two houses. GPS: N 34 12.1833' / W 118 7.3833'

THE HIKE

Rubio Canyon is part of the historic site of Professor Thaddeus S. C. Lowe's intricate rail system, debuting in 1893 as Mount Lowe Railway. The Rubio Pavilion and hotel was located at the lower terminal of the incline of the railway that traversed the hillside to the top of Echo Mountain. Passengers could board the "white chariots" at the pavilion for a thrilling ride up to any number of destinations along the Mount Lowe rail line. During its heyday, the pavilion boasted a complex system of stairways and walkways brilliantly lit by thousands of Japanese lanterns leading to nine of the magnificent waterfalls of Rubio Canyon. Unfortunately, the grand pavilion was short lived, because in 1909 a severe storm destroyed it and the hotel. What are left today are the concrete slabs of the foundation, easily visible along the trail.

The trailhead is located on an easement between two homes on Pleasantridge Drive and Rubio Vista Road; here the trail follows between the two houses toward the western ridge of Rubio Canyon. For the most part, there is very little

Rubio Canyon is rugged and beautiful at the same time. Allen Riedel

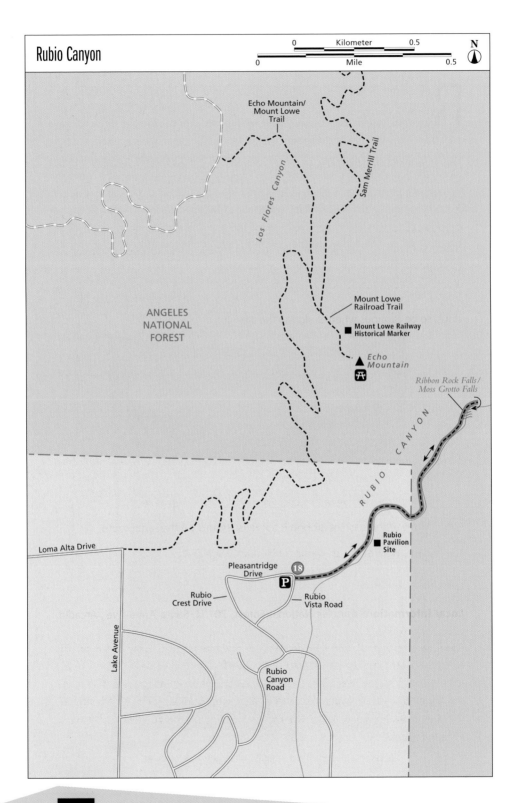

Rubio Canyon

Kilometer
0   0.5

Mile
0   0.5

N

Echo Mountain/
Mount Lowe
Trail

Los Flores Canyon

Sam Merrill Trail

ANGELES
NATIONAL
FOREST

Mount Lowe
Railroad Trail

Mount Lowe Railway
Historical Marker

▲ *Echo
Mountain*

*Ribbon Rock Falls/
Moss Grotto Falls*

RUBIO CANYON

Loma Alta Drive

Rubio
Pavilion
Site

Pleasantridge
Drive

18

P

Rubio
Crest Drive

Rubio
Vista Road

Lake Avenue

Rubio
Canyon
Road

shade along the trail, so during hot weather, it is advisable to prepare for extreme sun exposure.

At 0.5 mile you will begin your descent into the creek bed that the trail will ascend into the canyon. Here you will spot the first in a series of water pipes that follow along the trail. Just beyond an oak tree you will see the site of the Rubio Pavilion. Continue to veer right along the trail, which becomes a bit narrow in patches and requires some traversing, to the concrete foundation of the Rubio Pavilion.

From the foundation follow the creek bed north up into the canyon. Here the trail disappears and, depending on the time of year, may require some crisscrossing over water running down the canyon. At 0.75 mile you will find yourself at the base of charming Ribbon Rock Falls and just below Moss Grotto Falls. The beauty of Rubio Canyon is the dynamic nature of these falls. Prior to a prodigious landslide, there were several other falls in the lower canyon. Ribbon Rock Falls had, at one time, been obstructed by massive boulders as well. Due to the ever-changing nature of this area, it is advisable to note that some of the boulders may be capricious, so be cautious when exploring the area around the falls.

Today, Ribbon Rock Falls is once again flowing and provides for a delightful conclusion to this part of the trail. When you have had your fill of exploring the falls, head back down the creek bed toward the trail you came up on, and follow the same trail back to the trailhead.

MILES AND DIRECTIONS

0.0 Park on Pleasantridge Drive. Walk between the two houses on the signed trail.

0.5 Descend to the creek bed and follow the canyon upward.

0.75 Arrive at the base of Ribbon Rock Falls. Return via the same route.

1.5 Arrive back at the trailhead on Pleasantridge Drive.

HIKE INFORMATION

Local information: Angeles National Forest, 701 N. Santa Anita Ave., Arcadia, (626) 574-1613

Camping: Angeles National Forest campgrounds (first come, first served / 14-day stay maximum): Appletree, Bear, Big Rock, Blue Ridge, Cabin Flat Trail Camp, Chilao, Cooper Canyon Trail Camp, Cottonwood, Devore Trail Camp, Guffy, Horse Flats, Idlehour Trail Camp, Little Jimmy Trail Camp, Lupine, Manker Flats, Millard Trail Camp, Monte Cristo, Mountain Oak, Oak Flats, Peavine, Sawmill, South; www .fs.fed.us/r5/angeles

Local retailers: A-16 (Adventure 16), www.adventure16.com; REI, www.rei.com

Restaurants: Green Street Restaurant, 146 Shoppers Lane, Pasadena, (626) 577-7170; Matt Denny's Ale House, 145 E. Huntington Dr., Arcadia, (626) 462-0250; Din Tai Fung, 1108 S. Baldwin Ave., Arcadia, (626) 574-7068; Shogun, 470 N. Halsted St., Pasadena, (626) 351-8945; Robin's Woodfire BBQ, 395 N. Rosemead Blvd., Pasadena, (626) 351-8885; Big Mama's Rib Shack, 1453 N. Lake Ave., Pasadena, (626) 797-1792; Domenico's Italian Restaurant, 2411 E. Washington Blvd., Pasadena, (626) 797-6459; Mediterranean Garden Grill, 335 W. Foothill Blvd., Monrovia, (626) 301-0555; Peach Cafe, 141 E. Colorado Blvd., Monrovia, (626) 599-9092

> *Rubio Canyon was buried under countless tons of rock during a preventable accident while blasting in 1998. Heavy rains in 2004 uncovered five of the glorious waterfalls in the canyon.*

Learn how to spot poison oak before hiking! Monique Riedel

Eaton Canyon Falls

If you are looking for variety and challenge, Eaton Canyon is for you. This trail is a reasonably leisurely stroll that, at times, presents a moderate challenge and an even greater reward in the form of one of Southern California's most picturesque waterfalls and mirrored pools.

Start: At the end of Veranda Avenue in the Eaton Canyon Natural Area parking lot

Distance: 3.7 miles out and back

Hiking time: About 2.5 hours

Difficulty: Moderate for steep and loose footing and creek crossings

Trail surface: Paved road, dirt road, and packed dirt and rock

Nearest town: Pasadena

County: Los Angeles

Other trail users: None

Canine compatibility: Leashed dogs permitted

Trailhead facilities;amenities: Available

Land status: National forest

Fees and permits: None

Schedule: Open year-round, sunrise to sunset

Maps: USGS Mount Wilson, CA; www.ecnca.org/hiking_trails/ hiking_trails.html

Trail contact: Eaton Canyon Natural Area Park and Nature Center, 1750 N. Altadena Dr., Pasadena 91107; www.ecnca.org; (626) 398-5420

Finding the trailhead: From the intersection of I-10, I-5, and US 101, take I-5 north for 1.1 miles. Take exit 137B to merge onto CA 110/ Pasadena Freeway north. Drive for 6.6 miles to the end of the Pasadena Freeway. Continue north on Arroyo Parkway for 1.3 miles. Turn right onto Colorado Boulevard and drive for 2.6 miles. Turn left onto Sierra Madre Boulevard and drive for 0.4 mile. Turn left onto Altadena Drive and drive for 1.8 miles. Turn right onto Veranda Avenue into the signed parking lot for Eaton Canyon Park. GPS: N 34 10.65'/W 118 5.8'

E aton Canyon, formerly known as "El Precipio" by the Spanish due to its precipitous fissures and extreme terrain, is named for Judge Benjamin Eaton. Judge Eaton resided not far from Eaton Canyon at Fair Oaks Ranch House in the late 1800s and was one of the founders of the historic Mount Wilson Toll Road. Today, Eaton Canyon is governed by several different agencies and comprises 190 acres of land that lie between San Gabriel Peak and Mount Markham along the San Andreas Fault in the San Gabriel Mountains. The park offers a variety of activities, from challenging to leisurely.

Eaton Canyon has a visitor center you do not want to miss. The visitor center provides fantastic amenities including a restroom, gift shop, historical information, and an interactive learning center complete with live animals. This is a must-see for all ages. You won't be disappointed.

From the visitor center, follow the pavement to the north end of the parking area. The trailhead begins on the other side of a bright yellow gate. Follow the trail past the yellow gate; you are on Park Road Trail.

Park Road Trail is a very wide dirt path that resembles more of a road than a hiking trail. Continue into the creek bed and follow the trail over the creek. Depending on the season, the water level will vary. Beyond the creek, follow the trail veering to the left. This part of the trail consists of a wide, dusty path with patches of intermittent tree groves, but is predominantly open and exposed to sunlight. Follow this wide trail 1.3 miles to a bridge at the Mount Wilson Toll Road.

The rocky gorge of Eaton Canyon. Sierra Riedel

Continue under the bridge toward Eaton Falls Trail. Here the trail takes on a new appearance because you will be entering the canyon. It becomes narrower and uneven in constitution and is highly affected by the water level in the canyon, which will fluctuate with the season. The trail begins its windy course upward into the steep gorge of the canyon. Just underneath the bridge, a few feet up the canyon, you will come to the first of several creek crossings. There are strategically placed rocks and logs for crossings during high water, and the trail is easy to find on the other side of the creek bed. Continue upward into the canyon, following the intricate zigzag of the trail toward the falls for about 0.5 mile to Eaton Canyon Falls.

These falls are indubitably one of Southern California's most enchanting. John Muir is quoted as describing these falls as "a charming little thing, with a low, sweet voice, singing like a bird, as it pours from a notch in a short ledge, some thirty or forty feet into a round mirror-pool." The base of these falls is a popular destination for picknickers, sunbathers, and photographers, and, for the more adventuresome, swimmers. There are also other minor trails leading up to the top of the falls area and around the canyon ridge that are great for exploring.

When you have concluded your excursion, follow the same trail back down into the canyon to the parking area and visitor center.

MILES AND DIRECTIONS

0.0 Start from the visitor center in Eaton Canyon Park and walk north through the parking area along Veranda Avenue.

0.2 At the yellow gate cross over and walk north along the wide dirt path known as Park Road Trail. Stay on the main widest path.

1.3 Arrive at the bridge on Mount Wilson Toll Road. Continue on the Eaton Falls Trail, underneath the bridge. Follow the trail as it winds through the canyon.

1.8 Arrive at Eaton Canyon Falls. Return via same route.

3.7 Arrive back at the trailhead, visitor center, and parking area.

HIKE INFORMATION

Local information: Eaton Canyon Natural Area, 1750 N. Altadena Drive, Pasadena, (626) 398-5420; Angeles National Forest, 701 N. Santa Anita Ave., Arcadia, (626) 574-1613

Camping: Angeles National Forest campgrounds (first come, first served/14-day stay maximum): Appletree, Bear, Big Rock, Blue Ridge, Cabin Flat Trail Camp, Chilao, Cooper Canyon Trail Camp, Cottonwood, Devore Trail Camp, Guffy, Horse Flats, Idlehour Trail Camp, Little Jimmy Trail Camp, Lupine, Manker Flats, Millard

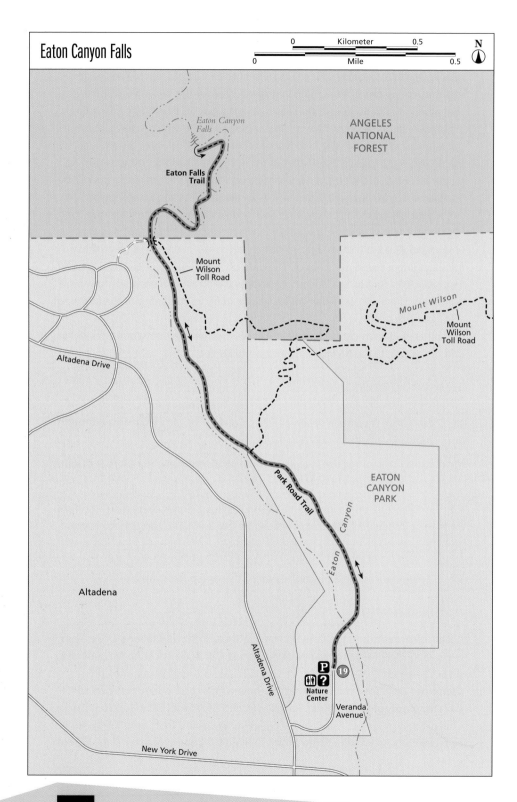

Eaton Canyon Falls

0 Kilometer 0.5

0 Mile 0.5

N

Eaton Canyon Falls

ANGELES NATIONAL FOREST

Eaton Falls Trail

Mount Wilson Toll Road

Mount Wilson

Mount Wilson Toll Road

Altadena Drive

Park Road Trail

Eaton Canyon

EATON CANYON PARK

Altadena

Altadena Drive

P
19
Nature Center

Veranda Avenue

New York Drive

Trail Camp, Monte Cristo, Mountain Oak, Oak Flats, Peavine, Sawmill, South; www.fs.fed.us/r5/angeles

Local retailers: A-16 (Adventure 16), www.adventure16.com; REI, www.rei.com

Restaurants: Green Street Restaurant, 146 Shoppers Lane, Pasadena, (626) 577-7170; Matt Denny's Ale House, 145 E. Huntington Dr., Arcadia, (626) 462-0250; Din Tai Fung, 1108 S. Baldwin Ave., Arcadia, (626) 574-7068; Shogun, 470 N. Halsted St., Pasadena, (626) 351-8945; Robin's Woodfire BBQ, 395 N. Rosemead Blvd., Pasadena, (626) 351-8885; Big Mama's Rib Shack, 1453 N. Lake Ave., Pasadena, (626) 797-1792; Domenico's Italian Restaurant, 2411 E. Washington Blvd., Pasadena, (626) 797-6459; Mediterranean Garden Grill, 335 W. Foothill Blvd., Monrovia, (626) 301-0555; Peach Cafe, 141 E. Colorado Blvd., Monrovia, (626) 599-9092

John Muir

John Muir, born in Scotland in 1838, is the founder of modern conservation and the Sierra Club. He is largely credited with being responsible for preserving wilderness in the western United States and for being the impetus for the foundation of Yosemite and Yellowstone National Parks. His writings and philosophies influenced presidents and other leaders.

As a young man, Muir was injured in an industrial accident and it was feared that he would not regain his sight. Immediately, he felt a sense of purpose, deciding that he would explore the wonders of the natural world and "study the inventions of God." He left his home and walked from Indiana to Florida, taking the most forested path he could find. In Florida he caught malaria and immediately booked transport to California. Upon arrival in California, Muir promptly traveled to Yosemite, where he found his life's passion. His was a kindred spirit with the natural world and he relished its magnificence, feeling a spiritual connection with nature and the beauty that surrounded him.

Muir's ideas differed from those of many of his contemporaries. To explain the scientific formation of Yosemite Valley, Muir argued for glaciation as the reason for the carved granite walls, whereas his chief rival, Josiah Whitney, head of the California Geological Survey, said that Yosemite was created by massive earthquakes. He also differed in his conservation strategies. Muir believed the forests to be a temple (though he saw a need for sustained use), whereas most of his contemporaries saw the forests as simply needing to be preserved for utilitarian purposes and nothing more.

Muir's ideas have influenced the very foundation with which we today look at nature. In the late 1800s civilization was encroaching upon the wildlands, but had not yet engulfed them. John Muir's voice was the centralizing force that led to the preservation of our national parks and wild areas; his leadership as a wilderness prophet was exactly what was needed at the right time for this nation and the world.

Sturtevant Falls

Amble down a charming trail rich with verdant foliage, indigenous wildlife, and rustic cabins from a bygone era. Experience an otherworldly appeal as you stroll through campsites reminiscent of fairytales and legends to a vibrant waterfall cascading from the crevice of a canyon wall.

Start: Chantry Flat Recreation Area

Distance: 3.5 miles out and back

Hiking time: About 2.5 hours

Difficulty: Easy, but with a few creek crossings

Trail surface: Paved road, dirt road, and singletrack dirt trail

Nearest town: Altadena

County: Los Angeles

Other trail users: Bicyclists

Canine compatibility: Leashed dogs permitted

Trailhead facilities/amenities: Located at the trailhead and along the hike; water must be filtered on trail

Land status: National forest

Fees and permits: Adventure Pass required for parking

Schedule: Open year-round; FR 2N40 open 6 a.m. to 8 p.m.

Maps: USGS Mount Wilson, CA; www.bigsantaanitacanyon.com/ Chantry_map.htm

Trail contact: Angeles National Forest, 701 N. Santa Anita Ave., Arcadia; www.fs.fed.us/r5/angeles; (626) 574-5200

Finding the trailhead: From the intersection of I-10, I-5, and US 101, take I-5 north for 3.6 miles. Take exit 139A for CA 2 North/Glendale Freeway north toward Glendale, driving for 3.5 miles. Take exit 17A to merge onto CA 134 east toward Pasadena, and drive for 5.3 miles. Continue on I-210 east for 6.4 miles. Take exit 32 for Santa Anita Avenue; turn left and drive 4.9 miles. Santa Anita Avenue becomes FR 2N40 and Santa Anita Canyon Trail/ Santa Anita Canyon Avenue. Park in the lot or along FR 2N40. GPS: N 34 11.7333'/W 118 1.35'

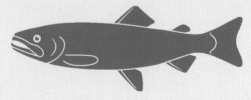

THE HIKE

The trail to Sturtevant Falls follows the Gabrielino National Recreation Trail, a classification assigned to existing trails that contribute to "health, conservation, and recreation goals" in the United States, for most of the route. Only the last portion follows the Sturtevant Falls Trail.

From the 1880s to the 1930s the "Great Hiking Era" boomed throughout the Angeles National Forest, causing an upswing in a need for trail accommodations as thousands of visitors were finding their way into the Big Santa Anita Canyon. Wilbur M. Sturtevant was one such hiking enthusiast, establishing Sturtevant's Camp in 1892, located in a shady grove in upper Big Santa Anita Canyon. Today, Sturtevant's Camp is the only remaining resort in the area. Private cabins can be seen nestled among alder trees and live oak groves along the trail's stream. These cabins are for recreational use only and are operated by private owners under a "special use permit" to keep "improvements" on federal land. While enjoying the charm and delight of these quaint cabins, be mindful and respectful of the owners' or occupants' privacy.

Shade cools the trail. Makaila Riedel

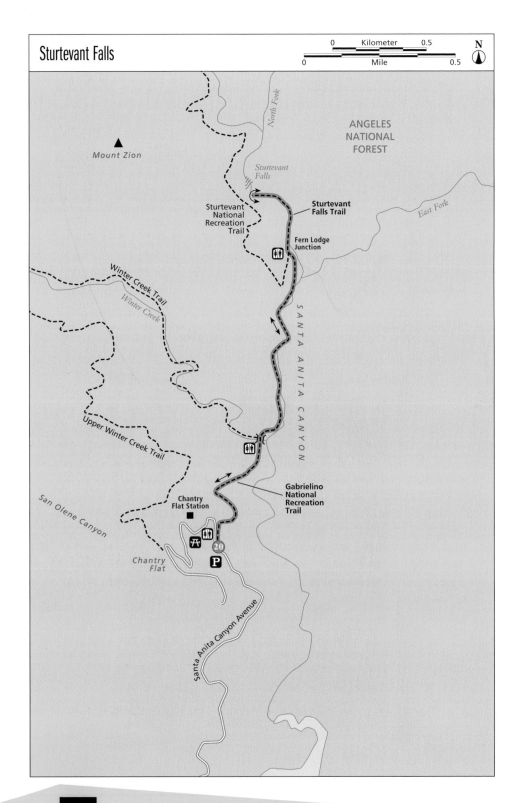

Sturtevant Falls

ANGELES
NATIONAL
FOREST

North Fork

Mount Zion

Sturtevant
Falls

Sturtevant
Falls Trail

East Fork

Sturtevant
National
Recreation
Trail

Fern Lodge
Junction

Winter Creek Trail

Winter Creek

S A N T A   A N I T A   C A N Y O N

Upper Winter Creek Trail

Gabrielino
National
Recreation
Trail

San Olene Canyon

Chantry
Flat Station

20

Chantry
Flat

P

Santa Anita Canyon Avenue

Parking at Chantry Flat is limited, so be prepared to find a spot along the narrow roadway leading into Chantry Flat. At the trailhead, there is a visitor kiosk and restrooms.

The first part of the trail is a wide, paved portion of the Gabrielino Trail. You will descend about 400 feet into Santa Anita Canyon via this road. At 0.5 mile you will arrive at a wooden footbridge crossing a stream and a rest area with restrooms. From here, follow the trail to the right at the junction with Winter Creek Trail and continue up Santa Anita Canyon to the north.

The trail begins to lose its lackluster appearance and emerges into a lush landscape teeming with vegetation, water, and wildlife. Here you will be greeted by the sounds of nature—several different species of birds, insects, and bubbling brooks. Where nature did not always provide conveniently placed rocks for a rippling stream, the County of Los Angeles has helped out by placing concrete weirs strategically along the creek, which when covered with moss and foliage add to the rustic appeal. At this juncture, the trail becomes narrow and follows the stream up into the canyon.

At 1.25 miles, at the Fern Lodge Junction, follow the trail straight up toward the falls. The trail to the left leads to a picnic area and campground. Just a few minutes past the junction, veer to the right at a cabin marked FIDDLERS CROSSING, and follow the easily definable trail over the creek. There are strategically placed rocks and boulders for crossing, but be prepared for a bit of adventure as water levels vary depending on season.

The trail winds back up to the left and to another similar creek crossing, which brings you to a shady grotto area canopied by trees and large boulders. Follow the trail straight uphill, veering to the right and into the alcove, where you will find the enchanting Sturtevant Falls.

Beginning at 50 feet up the canyon precipice, the falls provide a wondrous cascade into a shimmering pool at the base of the canyon wall. Large boulders, small rocks, and some shade trees offer a perfect ambience for those seeking to revel in the fragrant air and ethereal environment of Sturtevant Falls. When departing, be mindful that the last stretch of the hike requires a 400-foot ascent back up to Chantry Flat.

MILES AND DIRECTIONS

0.0 From the lower parking area, cross the road and head down the paved section of the Gabrielino Trail.

0.5 Turn right at the bridge and junction with the Winter Creek Trail, and follow Santa Anita Canyon north.

1.25 Turn right at Fern Lodge Junction and head to the base of Sturtevant Falls.

1.75 Arrive at the base of the falls. Return via the same route.

3.5 Arrive back at the trailhead at Chantry Flat.

HIKE INFORMATION

Local information: Angeles National Forest, 701 N. Santa Anita Ave., Arcadia, (626) 574-1613

Camping: Angeles National Forest campgrounds (first come, first served / 14-day stay maximum): Appletree, Bear, Big Rock, Blue Ridge, Cabin Flat Trail Camp, Chilao, Cooper Canyon Trail Camp, Cottonwood, Devore Trail Camp, Guffy, Horse Flats, Idlehour Trail Camp, Little Jimmy Trail Camp, Lupine, Manker Flats, Millard Trail Camp, Monte Cristo, Mountain Oak, Oak Flats, Peavine, Sawmill, South; www.fs.fed.us/r5/angeles

Local retailers: A-16 (Adventure 16), www.adventure16.com; REI, www.rei.com.

Restaurants: Green Street Restaurant, 146 Shoppers Lane, Pasadena, (626) 577-7170; Matt Denny's Ale House, 145 E. Huntington Dr., Arcadia, (626) 462-0250; Din Tai Fung, 1108 S. Baldwin Ave., Arcadia (626) 574-7068; Shogun, 470 N. Halsted St., Pasadena, (626) 351-8945; Robin's Woodfire BBQ, 395 N. Rosemead Blvd., Pasadena, (626) 351-8885; Big Mama's Rib Shack, 1453 N. Lake Ave., Pasadena, (626) 797-1792; Domenico's Italian Restaurant, 2411 E. Washington Blvd., Pasadena, (626) 797-6459; Mediterranean Garden Grill, 335 W. Foothill Blvd., Monrovia, (626) 301-0555; Peach Cafe, 141 E. Colorado Blvd., Monrovia, (626) 599-9092

Monrovia Canyon Falls

An easy jaunt through a primeval-looking riparian rainforest culminates at a charming waterfall resplendent with alluring flora and fauna at its bubbling crest.

Start: At the Monrovia Canyon Park middle parking lot
Distance: 2 miles out and back
Hiking time: About 1.5 hours
Difficulty: Easy, but with a few creek crossings
Trail surface: Paved road, dirt road, and singletrack dirt trail
Nearest town: Santa Anita
County: Los Angeles
Other trail users: None
Canine compatibility: Leashed dogs permitted
Trailhead facilities/amenities: All facilities available
Land status: City park, national forest
Fees and permits: Parking fee is charged

Schedule: Open year-round, 8 a.m. to 5 p.m., gate closes and locks at 5 p.m. sharp; closed Tues
Maps: USGS Azusa, CA; www .ci.monrovia.ca.us/images/content/community_life/bro_wild-guide_mcc.pdf
Trail contacts: Angeles National Forest, 701 N. Santa Anita Ave., Arcadia 91006; www.fs.fed.us/r5/angeles; (626) 574-5200. Monrovia Canyon Park, 1200 N. Canyon Blvd., Monrovia 91016; www .ci.monrovia.ca.us/community -life/parks/342-monrovia-canyon -park; (626) 256-8282

Finding the trailhead: From the intersection of US 101 and the CA 110 freeway, head north on CA 110. Drive for 8.1 miles to the conclusion of CA 110. Continue onto Arroyo Parkway for 1.3 miles. Turn right onto Colorado Boulevard; drive for 3.8 miles. Turn left onto Sierra Madre Villa Avenue and drive for 0.1 mile. Turn right to merge onto I-210 east. Drive for 2.8 miles. Take exit 32 for Santa Anita Avenue toward Arcadia. Turn left onto Santa Anita and drive for 0.2 mile. Turn right onto Foothill Boulevard. Drive for 2 miles. Turn left onto Canyon Boulevard and drive for 0.4 mile. Turn right to stay on Canyon Boulevard and continue for 0.8 mile to the parking lot and trailhead. GPS: N 34 10.5333'/W 117 59.4166'

THE HIKE

The Monrovia Canyon watershed is sustained by a variety of water sources high in the San Gabriel Mountains. The falls at Monrovia Canyon are a result of these springs nourishing the watershed at a 30-foot waterfall nestled in the canyon. The landscape and foliage surrounding the canyon are verdant any time of year and provide for a lush canopied traverse from the trailhead into the canyon to the streamside habitat at the base of the falls.

Parking at Monrovia Canyon Park is limited both in space and time. The area provides for a small number of vehicles and requires a fee. The gates are closed from 5 p.m. to 8 a.m. Therefore, if you are seeking a sunset or sunrise hike, it may be necessary to find parking in the residential area just outside the park entrance.

There is a nature center and restroom facilities in the parking area north of the trailhead. Begin on the trail behind the nature center. The trail starts out as a narrow

Monrovia Canyon Falls spills 30 feet over a double cascade. Michael Millenheft III

path following along a paved road, but quickly twists off the paved road and into the mouth of the canyon. Plant life and animal life are abundant any time of year. The path is well maintained but may still have some protruding poison oak during the spring months, so be wary of straying off the dirt trail.

Continue following the natural curve of the trail up into the canyon along a bubbling stream. The Los Angeles County water department has constructed a series of concrete weirs that provide added delight, with intermittent "waterfalls" along the route. At times, the trail widens and narrows along the canyon wall. The majority of the trail is canopied by overhanging trees of a variety of species, providing a good amount of shade from the sun.

At 0.75 mile, you will arrive at the aperture of Monrovia Falls. These 30-foot falls are dramatically set against large boulders and a canopy of trees. The boulders and rocks are plentiful and may be slippery or mossy, so caution is required when exploring the area around the falls. The pool at the base of the falls ranges from very shallow to moderate enough for wading. It is not uncommon to come upon fellow travelers wetting their feet in the pool or sitting on a rock dipping their toes in the cool mountain water. From the falls, return via the same trail, heading back down into the canyon and out to the trailhead by the parking area and nature center.

MILES AND DIRECTIONS

0.0   Begin your hike at the second parking lot, behind the nature center.

0.75   Arrive at Monrovia Canyon Falls. Return via the same route.

1.5   Arrive back at the trailhead and nature center.

HIKE INFORMATION

Local information: Angeles National Forest, 701 N. Santa Anita Ave., Arcadia 91006, (626) 574-1613

Camping: Angeles National Forest campgrounds (first come, first served / 14-day stay maximum): Appletree, Bear, Big Rock, Blue Ridge, Cabin Flat Trail Camp, Chilao, Cooper Canyon Trail Camp, Cottonwood, Devore Trail Camp, Guffy, Horse Flats, Idlehour Trail Camp, Little Jimmy Trail Camp, Lupine, Manker Flats, Millard Trail Camp, Monte Cristo, Mountain Oak, Oak Flats, Peavine, Sawmill, South; www .fs.fed.us/r5/angeles

Local retailers: A-16 (Adventure 16), www.adventure16.com; REI, www.rei.com

Restaurants: Green Street Restaurant, 146 Shoppers Lane, Pasadena, (626) 577-7170; Matt Denny's Ale House, 145 E. Huntington Dr., Arcadia, (626) 462-0250; Din Tai Fung, 1108 S. Baldwin Ave., Arcadia, (626) 574-7068; Shogun, 470

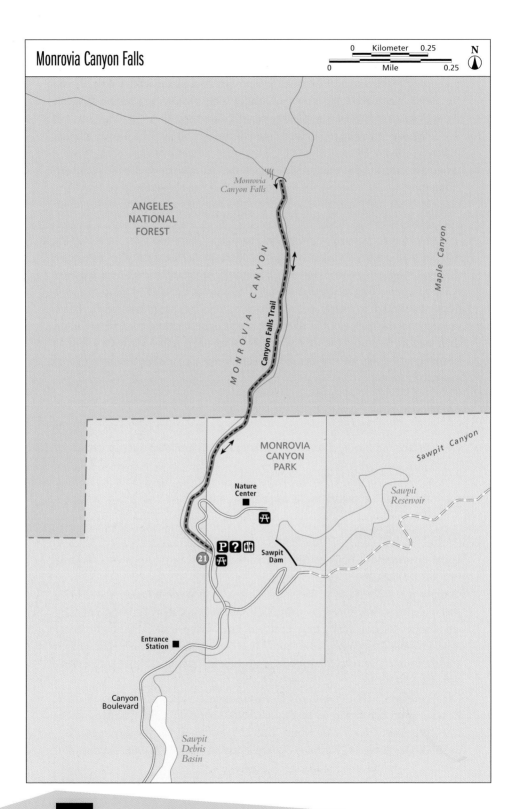

Monrovia Canyon Falls

0   Kilometer   0.25

0   Mile   0.25

N

Monrovia Canyon Falls

ANGELES
NATIONAL
FOREST

MONROVIA CANYON

Canyon Falls Trail

Maple Canyon

MONROVIA
CANYON
PARK

Sawpit Canyon

Nature
Center

*Sawpit
Reservoir*

P ? ⚧

21

Sawpit
Dam

Entrance
Station

Canyon
Boulevard

*Sawpit
Debris
Basin*

N. Halsted St., Pasadena, (626) 351-8945; Robin's Woodfire BBQ, 395 N. Rosemead Blvd., Pasadena, (626) 351-8885; Big Mama's Rib Shack, 1453 N. Lake Ave., Pasadena, (626) 797-1792; Domenico's Italian Restaurant, 2411 E. Washington Blvd., Pasadena, (626) 797-6459; Mediterranean Garden Grill, 335 W. Foothill Blvd., Monrovia, (626) 301-0555; Peach Cafe, 141 E. Colorado Blvd., Monrovia, (626) 599-9092

> ***Safety Tip: When hiking with children, hold hands at steep, narrow, or difficult sections.***

Creek crossings can be fairly simple, like this one, though swift moving and deep water should not be crossed. Allen Riedel

Twin Peaks

Some people call this one of the hardest "short" hikes in the Angeles National Forest. The summit view is incredible and made more rewarding by the difficulty of reaching it. Much of the hike wanders through towering pines and cedar, and outcroppings of granite make the region reminiscent of the Sierra Nevada. It is one of the more remote places to get to in the forest and a good introduction to "off-trail" hiking.

Start: Along CA 2, near Buckhorn Campground
Distance: 11 miles out and back
Hiking time: About 5.5 hours
Difficulty: Strenuous
Trail surface: Singletrack dirt trail
Nearest town: Wrightwood
County: Los Angeles
Other trail users: None
Canine compatibility: Leashed dogs permitted
Trailhead facilities/amenities: None

Land status: National forest
Fees and permits: Adventure Pass required for parking
Schedule: Open year-round
Maps: USGS Waterman Mountain, CA; www.peakbagging.com/CAPhotos/TwinPeaks.html
Trail contact: Angeles National Forest, 701 N. Santa Anita Ave., Arcadia 91006; www.fs.fed.us/r5/angeles; (626) 574-5200

Finding the trailhead: From the intersection of I-10, I-5, and CA 101, head north on I-5 and drive for 4.1 miles. Take exit 139A for CA 2/Glendale Freeway toward Glendale. Drive for 7.7 miles and take exit 21A to merge onto CA 2/I-210 east toward Pasadena. Drive for 1.2 miles. Take exit 20 for CA 2/Angeles Crest Highway toward La Canada Flintridge. Turn left onto CA 2 and drive 33.8 miles to a parking area on the left, just past the Mount Waterman Ski Area at mile marker 58.02.

CA 2 closes periodically due to storms, fire, fire danger, and rockslides, especially between Dawson Gap and Islip Saddle. While closures are in effect, use this alternate route: From the intersection of I-10, I-5, and CA 101, head east on I-10 for 40.9 miles and take exit 58A for I-15 north. Drive for 21.8 miles and take exit 131 for CA 138. Turn left onto CA 138 and drive for 8.6 miles. Turn left onto CA 2 and drive for 30.3 miles to a turnout just past the entrance to Buckhorn Campground and before the Mount Waterman Ski Area at mile marker 58.02.

GPS: N 34 20.65'/W 117 55.2666'

THE HIKE

This hike starts along the Waterman Mountain Trail. It is a little difficult to find the trailhead as there is no official parking except for pullout parking along the side of Angeles Crest Highway. The parking and trailhead are between the Mount Waterman Ski Area and the entrance to Buckhorn Campground. Watch on the south side of the road for the trailhead sign and for FR 3N03, as either will serve as the beginning of the hike.

Start out by hiking up the trail or the forest road, as the road crosses the trail in less than 0.1 mile. From the junction with the road the trail is easy to follow, climbing upward gently through towering pines and cedar. The forest is tranquil and beautiful in this section of the Angeles, and many newcomers and veteran hikers alike find this to be one of the finest trails in the woods. The trees are tall, providing shade for the entire route up to Waterman Mountain. It sits on the edge of the San Gabriel Wilderness, at nearly the halfway point along the Angeles Crest Highway, making this trail a destination and not just a place where people stop along the road and wander along the trail.

A view of Twin Peaks from Waterman Mountain. Allen Riedel

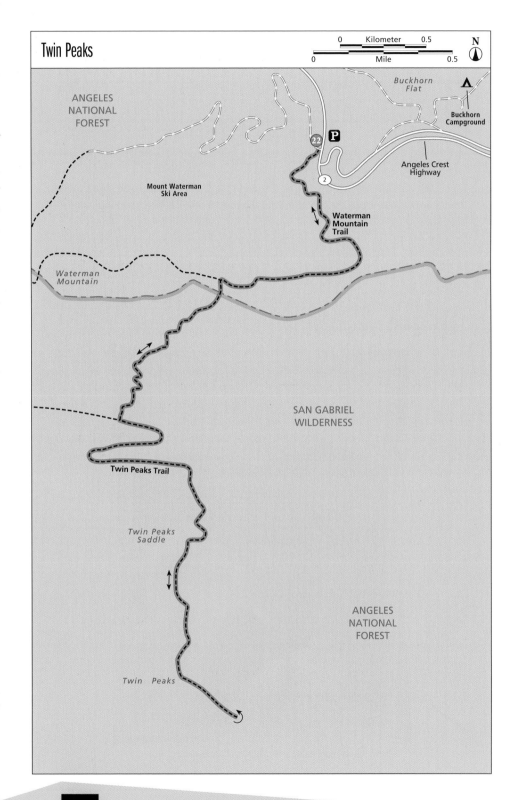

Twin Peaks

0 Kilometer 0.5
0 Mile 0.5

N

ANGELES
NATIONAL
FOREST

Buckhorn
Flat

Buckhorn
Campground

P

22

Mount Waterman
Ski Area

2

Angeles Crest
Highway

**Waterman
Mountain
Trail**

Waterman
Mountain

SAN GABRIEL
WILDERNESS

Twin Peaks Trail

Twin Peaks
Saddle

ANGELES
NATIONAL
FOREST

Twin Peaks

There are almost always other hikers along the first section of the route, although those numbers are greatly reduced at the connector to the Twin Peaks Trail. At 2.5 miles the trail meets the junction with the Twin Peaks Trail. Here, you begin a descent into Devils Canyon that drops 1,200 feet simply to reach the saddle between Waterman Mountain and the Twin Peaks massif itself. Although the route is signed and decently traversed for an "off-route" mountaineer's trail, it is still a difficult, foot-pounding descent. At just over 3 miles a trail departs on the right; keep left at the sign and descend toward Twin Peaks Saddle.

At the bottom (elevation 6,550 feet), there is another sign for the summit, which now towers 1,250 feet above. Due to the zigzag nature of parts of the trail and the sloping canyons on either side, getting an accurate trail GPS reading on this hike is difficult, but 11 miles is generally accepted as the true measure of its total distance. Continue straight up the mountain, watching the cairns (piles of stacked rocks) for the correct path to the top. The trail is pretty easy to follow and shouldn't provide much of a challenge to those who know what to look for.

At 5.2 miles, the trail veers decidedly east toward the summit block of East Twin. A little bit of scrambling is required to get up and over some of the rockier parts, but nothing that provides any sort of technical challenge. The views from the summit block are some of the best in the San Gabriel Mountains. Mount Baldy and the higher summits in the range can be seen to the east, and the rocky expanse of the San Gabriel Wilderness sits below, with the peaks of the front range of the San Gabriel Mountains making a pleasant tableau to the south.

Those making it to the top should enjoy a well-earned respite—after all, there is still the 1,200-foot descent back to the saddle and the 1,200-foot climb back to the Waterman Mountain Trail left for the hike out.

MILES AND DIRECTIONS

0.0 Begin by hiking along the Waterman Mountain Trail or FR 3N03.

2.5 Turn left at the junction onto the Twin Peaks Trail.

3.0 Stay left on the Twin Peaks Trail.

3.8 Arrive at Twin Peaks Saddle. Continue along the use trail to the summit.

5.2 Veer east toward the summit block.

5.5 Arrive on top of East Twin Peak. Return via the same route.

11.0 Arrive back at the trailhead and the parking area.

Local information: Angeles National Forest, 701 N. Santa Anita Ave., Arcadia, (626) 574-1613

Camping: Angeles National Forest campgrounds (first come, first served / 14-day stay maximum): Appletree, Bear, Big Rock, Blue Ridge, Cabin Flat Trail Camp, Chilao, Cooper Canyon Trail Camp, Cottonwood, Devore Trail Camp, Guffy, Horse Flats, Idlehour Trail Camp, Little Jimmy Trail Camp, Lupine, Manker Flats, Millard Trail Camp, Monte Cristo, Mountain Oak, Oak Flats, Peavine, Sawmill, South; www.fs.fed.us/r5/angeles

Local retailers: A-16 (Adventure 16), www.adventure16.com; REI, www.rei.com

Restaurants: Green Street Restaurant, 146 Shoppers Lane, Pasadena, (626) 577-7170; Matt Denny's Ale House, 145 E. Huntington Dr., Arcadia, (626) 462-0250; Din Tai Fung, 1108 S. Baldwin Ave., Arcadia, (626) 574-7068; Shogun, 470 N. Halsted St., Pasadena, (626) 351-8945; Robin's Woodfire BBQ, 395 N. Rosemead Blvd., Pasadena, (626) 351-8885; Big Mama's Rib Shack, 1453 N. Lake Ave., Pasadena, (626) 797-1792; Domenico's Italian Restaurant, 2411 E. Washington Blvd., Pasadena, (626) 797-6459

Twin Peaks sits at the geographical center of the San Gabriel Mountains in the middle of the San Gabriel Wilderness.

Devils Chair

Enjoy the remarkable tectonic scenery of Devil's Punchbowl Natural Area and its smooth, angular, uplifted sedimentary rocks. Hike high above through shrub forests of pinyon and Coulter pine, incense cedar, and the occasional Joshua tree for an awe-inspiring view of the Devils Punchbowl formation from the vista point known as the Devils Chair.

Start: At the end of Devils Punchbowl Road near Littlerock
Distance: 8-mile lollipop
Hiking time: About 5 hours
Difficulty: Strenuous
Trail surface: Singletrack dirt trail
Nearest town: Littlerock
County: Los Angeles
Other trail users: None
Canine compatibility: Leashed dogs permitted
Trailhead facilities/amenities: All facilities available at trailhead
Land status: National forest, Los Angeles county park
Fees and permits: None

Schedule: Open year-round, sunrise to sunset; visitor center closed Mon
Maps: USGS Valyermo, CA; www.devils-punchbowl.com/pages/map.html
Trail contacts: Devil's Punchbowl Natural Area/Los Angeles County Department of Parks and Recreation, 28000 Devils Punchbowl Rd., Pearblossom 93553; www.devils-punchbowl.com; (661) 944-2743. Angeles National Forest, 701 N. Santa Anita Ave., Arcadia 91006; www.fs.fed.us/r5/angeles; (626) 574-5200

Finding the trailhead: From the intersection of I-5, US 101, and I-10, head north on I-5 for 26.6 miles. Take exit 162 and merge onto CA 14, heading north toward Palmdale/Lancaster. Follow CA 14 for 29.5 miles. Take exit 30 for Angeles Forest Highway, and keep left at the fork to continue toward Sierra Highway, merging onto Sierra Highway. Drive for 5.8 miles, continuing straight as Sierra Highway becomes Pearblossom Highway. Make a slight right to continue on CA 138/Pearblossom Highway. Drive for 8.8 miles. Turn right onto 131st Street East/Longview Road. Drive for 2.2 miles. Turn left to continue on 131st Street East/Longview Road for 0.3 mile. Turn right to stay on 131st Street East/Longview Road and drive for 2.3 miles. Turn left onto Tumbleweed Road/Devils Punchbowl Road and drive for 3.1 miles to the parking area. GPS: N 34 24.8333'/W 117 51.5166'

From the parking area and visitor center, head out east onto the loop trail through the wondrous formations of the Devils Punchbowl. The loop trail heads straight through the smooth and vertically tilted sandstone rocks. Pictures and words hardly do any justice at all to the formations that loom from 50 feet to hundreds of feet overhead and seem to jut straight out of the earth at impossible angles. Their rugged beauty is undeniable.

The history of the Punchbowl is the story of the surrounding mountains and that of a tectonic California. The San Andreas Fault line runs straight through the region and is responsible for uncovering these slabs of rock. The same forces that uplifted the San Gabriel Mountains also pushed through the sandstone, and now these sentinels of stone stand for the enjoyment of all who come to visit. An intermittent creek flows alongside the loop trail and demonstrates that although this region is a desert, the mountains just to the north are tall and provide water and nutrients to the foothills nestled below.

From the loop, continue along the Burkhart Trail as it climbs up the mountain. The trail is shaded pretty well by pines for most of the route, though it is not advisable to hike in the summer due to extreme heat on this side of the desert. The elevation is not high enough to escape triple-digit temperatures in the summertime.

The uplifted sandstone at Devil's Punchbowl Natural Area towers 50 to 300 feet in the air. Allen Riedel

At just over 1 mile along the Burkhart Trail (2 miles for the total hike), a road splits to the left; continue to the left even though there are no signs that say to do so. In 0.5 mile another trail junction will note the presence of Devils Chair; turn onto the High Desert National Recreation Trail and from there the signs will be easy to follow for the rest of the hike.

At the next sign marked for Devils Chair, 2.7 miles into the total hike, turn left and enjoy the singletrack dirt trail for the remaining 2.8 miles. The trail makes its way up to the plateau above. The scenery is remarkably pleasant and the desert air is crisp and fresh. Most people will marvel at how forested the region is despite its arid nature.

The last 0.5 mile, before the chair, opens up onto a rocky promontory. The trail descends along an old iron railing and rickety stairs that have not been replaced for some time, and were probably built by the California Conservation Corps some-time in the 1940s or 1950s. Enjoy the spectacular view from the vista point at the chair and return via the same route.

MILES AND DIRECTIONS

0.0   Follow the trail from the right side of the parking lot by the visitor center. Turn left to follow the loop trail in a clockwise direction.

1.0   Return to the visitor center and continue southwesterly on the Burkhart Trail.

2.0   After a water tank, turn left onto the unsigned dirt road. Stay left at the split.

2.5   Stay straight at the trail junction and follow the signs for Devils Chair.

2.7   Turn left at the signed Devils Chair Trail.

4.5   Arrive at the overlook for Devils Chair. Return via same route.

8.0   Arrive back at the trailhead and parking area.

HIKE INFORMATION

Local information: Angeles National Forest, 701 N. Santa Anita Ave., Arcadia 91006, (626) 574-1613

Camping: Angeles National Forest campgrounds (first come, first served / 14-day stay maximum): Appletree, Bear, Big Rock, Blue Ridge, Cabin Flat Trail Camp, Chi-lao, Cooper Canyon Trail Camp, Cottonwood, Devore Trail Camp, Guffy, Horse Flats, Idlehour Trail Camp, Little Jimmy Trail Camp, Lupine, Manker Flats, Millard Trail Camp, Monte Cristo, Mountain Oak, Oak Flats, Peavine, Sawmill, South; www.fs.fed.us/r5/angeles

Local retailers: REI, www.rei.com

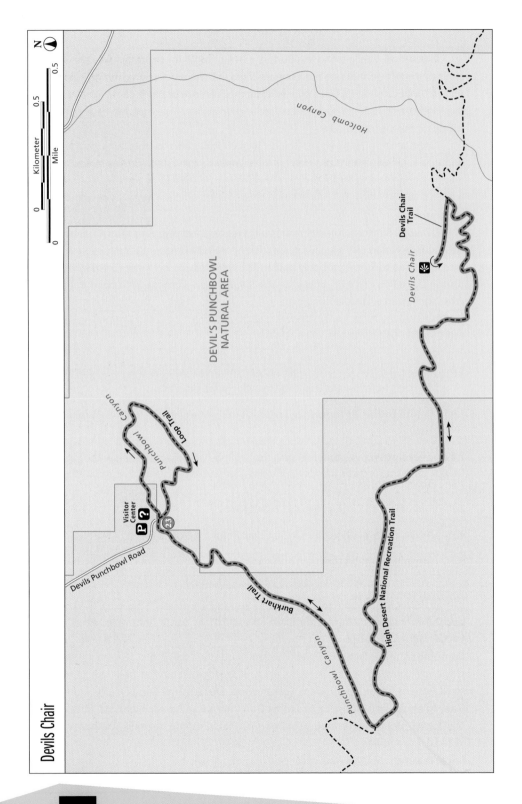

Devils Chair

Restaurants: Casa Ortega, 593 CA 138, Pinon Hills, (760) 868-6558; De Garcia's, 9595 Sheep Creek Rd., Phelan, (760) 868-3412; Mountain Top Cafe, 7637 CA 138, Phelan, (760) 249-4811; Charlie Brown Farms, 8317 Pearblossom Hwy., Littlerock, (661) 944-2606

> *The Devil's Punchbowl Natural Area's strange formations are caused by the uplift of tectonic faults, and the tilted rocks are sandstone eroded by flowing water.*

San Andreas Fault

The San Andreas Fault is the 810-mile sliding boundary between the Pacific Plate and the North American Plate that extends from the northwest part of California into Mexico and the Gulf of California. It has been responsible for the two major quakes in San Francisco: the 1906 disaster that nearly leveled and burned the entire city and the 1989 Loma Prieta Quake, or the World Series Quake, which caused substantial damage as well.

Everything to the west of the fault line is moving to the northwest, and the converse is true for the eastern side. Even though the plates only move a little more than an inch in each direction every year, the pressure exerted upon the tectonic plates is enough to cause major earthquakes when the two sides jar back into place. All of the mountain ranges of Southern California, from the Santa Lucias in Big Sur to the San Jacintos, were uplifted from the pressure and movement of the two plates. The fault is notable in that rocks on one side share no common geological component with the rocks on the other side of the fault line. One famous example is in the Pinnacles National Monument near Salinas, where the volcanic outcropping of rocks that makes up the park has a geologic twin in the remnants of the Neenach Volcano, which sits 200 miles to the south in the city of Lancaster.

Anyone wishing to see the power or the evidence of the fault line itself can travel to Devil's Punchbowl Natural Area, Vasquez, or Mormon Rocks, where colossal angular sedimentary rocks jut out from the earth's crust. The fault line is also visible from the ground in the Carrizo Plain in central California, and the familiar pictures in science books are taken here.

While the San Andreas Fault is not going to suddenly push California into the sea, it will, one day, after millions of years of movement, push Southern California into San Francisco—in fact , it has already done so. The geology at Point Reyes is the same as that of the Tehachapi Mountains, which sit several hundred miles to the south along the fault.

Mount Hawkins

This section of the Pacific Crest Trail, which heads into the high country of the Angeles National Forest, is one of the most beautiful sections of trail for hiking in Southern California. Starting from a popular trailhead at Islip Saddle, this route includes a peak that most people pass right on by, even though the views are spectacular. Mount Hawkins is an underrated and undervisited summit that is more than worth the effort.

Start: Islip Saddle
Distance: 8.5 miles out and back
Hiking time: About 5 hours
Difficulty: Strenuous
Trail surface: Singletrack dirt trail
Nearest town: Wrightwood
County: Los Angeles
Other trail users: None
Canine compatibility: Leashed dogs permitted
Trailhead facilities/amenities: Restrooms at trailhead and Little Jimmy Trail Camp, picnic area at camp, filterable water at Little Jimmy Spring
Land status: National forest
Fees and permits: Adventure Pass required for parking
Schedule: Open year-round
Maps: USGS Crystal Lake, CA; http://c0278592.cdn.cloudfiles. rackspacecloud.com/original /276832.jpg
Trail contact: Angeles National Forest, 701 N. Santa Anita Ave., Arcadia 91006; www.fs.fed.us/r5/ angeles; (626) 574-5200

Finding the trailhead: From the intersection of I-10, I-5, and US 101, head north on I-5 and drive for 4.1 miles. Take exit 139A for CA 2/Glendale Freeway, toward Glendale. Drive for 7.7 miles and take exit 21A to merge onto CA 2/I-210, heading east toward Pasadena. Drive for 1.2 miles. Take exit 20 for CA 2/Angeles Crest Highway, heading toward La Canada Flintridge. Turn left onto CA 2 and drive 39.5 miles to Islip Saddle. Park on the left.

CA 2 closes periodically due to storms, fire, fire danger, and rockslides, especially between Dawson Gap and Islip Saddle. When closures are in effect, use this alternate route: From the intersection of I-10, I-5, and US 101, head east on I-5 north for 3.8 miles. Take exit 139A for CA 2 North/Glendale Freeway toward Glendale, driving for 3.5 miles. Take exit 17A to merge onto CA 134 east toward Pasadena, driving for 5.3 miles. Continue onto I-210 and drive for 37.5 miles. Take the exit onto I-15 north and drive for 16.2 miles. Take exit 131 for CA 138 toward Palmdale/Silverwood Lake. Turn left onto CA 138 west and drive for 8.6 miles. Turn left onto CA 2 West/Angeles Crest Highway and drive for 24.6 miles to Islip Saddle. Park on the right. GPS: N 34 21.4166'/W 117 51.0666'

THE HIKE

From Islip Saddle, most hikers head to Mount Islip along the Pacific Crest Trail (PCT), and the trail is fairly popular. Even on weekdays, there are normally a few other people heading to and from the top. Some hikers take the route less traveled and trek on the desert side, heading toward Mount Williamson, a virtual twin hike and summit to Mount Islip. But only the very few take the trek to the top of Mount Hawkins. Overall, the distance for the entire trip is 2 miles greater and the elevation gain is steeper and greater, but then again, so are the elements of freedom, the vestiges of solitude, and the vistas that pack a much more exceptional punch.

The Angeles Crest Highway follows much of the route, albeit several hundred feet below the trail, so when the highway is open all the way through the mountains, there is considerably more noise on this trail—but mostly only when loud motorcyclists take to the mountains on Sunday. Midweek will barely give off an audible peep.

The Pacific Crest Trail (PCT) winds up toward Mount Hawkins. Allen Riedel

The trail begins at Islip Saddle. Cross the highway from the large parking lot and restrooms and begin heading up into the mountains. The beginning section of the trail switchbacks and heads steeply up through manzanita, whitethorn, and mountain chaparral for the first 0.5 mile. After that the route continues to gain elevation, but at a much slower pace, and the trail winds through a lovely forest of Jeffrey pine, sugar pine, and ponderosa pine trees.

The trail crosses an old dirt access road several times and there are signs along the way directing the hiker to Little Jimmy Camp, Little Jimmy Spring, and Mount Islip. Stay on the trail, not on the dirt road. Of course, the usual triangular-curved PCT trail sign can be seen on posts spaced fairly consistently along the way. At times, the highway can be also seen below and sometimes heard.

At 2 miles the trail enters Little Jimmy Trail Camp, named for "Little Jimmy" Swinnerton, a cartoonist who some say invented the comic strip. A favorite employee of William Randolph Hearst, he moved to the Southwest in 1906 after being diagnosed with tuberculosis. He frequented the campsite, drawing cartoons for guests and even carving a character on a tree there. He became such a regular that officials named the campsite after him.

Follow the trail through the lower section of camp toward Little Jimmy Spring and Windy Gap. Restrooms are available in the campsite. In seasons with normal precipitation, Little Jimmy Spring flows throughout the year, though it dries up considerably by end of summer and in dry years may only be a trickle. Improvements were made to the spring so that the water drips from a pipe, though it is still suggested to boil or filter the water before drinking.

At 2.25 miles, hikers will come to Windy Gap, a great viewpoint and a trail junction for those heading up to Mount Islip, heading down to Crystal Lake, or continuing along the PCT. Turn left and follow the PCT as it winds and switchbacks up the slope of Mount Hawkins. The trail gains 1,200 feet in the next 2 miles, and though it isn't severely steep, that is enough of a gain to make this a strenuous hike. Some remnants of the Curve Fire of 2002 will be visible on the higher reaches of the trail, and at 3.75 miles, the summit of Mount Hawkins sits 200 feet overhead as the trail passes it by.

At 4 miles the trail gains the crest and hikers must veer sharply right to take the use trail to the top of Mount Hawkins. The trail gains a short 100 feet to the summit, and the views are decidedly amazing. There is a view of Mount Baldy that is straight on, and the high desert can be seen below as well as the other high peaks in this section of the national forest.

The fire lookout on South Mount Hawkins burned down in the Curve Fire of 2002.

At 8,850 feet, Mount Hawkins is one of the tallest peaks in the forest and it is a great place to take in the sights. The two peaks to the south, Middle Hawkins and South Mount Hawkins also bear witness to the memory of a waitress, Nellie Hawkins, who worked at the Squirrel Inn at Crystal Lake in the very early twentieth century. Though information on her seems simply to point to her years serving customers, little else is known. One can only conjecture at her beauty and charm.

After enjoying the summit, return via the same route.

Little Jimmy Swinnerton

Little Jimmy Swinnerton (1875–1974), known by the names Little Jimmy, Swinny, and Swin, was an American cartoonist who was one of the first to develop newspaper cartoon strips. By some accounts, he was the first. His publication of *Little Bears and Tykes* in the *San Francisco Examiner* on June 1, 1892, predates the work of Richard F. Outcault, the man generally credited with the invention of the comic strip, by two full years.

The illustrations he created used word bubbles, distinct panels, and recurring main characters. His work made use of animals, and he is credited with creating the first humorous anthropomorphic animal cartoon character, Mr. Jack, after relocating to New York and writing for Hearst's *New York Journal American*.

In 1904 Swinnerton created *Little Jimmy*, the comic he is most remembered for. The character of Jimmy was a stereotypical young boy with a penchant for troublemaking. Little Jimmy earned his fair share of punishment by getting caught up in all sorts of shenanigans and forgetting the important things he needed to do. Little Jimmy appeared in nationwide daily syndication until the 1930s. Swinnerton continued to write a Sunday strip until he retired in 1958, when he suffered an accident that injured his hand.

Ironically, Swinnerton was told he had weeks to live when he contracted tuberculosis in 1906. He then moved West, alternating residences between Arizona and California, for the rest of his life. He disliked the heat of the desert summers and spent some time high in the San Gabriel Mountains at what is now known as Little Jimmy Trail Camp. It is reported that he carved a Little Jimmy character onto a tree there, and delighted visitors with personalized drawings of Little Jimmy, who by that time was well known to newspaper readers across the country.

Swinnerton outlived his doctor and the prognosis he received, surviving in Palm Springs to the ripe old age of ninety-eight.

Mount Hawkins

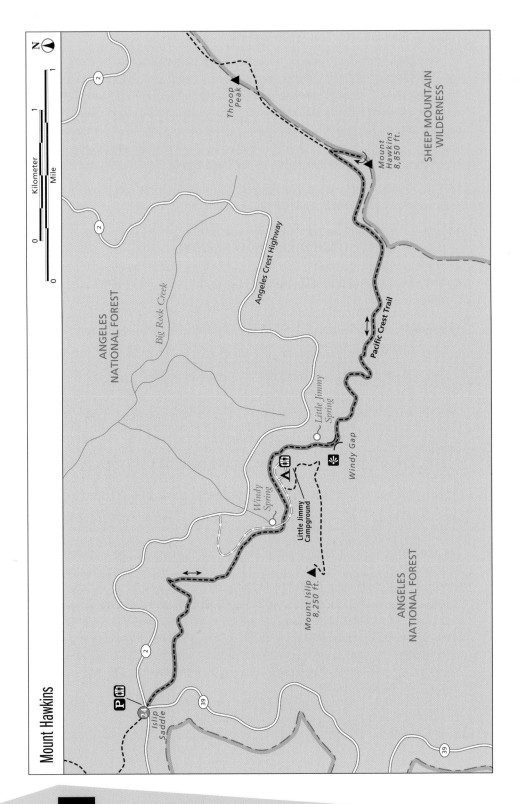

0.0   Start at Islip Saddle, cross the Angeles Crest Highway / CA 2, and hike along the Pacific Crest Trail (PCT).

0.75   Cross the fire road and continue along the PCT.

1.8   Cross the fire road again, then arrive at Little Jimmy Camp.

1.9   Arrive at the Little Jimmy Spring side trail. In another 250 feet you'll meet the Little Jimmy Spring use trail. Both lead to the spring.

2.5   Arrive at Windy Gap. Turn left to stay on the PCT.

3.75   Pass below the summit of Mount Hawkins.

4.0   Turn sharply right to take use trail back (south) to the summit of Mount Hawkins.

4.25   Arrive at the summit of Mount Hawkins. Return via same route.

8.5   Arrive back at the trailhead and the Islip Saddle parking area.

HIKE INFORMATION

Local information: Angeles National Forest, 701 N. Santa Anita Ave., Arcadia 91006, (626) 574-1613

Camping: Angeles National Forest campgrounds (first come, first served / 14-day stay maximum): Appletree, Bear, Big Rock, Blue Ridge, Cabin Flat Trail Camp, Chilao, Cooper Canyon Trail Camp, Cottonwood, Devore Trail Camp, Guffy, Horse Flats, Idlehour Trail Camp, Little Jimmy Trail Camp, Lupine, Manker Flats, Millard Trail Camp, Monte Cristo, Mountain Oak, Oak Flats, Peavine, Sawmill, South; www .fs.fed.us/r5/angeles

Local retailers: A-16 (Adventure 16), www.adventure16.com; REI, www.rei.com.

Restaurants: Mile High Pizza, 5996 Cedar, Wrightwood, (760) 249-4848; Yodeler, 6046 Park Dr., Wrightwood, (760) 249-6482; Evergreen Cafe and Raccoon Saloon, 1269 Evergreen Rd., Wrightwood, (760) 249-6393; Grizzly Cafe, 1455 CA 2, Wrightwood, (760) 249-6733; Mexico Lindo, 1253 Evergreen St., Wrightwood, (760) 249-4100; Mountain Top Cafe, 7637 CA 138, Phelan, (760) 249-4811; Blue Ridge Inn, 6060 Park Dr., Wrightwood, (760) 249-3440; Newcomb's Ranch, midway along Angeles Crest Highway / CA 2 between La Canada and Wrightwood, La Canada Flintridge, (626) 440-1001

Mount Lewis

A short but steep climb leads up a tree-lined hillside to a grand summit offering majestic and panoramic views of the San Gabriel Mountains and the Mojave Basin.

Start: Dawson Saddle, on the west side of the maintenance shed
Distance: 1 mile out and back
Hiking time: About 1 hour
Difficulty: Easy, but the trail is very steep
Trail surface: Singletrack dirt trail
Nearest town: Wrightwood
County: Los Angeles
Other trail users: None
Canine compatibility: Leashed dogs permitted

Trailhead facilities/amenities: None
Land status: National forest
Fees and permits: Adventure Pass required for parking
Schedule: Open year-round except during road closures
Maps: USGS Crystal Lake, CA
Trail contact: Angeles National Forest, 701 N. Santa Anita Ave., Arcadia 91006; www.fs.fed.us/r5/angeles; (626) 574-5200

Finding the trailhead: From the intersection of I-10, I-5, and CA 101, head north on I-5 and drive for 4.1 miles. Take exit 139A for CA 2/Glendale Freeway toward Glendale. Drive for 7.7 miles and take exit 21A to merge onto CA 2/I-210, heading east toward Pasadena. Drive for 1.2 miles. Take exit 20 for CA 2/Angeles Crest Highway toward La Canada Flintridge. Turn left onto CA 2 and drive 44.5 miles to a parking area on the left, next to the maintenance shed. Do not block the maintenance shed.

CA 2 closes periodically due to storms, fire, fire danger, and rockslides, especially between Dawson Gap and Islip Saddle. When closures are in effect, use this alternate route: From the intersection of I-10, I-5, and CA 101, head east on I-10 for 40.9 miles and take exit 58A for I-15 north. Drive for 21.8 miles and take exit 131 for CA 138. Turn left (west) onto CA 138 and drive for 8.6 miles. Turn left onto CA 2 and drive for 19.2 miles to Dawson Saddle, where again you should not block the maintenance shed. GPS: N 34 22.0833'/W 117 48.2'

THE HIKE

Mount Lewis is named for W. B. Lewis, one of the "Guardians of Yosemite" and the first superintendent of that park. The peak at Mount Lewis is a sizeable plateau carpeted with thick piles of leafy debris and fallen tree trunks and a 360-degree view of the Antelope Valley and neighboring peaks such as Mount Baden-Powell, Mount Islip, and Mount Hawkins.

At Dawson Saddle, you will find a narrow access trail leading up from the left side of a maintenance shed. The trail takes a minor switchback to the left, then goes right up a narrow path, almost vertically up the hillside. Since the trail is located in a dense forest of a variety of pine trees—Jeffrey and ponderosa—shade is a welcome comfort on the steep ascent.

The trail remains narrow for about half its distance, but widens as it reaches the summit of Mount Lewis. Since the ascent is steep and the elevation gain is 500 feet, you will want to take frequent breaks to soak in the beauty and ambience at different points along the climb. You will be able to take advantage of the different perspectives and angles of views of the Mojave Basin. On a clear day, you will see the distant mountain ranges of the Mojave Desert and the horizon toward Nevada.

At 0.5 mile you will arrive at the summit of Mount Lewis. The area atop the peak is spacious and lends itself to exploration and introspection, because there are unlimited viewpoints from which to observe the valley below. Fallen logs and

Mount Lewis is an easy climb to a high mountain summit. Allen Riedel

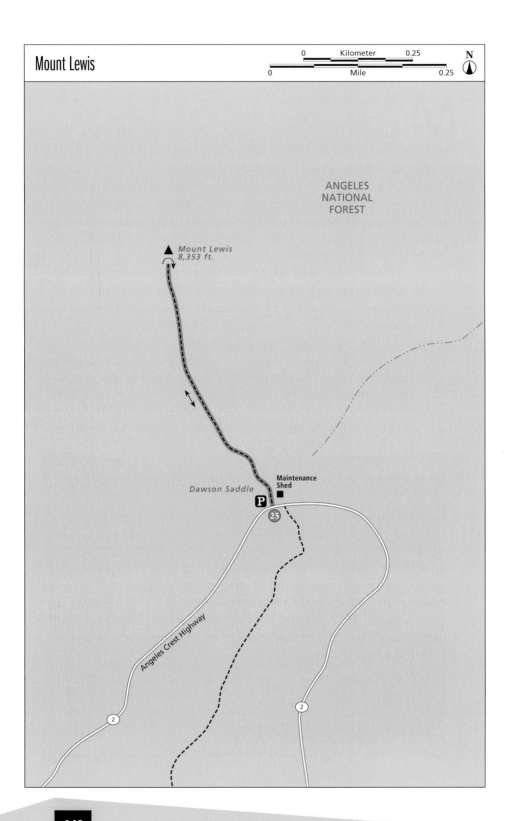

0   Kilometer   0.25

0   Mile   0.25

N

ANGELES
NATIONAL
FOREST

▲ *Mount Lewis*
8,353 ft.

Dawson Saddle

**Maintenance
Shed**

Ⓟ

25

Angeles Crest Highway

2

2

rocks seem to welcome you for a bit of rest after your steep jaunt up the hillside. This is not one of the more traveled trails; therefore it is not uncommon to be the only trail user on this hike. For those seeking solace and solitude, these are some of the attractive qualities of this intimate trail experience.

After you have reveled in the beauty and serenity of the summit, follow the same trail down toward Dawson Saddle. Footing on the descent is precarious at times, so be mindful of your downward journey to the parking area.

MILES AND DIRECTIONS

0.0 From the parking area, start up the use trail to the left (west) of the maintenance shed.

0.5 Arrive atop the summit of Mount Lewis.

1.0 After retracing your steps, reach the parking area.

HIKE INFORMATION

Local information: Angeles National Forest, 701 N. Santa Anita Ave., Arcadia 91006, (626) 574-1613

Camping: Angeles National Forest campgrounds (first come, first served / 14-day stay maximum): Appletree, Bear, Big Rock, Blue Ridge, Cabin Flat Trail Camp, Chilao, Cooper Canyon Trail Camp, Cottonwood, Devore Trail Camp, Guffy, Horse Flats, Idlehour Trail Camp, Little Jimmy Trail Camp, Lupine, Manker Flats, Millard Trail Camp, Monte Cristo, Mountain Oak, Oak Flats, Peavine, Sawmill, South; www.fs.fed.us/r5/angeles

Local retailers: A-16 (Adventure 16); www.adventure16.com. REI; www.rei.com.

Restaurants: Mile High Pizza, 5996 Cedar, Wrightwood, (760) 249-4848; Yodeler, 6046 Park Dr., Wrightwood, (760) 249-6482; Evergreen Cafe and Raccoon Saloon, 1269 Evergreen Rd., Wrightwood, (760) 249-6393; Grizzly Cafe, 1455 CA 2, Wrightwood, (760) 249-6733; Mexico Lindo, 1253 Evergreen St., Wrightwood, (760) 249-4100; Mountain Top Cafe, 7637 CA 138, Phelan, (760) 249-4811; Blue Ridge Inn, 6060 Park Dr., Wrightwood, (760) 249-3440; Newcomb's Ranch, midway along Angeles Crest Highway / CA 2 between La Canada and Wrightwood, La Canada Flintridge, (626) 440-1001

Safety Tip: Always be aware of surroundings and changing conditions. Don't take unnecessary risks. Turn around if you are not properly prepared; the mountains will be there another day.

Mount Baden-Powell

On this no-nonsense hike to the top of one of Southern California's most prominent summits, take in jaw-dropping ridgeline and mountain views, walk past trees older than the English language itself, and get a great workout in the process.

Start: Vincent Gap
Distance: 8.2 miles out and back
Hiking time: About 4.5 hours
Difficulty: Strenuous
Trail surface: Singletrack dirt trail
Nearest town: Wrightwood
County: Los Angeles
Other trail users: None
Canine compatibility: Leashed dogs permitted
Trailhead facilities/amenities: Restroom at trailhead, filterable water at spring

Land status: National forest
Fees and permits: Adventure Pass required for parking
Schedule: Open year-round
Maps: USGS Crystal Lake, CA; www.localhikes.com/HikeData .ASP?DispType=1&ActiveHike=0& GetHikesStateID=&ID=4031
Trail contact: Angeles National Forest, 701 N. Santa Anita Ave., Arcadia 91006; www.fs.fed.us/r5/ angeles; (626) 574-5200

Finding the trailhead: From the intersection of I-10, I-5, and US 101, head north on I-5 and drive for 4.1 miles. Take exit 139A for CA 2/Glendale Freeway toward Glendale. Drive for 7.7 miles and take exit 21A to merge onto CA 2/I-210, heading east toward Pasadena. Drive for 1.2 miles. Take exit 20 for CA 2/Angeles Crest Highway toward La Canada Flintridge. Turn left onto CA 2 and drive 51 miles to the parking area for Vincent Gap on the right.

CA 2 closes periodically due to storms, fire, fire danger, and rockslides, especially between Dawson Gap and Islip Saddle. When closures are in effect, use this alternate route: From the intersection of I-10, I-5, and US 101, head east on I-10 for 40.9 miles and take exit 58A for I-15 north. Drive for 21.8 miles and take exit 131 for CA 138. Turn left onto CA 138 and drive west for 8.6 miles. Turn left onto CA 2 and drive for 13.9 miles to the Vincent Gap parking area. GPS: N 34 22.4'/W 117 45.15'

THE HIKE

Mount Baden-Powell is an awesome mountain no matter which way you slice it. Sitting at 9,399 feet in elevation, it is the sixteenth-highest peak in Southern California. Because alternate routes to the top are longer in distance, this trip happens to be the most popular. The trail cuts back and forth, switchbacking forty-one times before reaching the summit and gaining 2,800 feet of elevation in the process. While not an easy distance or elevation gain, anyone with determination and a decent fitness level can make it to the summit.

The trail starts at the Vincent Gap parking area and is well marked. It is very easy to follow as there is only one designated junction on the trail. Head southwest up the Pacific Crest Trail (PCT) toward the summit. For the first 3 miles, the trail is very nicely shaded, passing through a mixed yellow pine forest of sugar, lodgepole, Jeffrey, and ponderosa pine with some white fir and incense cedar to boot.

Snow clings to this trail deep into summer due to its northern orientation, high elevation, and lack of direct sunlight. It is a favorite spot for novice glissading, with winter mountaineers practicing their craft with ice axe and crampons. The trail is also quite well used by Boy Scouts, casual hiking enthusiasts, backpackers, and tourists looking for a high mountain to climb just off the Angeles Crest Highway. There will be other people hiking along this trail every single day of the week, no matter what.

Views from the top of Mount Baden-Powell are expansive and broad. Allen Riedel

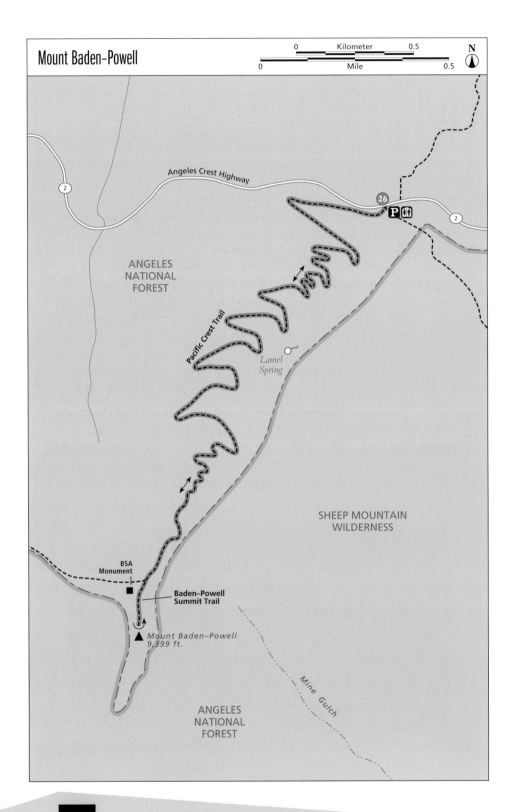

Mount Baden-Powell

0 Kilometer 0.5

0 Mile 0.5

N

Angeles Crest Highway

2

26

P

ANGELES
NATIONAL
FOREST

Pacific Crest Trail

Lamel
Spring

SHEEP MOUNTAIN
WILDERNESS

BSA
Monument

Baden–Powell
Summit Trail

▲ Mount Baden–Powell
9,399 ft.

Mine Gulch

ANGELES
NATIONAL
FOREST

At about 1.8 miles, a short side trail leads left for around 100 yards to Lamel Spring. Water should be treated, filtered, or boiled before using. Trees along the route begin to thin out a little beyond 3.1 miles, and the mountain ridgeline becomes the most visible trait. The steepness of the mountain in front can be seen firsthand and the switchbacks become less lengthy as the trail turns into more of a straight-up-the-mountain venture.

There is a short use trail that leads to a grove of limber pines at around 3.6 miles, but most people will want to bypass the trail and maybe visit on the way out. There are limber pines along the trail at this elevation anyway, and the largest one sits just ahead at the junction of the Baden-Powell Summit Trail and the PCT, which continues to the west just below the peak.

After reaching the giant limber pine at about 3.9 miles—the Wally Waldron Tree, estimated to be between 1,500 and 2,000 years old—the vistas of the upper reaches of the San Gabriels and Mount San Antonio really open up. Turning around and looking north into the high desert valleys is also breathtaking, provided there isn't any smog. From this point, it is a short jaunt to the top. Stay on the Baden-Powell Summit Trail, where a marker dedicated to Lord Baden-Powell, the founder of the Boy Scouts, was erected in 1957, listing some cardinal virtues and the dedication to service to others that all scouts are supposed to stand for.

Once on top, those looking for a little isolation can continue hiking south along Baden-Powell's large hogback. Any elevation lost will have to be regained on the way out, but getting as short a distance as 0.25 mile away from the summit will thin out any crowds and leave any hiker feeling like the summit belongs to him or her in its entirety.

Enjoy the views and return via the same route. The way down is just that—all downhill.

MILES AND DIRECTIONS

0.0 From the Vincent Gap parking area, head southwest up the Pacific Crest Trail.

1.8 Continue straight at the junction with the Lamel Spring trail.

3.6 A small use trail leads to a grove of limber pines, the oldest trees in Southern California.

3.9 Continue up straight and left at the turnoff for Baden-Powell Summit Trail.

4.1 Arrive at the summit. Return via the same route.

8.2 Arrive back at the trailhead and parking area.

HIKE INFORMATION

Local information: Angeles National Forest, 701 N. Santa Anita Ave., Arcadia 91006, (626) 574-1613

Camping: Angeles National Forest campgrounds (first come, first served / 14-day stay maximum): Appletree, Bear, Big Rock, Blue Ridge, Cabin Flat Trail Camp, Chilao, Cooper Canyon Trail Camp, Cottonwood, Devore Trail Camp, Guffy, Horse Flats, Idlehour Trail Camp, Little Jimmy Trail Camp, Lupine, Manker Flats, Millard Trail Camp, Monte Cristo, Mountain Oak, Oak Flats, Peavine, Sawmill, South; www .fs.fed.us/r5/angeles

Local retailers: A-16 (Adventure 16), www.adventure16.com; REI, www.rei.com

Restaurants: Mile High Pizza, 5996 Cedar, Wrightwood, (760) 249-4848; Yodeler, 6046 Park Dr., Wrightwood, (760) 249-6482; Evergreen Cafe and Raccoon Saloon, 1269 Evergreen Rd., Wrightwood, (760) 249-6393; Grizzly Cafe, 1455 CA 2, Wrightwood, (760) 249-6733; Mexico Lindo, 1253 Evergreen St., Wrightwood, (760) 249-4100; Mountain Top Cafe, 7637 CA 138, Phelan, (760) 249-4811; Blue Ridge Inn, 6060 Park Dr., Wrightwood, (760) 249-3440; Newcomb's Ranch, midway along Angeles Crest Highway / CA 2 between La Canada and Wrightwood, La Canada Flintridge, (626) 440-1001

Trail Sign showing the distances to popular trailheads and destinations within the Angeles National Forest. Allen Riedel

Lord Baden-Powell

Robert Stephenson Smyth Baden-Powell (1857–1941) was born the eighth of ten children to a reverend father who was also a professor at Oxford University. His father passed on when Baden-Powell (or BP, as he was known for short) was only three years old. As a young boy, he spent his time hunting and exploring in the woods, avoiding his siblings and teachers by remaining out of sight.

The monument atop Mount Baden-Powell to Lord Baden Powell, founder of the Boy Scouts, of course. Allen Riedel

He joined the military and embarked on campaigns in India and Africa. In Africa, he led reconnaissance missions deep into enemy territory, and this was the fundamental experience that led him to formulate his ideas on scouting. He first wrote of scouting in *Aids to Scouting,* from a military standpoint, to train young men entering into service in the army. His idea was to help young men understand and interpret their surroundings and others around them, equip them with the ability to survive, and use their powers of independent thought to solve problems. The manual became a bestseller and gave BP the idea to revise the work for all young men. Teachers across the country had begun to use the manual for instructing young boys.

Baden-Powell saw what he thought was a decline in the physical prowess of young boys, and he abhorred laziness. He wanted to instruct them in the ways of being a good citizen and helping others. The motto was to "be prepared," with an emphasis on being "good" and just to fellow citizens. Scouts were to value honor, duty, loyalty, helpfulness, courtesy, obedience, and thrift. Baden-Powell was a gifted artist and musician; he was also known as an excellent storyteller. He died and was buried in Kenya in 1941.

Big Horn Mine

A hardy ten-stamp mill stands intact on the stalwart slopes of Mount Baden-Powell. Follow an old wagon route to the mine and enjoy the scenery of Mount Baldy and the rugged East Fork of the San Gabriel River.

Start: Vincent Gap
Distance: 3.8 miles out and back
Hiking time: About 2 hours
Difficulty: Easy
Trail surface: Dirt and gravel trail
Nearest town: Wrightwood
County: Los Angeles
Other trail users: None
Canine compatibility: Leashed dogs permitted
Trailhead facilities/amenities: Restrooms available at trailhead
Land status: National forest

Fees and permits: Adventure Pass required for parking
Schedule: Open year-round
Maps: USGS Crystal Lake, CA and Mount San Antonio, CA; www .localhikes.com/HikeData.ASP ?DispType=1&ActiveHike=0 &GetHikesStateID=&ID=4677
Trail contact: Angeles National Forest; 701 N. Santa Anita Ave., Arcadia 91006 www.fs.fed.us/r5/ angeles; (626) 574-5200

Finding the trailhead: From the intersection of I-10, I-5, and US 101, head north on I-5 and drive for 4.1 miles. Take exit 139A for CA 2/Glendale Freeway toward Glendale. Drive for 7.7 miles and take exit 21A to merge onto CA 2/I-210, heading east toward Pasadena. Drive for 1.2 miles. Take exit 20 for CA 2/Angeles Crest Highway toward La Canada Flintridge. Turn left onto CA 2 and drive 51 miles to the parking area for Vincent Gap on the right.

CA 2 closes periodically due to storms, fire, fire danger, and rockslides, especially between Dawson Gap and Islip Saddle. When closures are in effect, use this alternate route: From the intersection of I-10, I-5, and US 101, head east on I-10 for 40.9 miles and take exit 58A for I-15 north. Drive for 21.8 miles and take exit 131 for CA 138. Turn left onto CA 138 and drive for 8.6 miles. Turn left onto CA 2 and drive west for 13.9 miles to the Vincent Gap parking area. GPS: N 34 22.4'/W 117 45.15'

THE HIKE

The historic Big Horn Mine rests on the shoulder of mighty Mount Baden-Powell. The claim originally took shape in 1896, when old mountain man/prospector/hermit/Civil War fighter Charles Vincent (Dougherty) found gold while hunting for bighorn sheep on the side of the mountain and discovered a vein. Vincent began to work the mine, digging tunnels, but had no way to transport the gold ore, so he ended up selling the claim in 1901. Then the stamp mill was erected and the mine was enlarged to a massive endeavor. The mine became the largest in Los Angeles County. And, yes, Vincent Gap, Vincent Saddle, and Vincent Gulch are all named after the man who founded the mine.

The mine was a towering complex, with six levels and miles of tunnel, though the exact extent is somewhat disputed. Spelunkers will no doubt scream with delight at the prospect of entering and exploring an old mine shaft, let alone an

Rusted—but fascinating—machinery from the Big Horn Mine. Allen Riedel

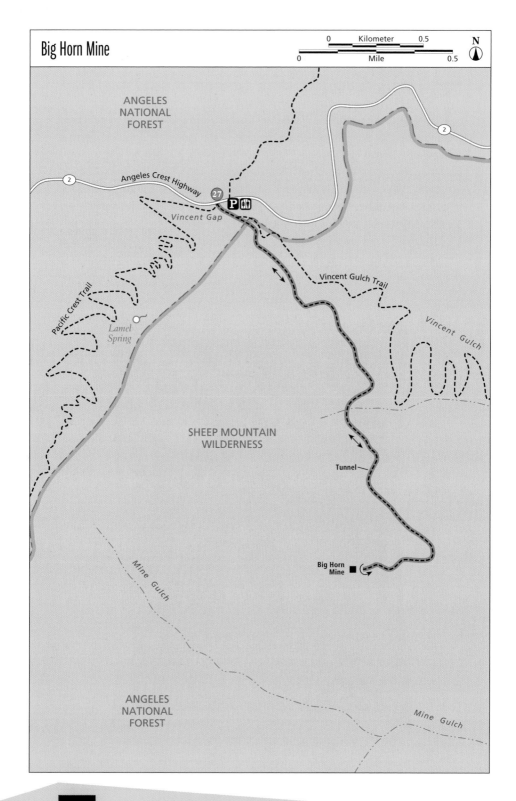

Big Horn Mine

Angeles Crest Highway

Vincent Gap

Pacific Crest Trail

Lamel
Spring

Vincent Gulch Trail

Vincent Gulch

ANGELES
NATIONAL
FOREST

SHEEP MOUNTAIN
WILDERNESS

Tunnel

Big Horn
Mine

Mine Gulch

ANGELES
NATIONAL
FOREST

Mine Gulch

extensive network. The mine itself is inundated with water in many spots, and the old ladders are soggy and waterlogged. Deep shafts filled with water are everywhere, and the mine entrance has been closed off by the forest service and property owners on several occasions. It is unsafe to explore, although maps can be found online. Many of the tunnels lead in circles, and even the official maps of the mine make it look rather labyrinthine.

At one time, the mine was thought to have been the most lucrative in Southern California, but it did not end up as such. Still, the beauty of the mill sitting on the mountain slope is fascinating and will be of great interest to almost anyone who visits. It is fairly easy to reach and the hike is not difficult, but there are a few places where the old road has washed out, and getting to the stamp mill requires a leap over a small drainage area that may be difficult for very young children.

The hike is straightforward for the most part. Look for the ROAD CLOSED sign and gate, and follow the old wagon road for the entire route. At just more than 0.1 mile there is a sign for the Sheep Mountain Wilderness, and the trail leading to Vincent Gulch follows on the left just beyond that. A little less than halfway into the hike, the main mineshaft entrance sits to the right. It is closed up and welded shut, though water drips and seeps from the old mine. Stay on the old wagon road and continue the entire 1.9 miles to the stamp mill.

The views into the East Fork of the San Gabriel River and of the Devils Backbone along the backside of Mount Baldy are fantastic; the high mountain air is fresh and invigorating. It's a great place to ponder the history of the mountains, and what life must have been like for the lone mountain man who eked out his existence in his tiny cabin nearby. There is much to enjoy on this hike.

MILES AND DIRECTIONS

0.0 Start on the old wagon road headed toward Vincent Gulch, past the gate with the ROAD CLOSED sign

0.1 Reach the Sheep Mountain Wilderness boundary and the junction with Vincent Gulch Trail. Continue toward Big Horn Mine.

0.6 Reach the main entrance to the mine (closed).

1.9 Arrive at the stamp mill. Return via the same route.

3.8 Arrive back at the trailhead and the Vincent Gap parking area.

HIKE INFORMATION

Local information: Angeles National Forest, 701 N. Santa Anita Ave., Arcadia 91006, (626) 574-1613

Camping: Angeles National Forest campgrounds (first come, first served / 14-day stay maximum): Appletree, Bear, Big Rock, Blue Ridge, Cabin Flat Trail Camp, Chilao, Cooper Canyon Trail Camp, Cottonwood, Devore Trail Camp, Guffy, Horse Flats, Idlehour Trail Camp, Little Jimmy Trail Camp, Lupine, Manker Flats, Millard Trail Camp, Monte Cristo, Mountain Oak, Oak Flats, Peavine, Sawmill, South; www .fs.fed.us/r5/angeles

Local retailers: A-16 (Adventure 16), www.adventure16.com; REI, www.rei.com

Restaurants: Mile High Pizza, 5996 Cedar, Wrightwood, (760) 249-4848; Yodeler, 6046 Park Dr., Wrightwood, (760) 249-6482; Evergreen Cafe and Raccoon Saloon, 1269 Evergreen Rd., Wrightwood, (760) 249-6393; Grizzly Cafe, 1455 CA 2, Wrightwood, (760) 249-6733; Mexico Lindo, 1253 Evergreen St., Wrightwood, (760) 249-4100; Mountain Top Cafe, 7637 CA 138, Phelan, (760) 249-4811; Blue Ridge Inn, 6060 Park Dr., Wrightwood, (760) 249-3440; Newcomb's Ranch, along Angeles Crest Highway / CA 2 midway between La Canada and Wrightwood, La Canada Flintridge, (626) 440-1001

Ten Stamp Mill remains at the Big Horn Mine. Allen Riedel

Charles Tom Vincent

Charles Tom Vincent (1838–1926), aka Charles Vincent Dougherty, was an irascible old miner/mountain man who lived a solitary life on the steep slopes of what is now Mount Baden-Powell. Vincent was a man of extraordinary skill who was rumored to have killed three grizzly bears while they were in the process of attacking him.

What is known for sure is that Vincent established the claim for the Big Horn Mine, which sits just below the saddle and above the gulch that was named for him in the Angeles National Forest. It is purported that he found gold one day while out hunting for bighorn sheep. The mine became the biggest in Los Angeles County, spanning six levels and including several miles of tunnels, but it was hardly the most profitable mine. Vincent eked out the puny sum of $200,000, a small amount for gold mines in the heyday of mining. Vincent was unable to move the ore and sold his claim to the California Mining Company in 1901.

He lived in a fairly solitary manner for the remainder of his days, befriending only Bob Pallett and Dr. Lee Nobel and his wife, Dorothy. Pallett delivered the mail to Vincent, and the trio would stop in from time to time to check on the old man. He regaled them with stories of his time in the forest, his days in the Union Army, and of the battle of Gettysburg, where he was wounded. Vincent was a member of the Eighth Ohio Infantry, F Company.

With his friends, Vincent shared the story of his life. Apparently Vincent and a friend named Lockwood, who had registered for the army with him, set out west with ideas of making it rich prospecting for gold. Vincent and his friend found an Arizona claim, filed on it, and then, out of nowhere, left the claim behind and emigrated to California. Vincent would not reveal the details of why he left such a rich claim . . . until his deathbed, that is.

As Vincent lay dying, he pleaded with the doctor to have him buried in the Los Angeles National Cemetery with other soldiers. But in order to do that he had to release his real name, Charles Vincent Dougherty. Vincent had been hiding out in the Angeles National Forest since right after the Civil War. He and his friend, Lockwood, were about to become the victims of claim jumpers, who were planning to take the claim and kill the men who had staked it. Before the scoundrels could pull off their plot, Vincent and Lockwood snuck up on the three men and shot them dead. They were so worried about Western justice that they fled the scene without ever letting their side of the story be known. Vincent believed up until his dying days that he was a fugitive wanted for murder, so he changed his name and lived the life of a hermit. As it turned out, there was no connection to his name anywhere, no warrant for his arrest, and no search for justice of any kind.

Dawson Peak

The Devil's Backbone is the colloquial moniker of the trail up the knifelike ridgeline to Mount San Antonio. The "other Devils Backbone" follows a mountaineer use trail on the backside of Mount Baldy and traverses the second- and third-highest peaks in the Angeles National Forest. The way is steep, no-nonsense, not overused, and not for the timid or the acrophobic. Breathtaking views are the norm and scrambling over loose rock is guaranteed, as well as high-mountain adventure.

Start: Guffy Campground (if the gate is locked), or the pullout at the base of Pine Mountain
Distance: 8.3 miles out and back (if the road to the Pine Mountain trailhead is open, the hike can be 4.5 miles out and back)
Hiking time: About 4 or 6 hours
Difficulty: Strenuous
Trail surface: Dirt road and dirt use trail
Nearest town: Wrightwood
County: Los Angeles
Other trail users: None
Canine compatibility: Leashed dogs permitted

Trailhead facilities/amenities: Restroom and picnic facilities at Guffy, no water on trail
Land status: National forest
Fees and permits: Adventure Pass required for parking
Schedule: Open year-round; the road may be closed due to snow and/or dangerous fire conditions
Maps: USGS Mount San Antonio, CA
Trail contact: Angeles National Forest, 701 N. Santa Anita Ave., Arcadia 91006; www.fs.fed.us/r5/angeles; (626) 574-5200

Finding the trailhead: From the intersection of I-10, I-5, and US 101, head north on I-5 and drive for 4.1 miles. Take exit 139A for CA 2/Glendale Freeway toward Glendale. Drive for 7.7 miles and take exit 21A to merge onto CA 2/I-210, heading east toward Pasadena. Drive for 1.2 miles. Take exit 20 for CA 2/Angeles Crest Highway toward La Canada Flintridge. Turn left onto CA 2, drive 54.3 miles, and turn right onto East Blue Ridge Truck Trail/FR 3N06. Drive for 5.1 miles to Guffy Campground, and follow the directions below to the trailhead.

CA 2 closes periodically due to storms, fire, fire danger, and rockslides, especially between Dawson Gap and Islip Saddle. When closures are in effect, use this alternate route: From the intersection of I-10, I-5, and US 101, head east on I-10 for 40.9 miles and take exit 58A for I-15 north. Drive for 21.8 miles and take exit 131 for CA 138. Turn left onto CA 138 and drive for 8.6 miles. Turn left onto CA 2 and drive for 10.6 miles. Turn left onto East Blue Ridge Truck Trail / FR 3N06 and drive for 5.1 miles to Guffy Campground. If the gate is locked, park alongside the road, but do not block the gate. If the gate is not locked, keep right and continue 0.5 mile. Veer left and continue on FR 3N06 for another 1.6 miles to the turnout on the left at the base of Pine Mountain. The trail heads down and then straight up the mountain from here. There is no trailhead sign, but a Sheep Mountain Wilderness sign sits just below the roadway along the use trail. GPS: N 34 20.45' / W 117 39.4833'

THE HIKE

At times, the road that leads to Pine Mountain is open, and at others it is closed. There hardly seems to be rhyme or reason for the closed or open nature of the road, but if hiking this trail, you must be prepared to find the gate closed (and be ready for an additional 3.8 miles round-trip of hiking for a total

Views of Mount Baden-Powell in the distance. Allen Riedel

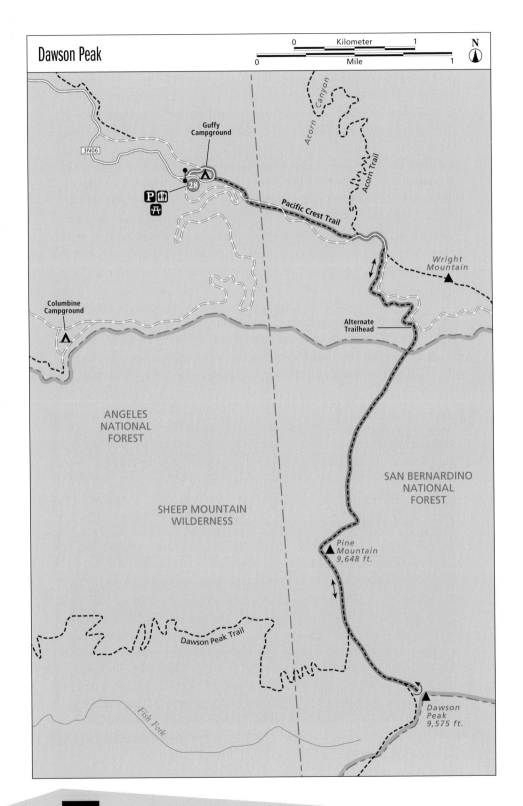

Dawson Peak

0 ——— Kilometer ——— 1
0 ——— Mile ——— 1

N

Guffy
Campground

3N06

28

P

Acorn Canyon

Acorn Trail

Pacific Crest Trail

Wright
Mountain

Alternate
Trailhead

Columbine
Campground

ANGELES
NATIONAL
FOREST

SAN BERNARDINO
NATIONAL
FOREST

SHEEP MOUNTAIN
WILDERNESS

Pine
Mountain
9,648 ft.

Dawson Peak Trail

Fish Fork

Dawson
Peak
9,575 ft.

of 8.3) or be happily surprised if it is open for an out-and-back of 4.5. The description provided here and in the Miles and Directions begins from Guffy Campground and assumes the gate is locked.

The route out of Guffy Campground is rather pedestrian, a simple walk along FR 3N06 or along the PCT. It is better to take the PCT, though the trail and road cross each other so frequently, either route is a viable option. Hike east from the very small one-car pullout parking area next to the locked gate toward Guffy Campground. Head behind the restrooms and find the Pacific Crest Trail just below the ridge. Follow it southeast. The trail intersects with the road multiple times. Follow the trail to the intersection with the Acorn Trail at 1.1 miles. Just beyond this junction the PCT enters the roadway again. Stay on the road and veer right at the fork at 1.5 miles, leaving the PCT. Take the lower section of roadway and follow it to the turnout parking area at 1.9 miles. The trailhead is easy to spot as Pine Mountain looms large in the foreground, and below the roadway there is a gray sign marker for Sheep Mountain Wilderness. The trail is also noticeable, heading straight up the edge of the ridgeline to the top of Pine Mountain at 9,648 feet—the second-tallest mountain in the Angeles National Forest. If the road is open, the route begins here, cutting off 3.8 miles from the entire trip.

From this point, hike downhill sharply for 0.1 mile. The unsigned use trail, also called the "other Devil's Backbone," heads up from here, gaining a whopping 1,500 feet of elevation in just over 1 mile. The route is clearly defined and easy to follow, despite being simply a mountaineer's route. The views are spectacular, the scree is loose in spots, the drops on either side of the ridge are heart-clenching and possibly quite terrifying for anyone without a good sense of balance and/or a fear of heights.

After 1.2 miles of hiking from the road, reach the summit of Pine Mountain, which is wide open, rounded, and large. There is no good 360-degree viewpoint from the top, but there are several spots to rest and get at least a 290-degree view.

From atop Pine Mountain, the trail heads off toward the venerable Mount Baldy; the hump in the middle is Dawson Peak. While this section of trail isn't nearly as frequented as the route up Pine Mountain, it is still very easy to follow as it heads along the ridgeline, and it is the simplest route straight up the mountain.

The trail loses nearly 600 feet of elevation to the saddle between Pine Mountain and Dawson Peak in a little less than 0.5 mile. This elevation must be gained again on the way back, of course. An old logging road designated as Dawson Peak Trail (8W32) crosses the trail just above the saddle; continue straight up the mountain.

Abruptly, the path begins climbing again, gaining 500 feet in roughly 0.75 mile. The route is a bit gentler, but still tough after scrambling up Pine Mountain. And the view from on top of Dawson Peak, although at a lower elevation (9,575 feet), is better. From the summit block, it is possible to look 360 degrees, albeit with some trees blocking the way. Mount Baldy and Mount Harwood are up close and personal. It feels as if you could reach out and touch them. The Cajon Pass and the big mountains of the San Bernardino National Forest, San Jacinto and San Gorgonio, are also seemingly a stone's throw away. Enjoy the vantage point—there is none other like it in Southern California, and it should be yours and yours alone. If there does happen to be a like-minded individual hiking on the same day as you, it might be wise to strike up a conversation. You may just have found a friend for life.

From the summit, the route up Mount Baldy can be discerned for the brutal butt-kicker it is. Some may want to continue on, losing 700 feet to the next saddle and then gaining 1,300 feet to the top of Old Baldy, but most will be content sitting on top of out-of-the-way Dawson Peak. Head back along the same route to whichever parking area you started from.

MILES AND DIRECTIONS

0.0 Start hiking eastward from the roadway toward the restrooms at Guffy Campground.

0.2 Below the restrooms along the ridgeline, meet up with the Pacific Crest Trail. Turn right and head east.

1.1 At the junction with Acorn Trail, stay straight and join FR 3N06.

1.2 Stay on the road as it turns right (south).

1.3 Stay right at the fork.

1.9 At the turnout and lower parking area, join the use trail as it leads toward the summit of Pine Mountain. A Sheep Mountain Wilderness sign is visible below the roadway.

3.2 Reach the summit of Pine Mountain. Continue south along the trail.

3.6 Continue straight up toward Dawson Peak at the junction with the old Dawson Peak Trail (8W32).

4.1 Reach the summit of Dawson Peak. Return via the same route.

8.3 Arrive back at the Guffy Campground trailhead and parking area.

HIKE INFORMATION

Local information: Angeles National Forest, 701 N. Santa Anita Ave., Arcadia 91006, (626) 574-1613

Camping: Angeles National Forest campgrounds (first come, first served / 14-day stay maximum): Appletree, Bear, Big Rock, Blue Ridge, Cabin Flat Trail Camp, Chilao, Cooper Canyon Trail Camp, Cottonwood, Devore Trail Camp, Guffy, Horse Flats, Idlehour Trail Camp, Little Jimmy Trail Camp, Lupine, Manker Flats, Millard Trail Camp, Monte Cristo, Mountain Oak, Oak Flats, Peavine, Sawmill, South; www .fs.fed.us/r5/angeles

Local retailers: A-16 (Adventure 16), www.adventure16.com; REI, www.rei.com

Restaurants: Mile High Pizza, 5996 Cedar, Wrightwood, (760) 249-4848; Yodeler, 6046 Park Dr., Wrightwood, (760) 249-6482; Evergreen Cafe and Raccoon Saloon, 1269 Evergreen Rd., Wrightwood, (760) 249-6393; Grizzly Cafe, 1455 CA 2, Wrightwood, (760) 249-6733; Mexico Lindo, 1253 Evergreen St., Wrightwood, (760) 249-4100; Mountain Top Cafe, 7637 CA 138, Phelan, (760) 249-4811; Blue Ridge Inn, 6060 Park Dr., Wrightwood, (760) 249-3440; Newcomb's Ranch, midway along Angeles Crest Highway / CA 2 between La Canada and Wrightwood, La Canada Flintridge, (626) 440-1001

> *Safety Tip: When hiking at high altitude (8,000–12,000 feet), be watchful for signs of altitude illness. If you or a member of your party suffers from headache, nausea, and fatigue, descend immediately.*

Mount Baldy

There is an "easy" route to climb Mount Baldy, a moderate way, and a straight-out difficult trek. This trail follows the Bear Canyon Trail from Mount Baldy Village, gaining 6,000 feet of elevation in 6 miles. It is one of the toughest hikes in the Angeles National Forest that doesn't require special skills. The views are magnificent, the traffic infrequent, and the workout unmatched.

Start: Mount Baldy Schoolhouse Visitor Center
Distance: 12 miles out and back
Hiking time: About 8 to 12 hours
Difficulty: Extremely strenuous
Trail surface: Singletrack dirt trail
Nearest town: Mount Baldy
County: Los Angeles
Other trail users: None
Canine compatibility: Leashed dogs permitted
Trailhead facilities/amenities: restrooms and water at visitor center
Land status: National forest

Fees and permits: Adventure Pass required for parking
Schedule: Open year-round; gate locked after 4 p.m.—do not park at visitor center
Maps: USGS Mount San Antonio, CA
Trail contact: Angeles National Forest, 701 N. Santa Anita Ave., Arcadia 91006; www.fs.fed.us/r5/angeles; (626) 574-5200

Finding the trailhead: From the intersection of I-5, US 101, and I-10, take I-10 east for 12.1 miles. Take exit 31B to merge onto I-605 north. Drive for 5.4 miles. Take exit 27A to merge onto I-210 east. Drive for 15.5 miles. Take exit 52 toward Baseline Road. Turn left onto Baseline Road and drive for 0.2 mile. Turn right onto Padua Avenue. Drive for 1.8 miles. Turn right onto Mount Baldy Road and drive for 7.4 miles to the Mount Baldy Visitor Center. Park just off Bear Canyon Drive in the parking lot 100 yards south of the visitor center. GPS: N 34 14.2666' / W 117 39.4666'

THE HIKE

From the parking area just south of the Mount Baldy Visitor Center, walk north-west up Bear Canyon Drive to where the Bear Canyon Trail begins at the signed trailhead. The first 2 miles along the trail gain 1,000 feet of elevation. This is a steep trail—usually 1,000 feet gained in a mile is about as tough as trails maintained by the forest service get. But after the second full mile, the trail gets even steeper and heads practically straight up the mountain, gaining a monstrous 1,600 feet in the next mile, even with switchbacks. From there it levels off some, but make no mistake, this trail is a workout, a true leg-burner.

The trail follows lovely Bear Canyon, which is shaded for a good portion of the early hike by old oaks and scattered pines. There are quite a few forest cabins along the trail, like on some other routes in the Angeles National Forest. Most of the owners seem to take pride in their uniqueness and most seem well cared for. The last cabin sits just about 1 mile up the trail; at the last cabin, stay to the right on Bear Canyon Trail and follow it the rest of the way up the mountain. There aren't any confusing junctions or unsigned trails beyond this point.

After 1.75 miles, the marshy fern-lined meadow area known as Bear Flat comes into view. A sign with a goofy bear marks the location. From here, the trail takes on a whole different level of intensity. First the trail exits the shady confines of the can-yon and begins to climb and switchback up the mountain. There is less tree cover,

View from the trail near the summit on Mount Baldy. Allen Riedel

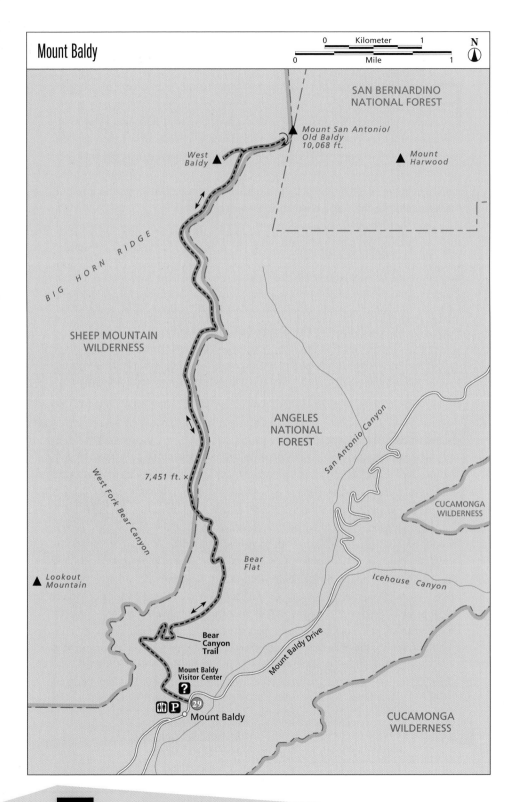

Mount Baldy

0 Kilometer 1
0 Mile 1

N

SAN BERNARDINO
NATIONAL FOREST

*Mount San Antoniol
Old Baldy*
10,068 ft.

▲ *Mount*
Harwood

West
Baldy ▲

B I G   H O R N   R I D G E

SHEEP MOUNTAIN
WILDERNESS

ANGELES
NATIONAL
FOREST

San Antonio Canyon

CUCAMONGA
WILDERNESS

7,451 ft. ×

West Fork Bear Canyon

Bear
Flat

Icehouse Canyon

▲ *Lookout*
Mountain

Bear
Canyon
Trail

Mount Baldy
Visitor Center
?

Mount Baldy Drive

🚻 P 29 Mount Baldy

CUCAMONGA
WILDERNESS

and if the sun is shining directly on the south-facing slope, it can get very hot. A fire in 2008 burned off some of the ground cover here, but spared the canyon, most of the pines, and the upper reaches of the mountain. Evidence of the fire is omnipresent, but the recovery of the mountain chaparral and manzanita hardly shows any signs at all. Views into Icehouse Canyon open up, and soon so will views into the entire Southern California basin.

The trail works its way back under pines, which are mostly tall and isolated to begin with, but eventually become evenly spaced along the trail, providing shade intermittently with ample spots for respite from the sun.

At 2.5 miles the trail hits the West Baldy ridgeline, near the prominence marked 7,451 feet on the topo map. Views open up into Cattle Canyon below and across to Big Horn Ridge, which meets the trail and West Baldy Ridge 2 miles and 2,000 feet ahead and above. The route follows the steep ridgeline for the remaining 2,500 feet to the top.

The trail seems to climb incessantly, but the views get continually better and better. From the notch above Big Horn Ridge, the summit of Mount Baldy and the closer West Baldy can be seen. The route traverses a few hundred feet below the summit of West Baldy and eventually meets the saddle between the two peaks. Turn left and take the small 0.2-mile use trail to the summit of West Baldy. Hardly anyone does; most people only go for the gusto of Mount Baldy itself. But the peak is way less crowded and the views are nearly as remarkable. Take a short break, head back to the main trail, and continue the remaining 0.4 mile to the summit of Mount Baldy.

Mount Baldy was so named due to its lack of tree cover and hence its "bald" appearance, especially in winter when snow caps the peak for a good portion of the darker months. Its true name is Mount San Antonio, but hardly anyone calls it that; others, including the USGS topo map of the region, refer to it as "Old Baldy."

There will more than likely be other hikers atop the peak—it is a popular destination with other trails leading to the summit. If you planned your trip on a weekend, some hikers will have even taken a ski lift to a point a mere 2,000 feet below the top to begin hiking to the same destination. While still not an easy trip up, these hikers likely won't be as tired as you and your party—but they have earned it just as well. Relish the knowledge that your trip has followed the truly intrepid route. From the summit, take the trail back to Mount Baldy Village.

Caution: The summit of Mount Baldy is quite large and open. Many visitors have lost their bearings on top and taken the wrong trail back to the bottom. Pay attention to your surroundings and be wary that temperatures and weather pat-

Mount Baldy, also known as Mount San Antonio, is the highest point in Los Angeles County at 10,046 feet.

terns can shift rapidly at such high altitudes. Do not continue climbing in storms unless you are prepared for them and knowledgeable in methods of route finding/winter mountaineering. Mount Baldy's proximity to the sunny beaches of Los Angeles doesn't make it safer than other high-altitude mountains. Paradoxically, it only makes it more dangerous, because people underestimate its potential for tragedy. Many have paid for this hubris with their lives. If weather conditions turn bad, turn back. Don't overestimate your abilities or of those in your party.

MILES AND DIRECTIONS

0.0 Start up Bear Canyon Drive 100 yards south of Mount Baldy Visitor Center.

1.0 Reach the last cabin and take the right fork in the trail.

1.75 Reach Bear Flat.

5.6 Turn left onto the West Baldy use trail.

5.8 Arrive on the summit of West Baldy. Return to the main trail.

6.0 Turn left onto the main trail and head for the summit of Mount Baldy.

6.4 Arrive at the summit of Mount Baldy. Follow the main trail back.

12.0 Arrive back at the trailhead and parking area.

HIKE INFORMATION

Local information: Angeles National Forest, 701 N. Santa Anita Ave., Arcadia 91006, (626) 574-1613

Camping: Angeles National Forest campgrounds (first come, first served / 14-day stay maximum): Appletree, Bear, Big Rock, Blue Ridge, Cabin Flat Trail Camp, Chilao, Cooper Canyon Trail Camp, Cottonwood, Devore Trail Camp, Guffy, Horse Flats, Idlehour Trail Camp, Little Jimmy Trail Camp, Lupine, Manker Flats, Millard Trail Camp, Monte Cristo, Mountain Oak, Oak Flats, Peavine, Sawmill, South; www.fs.fed.us/r5/angeles

Local retailers: A-16 (Adventure 16), www.adventure16.com; REI, www.rei.com

Restaurants: Mile High Pizza, 5996 Cedar, Wrightwood, (760) 249-4848; Yodeler, 6046 Park Dr., Wrightwood, (760) 249-6482; Evergreen Cafe and Raccoon Saloon, 1269 Evergreen Rd., Wrightwood, (760) 249-6393; Grizzly Cafe, 1455 CA 2, Wrightwood, (760) 249-6733; Mexico Lindo, 1253 Evergreen St., Wrightwood, (760) 249-4100; Mountain Top Cafe, 7637 CA 138, Phelan, (760) 249-4811; Blue Ridge Inn, 6060 Park Dr., Wrightwood, (760) 249-3440; Newcomb's Ranch, midway along Angeles Crest Highway / CA 2 between La Canada and Wrightwood, La Canada Flintridge, (626) 440-1001

Timber Mountain

Icehouse Canyon is a lovely sylvan glen that leads into the rugged Cucamonga Wilderness. Hikers of all ages will enjoy the splendor of the mixed oak and pine forest, the cabins in the woods, the flowing creek, and the towering summits that reach high above the confines of the canyon. Timber Mountain is the first in a line of mountains called the Three-Tee's: Timber, Telegraph, and Thunder. Timber Mountain is the closest peak to Icehouse Saddle.

Start: Icehouse Canyon Trailhead
Distance: 9 miles out and back
Hiking time: About 5 hours
Difficulty: Strenuous
Trail surface: Singletrack dirt trail
Nearest town: Mount Baldy
County: San Bernardino
Other trail users: None
Canine compatibility: Leashed dogs permitted
Trailhead facilities/amenities: Restrooms at trailhead, filterable water at Columbine Spring
Land status: National forest

Fees and permits: Wilderness permit required; Adventure Pass required for parking. Wilderness permits can be acquired at the Mount Baldy Visitor Center, Mount Baldy Road, Mount Baldy 91759; (909) 982-2829.
Schedule: Open year-round
Maps: USGS Cucamonga Peak, CA and Mount San Antonio, CA
Trail contact: Angeles National Forest, 701 N. Santa Anita Ave., Arcadia 91006; www.fs.fed.us/r5/angeles; (626) 574-5200

Finding the trailhead: From the intersection of I-5, US 101, and I-10, take I-10 east for 12.1 miles. Take exit 31B to merge onto I-605 north. Drive for 5.4 miles. Take exit 27A to merge onto I-210 east. Drive for 15.5 miles. Take exit 52 toward Baseline Road. Turn left onto Baseline Road and drive for 0.2 mile. Turn right onto Padua Avenue. Drive for 1.8 miles. Turn right onto Mount Baldy Road and drive for 8.9 miles. Turn right onto Ice House Canyon Road. Drive for 0.1 mile and park in the lot. GPS: N 34 15'/W 117 38.3166'

cehouse Canyon is a lovely slice of the Southern California mountains, and it is an incredibly popular region as well. In fact, the canyon is one of the most popular hiking destinations in all of the Angeles National Forest. Even though there are a lot of visitors, the area still seems remote. It is a large enough region to accommodate everyone, but this is not the hike to take if you are looking for solitude.

The Icehouse Canyon Trail begins up a gated road, which eventually turns into a dirt road that narrows until it becomes simply a dirt path. Forest cabins line the road and eventually dot the trail as well. This is a common occurrence in the Angeles National Forest, as there are quite a few cabin-lined trails and canyons. Most of the woodland homes are well taken care of and some are absolutely beautiful.

The route follows the powerful unnamed stream that flows through Icehouse Canyon and floods the spillway at the San Antonio Dam, just north of the community of Upland. At high runoff, the creek can be a raging torrent, making crossings dangerous, but normally its flow is strong and the area is lush year-round, which gives the canyon its genuine appeal. The trail gains a steady 700 feet per mile, which isn't necessarily an easy hike, but it is manageable for most people, and a lot of parents bring their children along to play in the forest and the stream when it is gently flowing. The route is luxuriant, and those who come here generally return time and time again.

The trail winds up Icehouse Canyon toward Timber Mountain. Allen Riedel

At 1 mile, the trail junctions with the Chapman Trail, though it is not marked on the USGS topo map. The Chapman Trail is a semicircle loop that ascends and rejoins the Icehouse Canyon Trail, gaining elevation less rapidly but also covering more distance. (**Option:** Taking the Chapman Trail one way will add an additional 1.7 miles to the total hike distance.)

After the junction, the hike leaves the mountain cabins behind, though some large ruins still exist farther up the canyon, and the trail continues to follow the lovely sylvan stream. Some reworking of the trail has been completed over the past few years, and improvements have been made to curb erosion along the trail.

As the trail ascends, the surrounding woods become a pine forest and the trail wanders away from the stream, even though the creek is never more than a hundred or so yards lower in the canyon. At 1.8 miles, the trail enters the Cucamonga Wilderness and there is a sign to mark this boundary, along with an interpretative informational kiosk. The next trail junction occurs at the Columbine Spring, an ice-cold freshwater source that pours from out of the rock year-round. A short spur trail of less than 0.1 mile leads to the spring and back.

Mile markers indicate distance along the Icehouse Canyon Trail; the Chapman Trail rejoins the main route just before the 3-mile marker. The saddle is another 0.5 mile beyond. The saddle is a cool spot for a rest—taking in the fresh mountain air, looking over the various canyons that drop off below—complete with a four-way trail junction.

Trails lead to all parts of the wilderness from the saddle. Follow the route that is labeled the Three Tee's Trail. The summit of Timber Mountain is listed as being another 0.9 mile. There will be foot traffic at the saddle, but there is a good chance that taking a step onto the Three Tee's Trail will lead to solitude. At the very least, there will no longer be the mass of people found lower in Icehouse Canyon.

From the junction, the trail to Timber Mountain climbs steeply up the slope. It drops just to the west of the summit, and a use trail departs to the right at 4.25 miles, leading to the summit. In another 0.25 mile the trail reaches the summit of Timber Mountain.

At 8,308 feet Timber Mountain is tall enough to command outstanding views of the surrounding countryside, mountains, and wilderness. There are trees on top, so hikers have to move around to get in all the differing views. An illegible sign marks the summit, along with a metal sign featuring Mount Chapman.

After taking in the views, return via the same route, or take the Chapman loop back to the parking area for Icehouse Canyon.

Hiking Tip: To avoid rattlesnakes, don't put your hands into places you can't see into. Back away and give a wide berth to rattlesnakes on the trail. At best, rattlesnakes can strike between one-half and two-thirds their total body length.

Timber Mountain

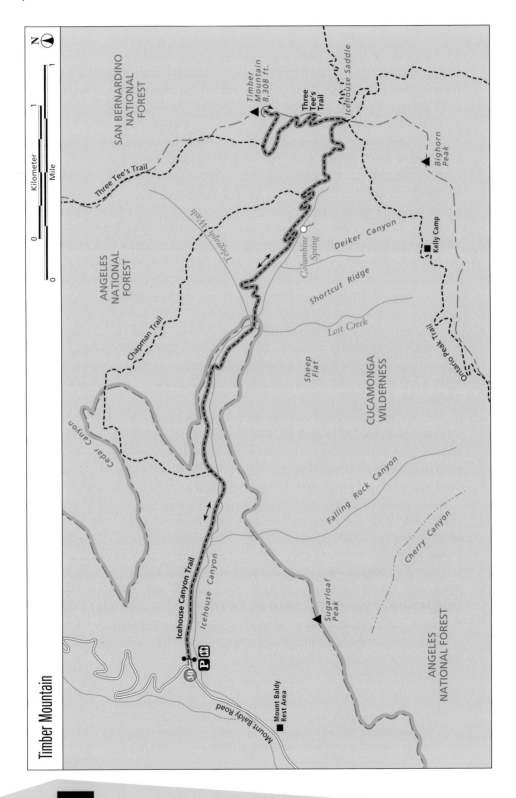

N

Kilometer
Mile

SAN BERNARDINO
NATIONAL
FOREST

ANGELES
NATIONAL
FOREST

Three Tee's Trail

Telegraph Wash

Chapman Trail

Cedar Canyon

Icehouse Canyon Trail

Icehouse Canyon

Mount Baldy Road

Mount Baldy
Rest Area

30

P

Timber
Mountain
8,308 ft.

Three
Tee's
Trail

Icehouse Saddle

Bighorn
Peak

Columbine
Spring

Deiker Canyon

Kelly Camp

Shortcut Ridge

Lost Creek

Sheep
Flat

CUCAMONGA
WILDERNESS

Ontario Peak Trail

Falling Rock Canyon

Cherry Canyon

Sugarloaf
Peak

ANGELES
NATIONAL FOREST

0.0   Start by hiking east along the road from the Icehouse Canyon parking lot.

0.1   The road becomes a dirt road and then a trail.

1.0   At the junction with the Chapman Trail, continue straight.

1.8   Enter the Cucamonga Wilderness.

2.5   Continue straight at the spur trail to Columbine Spring.

2.8   Continue right at second junction with the Chapman Trail.

3.5   Arrive at Icehouse Saddle. Turn left and take the Three Tee's Trail.

4.25 Turn right onto the Timber Mountain use trail.

4.5   Arrive on top of Timber Mountain. Return via the same route.

9.0   Arrive back at the trailhead.

HIKE INFORMATION

Local information: Angeles National Forest, 701 N. Santa Anita Ave., Arcadia 91006, (626) 574-1613

Camping: Angeles National Forest campgrounds (first come, first served / 14-day stay maximum): Appletree, Bear, Big Rock, Blue Ridge, Cabin Flat Trail Camp, Chilao, Cooper Canyon Trail Camp, Cottonwood, Devore Trail Camp, Guffy, Horse Flats, Idlehour Trail Camp, Little Jimmy Trail Camp, Lupine, Manker Flats, Millard Trail Camp, Monte Cristo, Mountain Oak, Oak Flats, Peavine, Sawmill, South; www .fs.fed.us/r5/angeles

Local retailers: A-16 (Adventure 16), www.adventure16.com; REI, www.rei.com

Lodging/restaurants: Mile High Pizza, 5996 Cedar, Wrightwood, (760) 249-4848; Yodeler, 6046 Park Dr., Wrightwood, (760) 249-6482; Evergreen Cafe and Raccoon Saloon, 1269 Evergreen Rd., Wrightwood, (760) 249-6393; Grizzly Cafe, 1455 CA 2, Wrightwood, (760) 249-6733; Mexico Lindo, 1253 Evergreen St., Wrightwood, (760) 249-4100; Mountain Top Cafe, 7637 CA 138, Phelan, (760) 249-4811; Blue Ridge Inn, 6060 Park Dr., Wrightwood, (760) 249-3440; Newcomb's Ranch, midway along Angeles Crest Highway / CA 2 between La Canada and Wrightwood, La Canada Flintridge, (626) 440-1001

Etiwanda Peak

The hike to Etiwanda Peak combines a trek up the Middle Fork of Lytle Creek and an epic adventure from Icehouse Saddle deep into the Cucamonga Wilderness to Cucamonga Peak—and ultimately to remote Etiwanda Peak, where views into the Southern California basin are incredible and the serenity is sublime.

Start: Middle Fork Lytle Creek trailhead

Distance: 16.5 miles out and back

Hiking time: About 8 to 12 hours

Difficulty: Extremely strenuous

Trail surface: Singletrack dirt trail

Nearest town: Lytle Creek

County: San Bernardino

Other trail users: None

Canine compatibility: Leashed dogs permitted

Trailhead facilities/amenities: None

Land status: National forest

Fees and permits: Wilderness permit required; Adventure Pass required for parking. Obtain your wilderness permit at Lytle Creek Ranger Station, 1209 Lytle Creek Rd., Lytle Creek 92358; (909) 382-2851.

Schedule: Open year-round; the road closes during inclement weather

Maps: USGS Cucamonga Peak, CA and Devore, CA; http://c0278592 .cdn.cloudfiles.rackspacecloud .com/original/405624.jpg

Trail contacts: Angeles National Forest, 701 N. Santa Anita Ave., Arcadia 91006; www.fs.fed.us/ r5/angeles, (626) 574-5200. San Bernardino National Forest, 602 S. Tippecanoe Ave., San Bernardino 92408; www.fs.fed.us/r5/san bernardino/; (909) 382-2600 or (909) 382-2851

Finding the trailhead: From the intersection of I-5, US 101, and I-10, take I-10 east for 38.6 miles. Take exit 58A to merge onto I-15 north/Ontario Freeway, and continue for 10.7 miles. Take exit 119 for Sierra Avenue and turn left. Drive for 6.5 miles on Sierra Avenue/ Lytle Creek Road. Turn left onto Middle Fork Road. Drive for 2.8 miles. Park in the lot at the end of the road. GPS: N 34 15.2' / W 117 32.4333'

THE HIKE

Lytle Creek marks the eastern boundary of the San Gabriel Mountains; its waters flow from the highest peaks in the range, draining down the steep eastern slopes through lovely wooded canyons. All forks of Lytle Creek are lovely, but the Middle Fork is the standout. In fall the foliage displays some of the best autumn color in all of Southern California. In spring the wildflowers bloom in abundance. The canyon also happens to be one of the best places to see some of the remaining bighorn sheep in the range, as well as other wildlife. Backcountry camping options exist in several spots along the trail, and the hiking is some of the best anywhere—no doubt about it.

This hike is an epic journey and not for the faint of heart, beginners, or the uninitiated. The trail begins in a portion of the canyon that was severely burned during the devastating Old Fire of 2003, and it climbs over 1 mile in elevation to two spectacular summits. At the lower elevations though, it seems to be little more than a dry, dusty wash filled with yucca and other desert shrubs. While some of the canyon's beauty was destroyed in the fire, most of the upper reaches of the canyon survived unscathed.

The trail comes to a junction at 0.6 mile. Both trails meet up and cover about the same amount of distance, so take the one on the left, which dips down into Middle Fork of Lytle Creek and passes the Stone House Crossing campsite. Here,

On top of Etiwanda Peak you can see for miles, and then some. Allen Riedel

Etiwanda Peak

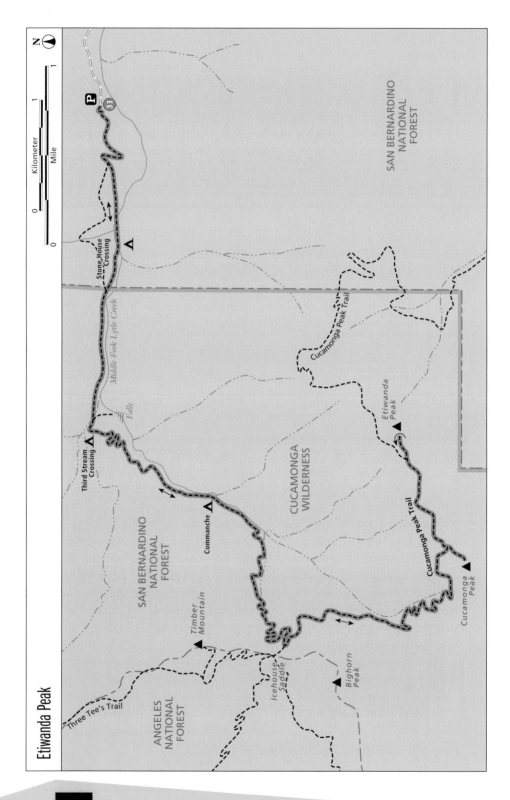

the forest starts off as a mixed pine and deciduous forest and quickly elevates into an alpine wonderland.

The trail meets up with the spur trail again at 1.4 miles. Continue straight up into the canyon. At 2 miles a small use trail leads into a steep and obviously spectacular drainage. (Option: Many people will want to scramble the short 0.15 mile over rocks up into the side canyon. The scramble is a bit challenging, but definitely worth the extra effort. A lovely 30-foot waterfall plunges over a cliff into a deep pool, and there are more waterfalls up the dramatic gorge, but those without mountaineering experience will want to return to the main trail after visiting the first fall and continue up the mountain.)

At the Third Stream Crossing campsite, the trail makes a 90-degree turn to the left (southwest) and begins to climb more steeply and enter the pine wonderland. Continue up the mountain along the trail and pass the Commanche campsite at 3.7 miles.

The trail continues to climb sharply until it levels off at Icehouse Saddle at 5.2 miles. The saddle is the major intersection for five trails in the Cucamonga Wilderness. It is well signed and easy to follow. Turn left and follow the Cucamonga Peak Trail as it drops 200 feet before beginning to climb again at a rate of 1,500 feet in 1.5 miles to the top of Cucamonga Peak. The narrow route follows along the side of the slope of the mountain.

At 7 miles, turn right on the Cucamonga Peak use trail. It is a small mountaineer's trail marked with an old wooden sign that seems to be barely hanging on. In another steep 0.25 mile, the trail tops out on the apex of Cucamonga Peak. The views down into Los Angeles and beyond are breathtaking.

Take a rest. Those who are exhausted may want to call it a day, but for those wanting to reach a peak that is rarely visited, along a trail that is traversed more by bighorn sheep and Bigfoot than homo sapiens, head back down to the main trail and turn right along one of the least-traveled paths, the Cucamonga Peak Trail as it leads to San Sevaine Flats in the Angeles National Forest. It is another 0.8 mile to the use trail to the summit of Etiwanda Peak. The trail loses another 600 feet before it begins climbing up to Etiwanda. The small use trail veers off the main trail to the right and quickly gains the summit block of Etiwanda Peak. Atop the mountain, the views are fairly similar to those on Cucamonga, but the summit block is much smaller and seemingly more intimate. A summit register has only a few entries in it, and there is solitude and serenity on the top.

The trail back leads 300 feet up to Cucamonga Peak Trail, and from there the route is mostly downhill all the way back to the Middle Fork of Lytle Creek.

MILES AND DIRECTIONS

0.0   Begin by hiking west up the Middle Fork of Lytle Creek.

0.6   Continue straight at the junction with the spur trail, heading into the creek bed.

1.0   Arrive at Stone House Crossing campsite. Continue straight.

1.4   Continue straight at the second junction with the spur trail.

2.0   A use trail leads to spectacular falls on the left. Continue straight.

2.1   Reach the Third Stream Crossing campsite. The trail turns south, heading up to Icehouse Saddle.

3.7   Reach Commanche campsite.

5.2   Arrive at Icehouse Saddle. Turn left and follow the Cucamonga Peak Trail.

7.0   Turn right onto the Cucamonga Peak use trail.

7.25 Arrive atop Cucamonga Peak. Return to the main trail.

7.5   Turn right onto the Cucamonga Peak Trail, heading east toward Etiwanda Peak.

8.3   Veer right and continue straight onto the use trail for Etiwanda Peak.

8.5   Arrive atop Etiwanda Peak. Return via the same route.

16.5 Arrive back at the trailhead and parking area.

HIKE INFORMATION

Local information: Angeles National Forest, 701 N. Santa Anita Ave., Arcadia 91006, (626) 574-1613

Camping: Angeles National Forest campgrounds (first come, first served / 14-day stay maximum): Appletree, Bear, Big Rock, Blue Ridge, Cabin Flat Trail Camp, Chilao, Cooper Canyon Trail Camp, Cottonwood, Devore Trail Camp, Guffy, Horse Flats, Idlehour Trail Camp, Little Jimmy Trail Camp, Lupine, Manker Flats, Millard Trail Camp, Monte Cristo, Mountain Oak, Oak Flats, Peavine, Sawmill, South; www.fs.fed.us/r5/angeles

Local retailers: A-16 (Adventure 16), www.adventure16.com; REI, www.rei.com

Restaurants: Mile High Pizza, 5996 Cedar, Wrightwood, (760) 249-4848; Yodeler, 6046 Park Dr., Wrightwood, (760) 249-6482; Evergreen Cafe and Raccoon Saloon, 1269 Evergreen Rd., Wrightwood, (760) 249-6393; Grizzly Cafe, 1455 CA 2, Wrightwood, (760) 249-6733; Mexico Lindo, 1253 Evergreen St., Wrightwood, (760) 249-4100; Mountain Top Cafe, 7637 CA 138, Phelan, (760) 249-4811; Blue Ridge Inn, 6060 Park Dr., Wrightwood, (760) 249-3440; Newcomb's Ranch, midway along Angeles Crest Highway / CA 2 between La Canada and Wrightwood, La Canada Flintridge, (626) 440-1001

Honorable Mentions

C. Waterman Mountain

Waterman Mountain is a comfortable climb just to the north of Twin Peaks. It can serve as a great introduction to hiking in general, as it climbs through lovely forest to the top of a rounded summit with some nice views to the south. It isn't too long or too short, but just about the perfect-size outing with enough elevation gain to keep the interest of even those in top physical shape. A ski area on the north side of the mountain is entirely out of view for the trip up the trail. The summit sits right in the middle of the Angeles National Forest on the edge of the San Gabriel Wilderness; it is one of the tall mountains of the back range. It is also one of the twenty-one peaks in the San Gabriel Mountains above 8,000 feet, standing 38 feet above that marker.

Even though the trailhead is not very well marked, it is easy to ferret out. The trail is fairly popular and a favorite of many who visit the forest. Granite-lined and forested with towering pines, it feels more like the northern forests of the Sierra Nevada. A little too long for very young children—the hike is 6 miles round-trip with a 1,300-foot elevation gain—the trail can serve as a great first summit for those who are a bit older. The mountain was originally named Lady Waterman's Peak for the wife of a forest supervisor who stacked a pile of rocks on top of the summit. Liz Waterman was the first known woman to have crossed the San Gabriel Mountains. Mapmakers removed her name, even though her husband lobbied for the rest of his life to have the appellation reapplied. The trailhead is close to the middle of the Angeles Crest Highway, located next to the parking area at mile marker 58.02.

D. Mount Islip

Mount Islip is a great high peak, rising to 8,250 feet near the eastern end of the San Gabriel Mountains. The trail begins at Islip Saddle, a parking area and trail junction for the Pacific Crest Trail (PCT) in the Angeles National Forest. The trail climbs gently around the base of the mountain through desertlike chaparral to the Little Jimmy Camp and Little Jimmy Spring, following the PCT along the same route as the trip to Mount Hawkins. Hikers can take two trails up to the summit. One starts from the back end of the camp, or hikers can simply follow the trail to Windy Gap, another fantastic trail junction of the high Angeles forest. The route then steeply climbs up the side of the mountain through remnants of the 2002 Curve Fire, which burned a good portion of the eastern edge of the San Gabriel range. The views are fairly outstanding along the way for the entire route. Once on top, the rocky summit of Mount Baldy is visible, and the walls of an old stone lookout structure from the 1920s remain on the summit. Climbing on mostly north-facing slopes, the trail ascends through a nice yellow pine forest with a round-trip total mileage of 6 miles.

E. Mount Williamson

Mount Williamson is the twin summit to Mount Islip, on the north across Islip Saddle. Both peaks sit high above the Angeles Crest Highway at almost the same elevation, with Williamson being only 6 feet shorter at 8,244 feet above sea level. Although the two summits start from the same trailhead, they could hardly be any more different. Both are obviously arid Southern California peaks, but Mount Williamson is slightly north and much closer to the dry Mojave Desert and the Victor Valley; the vegetation clearly shows this distinction. The Pacific Crest Trail (PCT) climbs along its south-facing slopes, and although there are tall pines along this route, the vegetation is much sparser and the trail seems quite a bit rockier.

The summit is one of the strangest of all of the Southern California peaks. All three bumps along the summit ridge seem higher, giving a grass-is-greener effect when on top. The middle bump is actually the tallest, even though it is hard to tell when standing atop it. The summit was named for a lieutenant, Robert S. Williamson, in the US Army Corps of Engineers. Williamson was sent with his men to find a feasible site for a railroad to enter Southern California. Their Pacific Railroad Survey of 1853, on the backside of the San Gabriel and San Bernardino Mountains, led to the modern-day Cajon Pass and the railroad tracks that run through there, which are also clearly visible from the top. The round-trip total mileage is 6 miles.

F. Cooper Canyon Falls

The waterfalls at Cooper Canyon are some of the loveliest in all of the San Gabriel Mountains. The front side of the range is teeming with waterfalls; it is hardly exaggeration to say that there is one in nearly every canyon. Cooper Canyon is different though. The canyons on the front side of the range are undoubtedly pretty, with their riparian splendor and falls that flow all year (or at least for most of the year), providing water to nourish the lush vegetation. Here, in the middle of the high country, pines and incense cedar are more natural than the oaks and sycamores that grow in the lower elevations. Hiking from Buckhorn Campground along the High Desert National Recreation Trail is like hiking in some faraway distant mountain heights. Tall trees tower overhead and Cooper Creek babbles in the undergrowth. As the trail drops toward the final destination, there are actually two other sets of waterfalls along the way—smaller, of course, than the third and final set. Hiking in from the Cooper Canyon Trail Camp circumvents the first two sets and ends up near the falls at the junction of the Pacific Crest Trail (PCT) and the High Desert Trail. The final falls are a spectacular 35 feet in height, dropping over a precipice and directly into a wading pool. Some of the trail was damaged in the Station Fire of 2009; check with the forest service before attempting to hike to the falls. Be prepared for the hike back out of the canyon, because the trail gains 1,000 feet back to Buckhorn Campground and 800 feet back to Cooper Canyon Trail Camp. From Buckhorn Campground the trail is a round-trip of 3 miles.

San Bernardino
National Forest

The San Gorgonio Wilderness is the premier unspoiled forest in Southern California (hikes 33, 34). Allen Riedel

The San Bernardino National Forest has the distinction of being the most heavily populated forest region in the United States. Its borders stretch from Mount Baldy in the west to the Coachella Valley in the east and the Salton Sink in the south. The highest mountain in Southern California, San Gorgonio, resides at 11,499 feet within the boundaries of the forest. The area provides several popular skiing destinations for all of Southern California, and the forest has been home to many memorable scenes from both the small screen and the silver screen. A recreation

> **The San Bernardino National Forest is the most heavily populated forest in the United States.**

mecca, the forest offers climbing, hiking, skiing, boating, fishing, camping, winter mountaineering, and more.

The ecology of the forest is varied, ranging from high desert in the far north to foothills and alpine forests. There is also a broad variety of scenery, flora, and fauna. The mountaintops are some of the highest in the United States, and the wilderness areas are without a doubt some of the greatest in the world. The forest has creeks, hot springs, towering peaks, alpine lakes, and world-class resorts. Many species of animals reside within the forest, including endangered desert bighorn sheep and black bear. Wildflowers are amazing in the spring, and the region is also home to Southern California's only stand of quaking aspen.

Created by the uplift of the San Andreas Fault and the pressure between the Pacific and North American tectonic plates, the mountains are relatively young and growing. The range is known as a transverse range for its east/west orientation, and because of this the area has fallen victim to a rash of wildfires in the recent decades. Due to the position of the Earth, the sun shines on the southern-facing mountains all day long, even in winter, melting away snow at a tremendous rate and leaving the mountains exposed to extreme dryness. Coupled with the nonnative grasses that have invaded the continent since the arrival of the Spanish, the dryer areas react like a tinderbox, and conflagrations are likely during the dry season and droughts.

Due to the effects of fire suppression as a means of forest management for the past century, plus a decade of drought conditions, the forest has grown unhealthy, with more trees living in areas without the proper nutrients to survive. A bark beetle infestation has weakened and killed many trees in the forest, leaving the region further susceptible to fire, and the forest's survival has even been called into question by the United States Congress.

Despite that, the region is exquisitely beautiful, overflowing with glorious scenery, wonderful history, and wildlands filled with woodland creatures. Streams, lakes, peaks, and even wondrous waterfalls grace the mountains. The area is so captivating that most visitors will feel a pull to remain and wish that they could call the region home.

Local organizations: San Gorgonio Wilderness Association, 34701 Mill Creek Rd., Mentone, CA 92359, (909) 382-2881; San Bernardino National Forest Association, (909) 382-4802; Big Bear Discovery Center, (909) 866-3437; Children's Forest, (909) 382-2777; Pacific Crest Trail Association, (916) 285-1846; Off Highway Vehicle Volunteer Program, (909) 382-4011; Fire Lookout Hosts, (909) 225-1025 or (909) 382-2881; Friends of the Desert Mountains, (760) 568-9918; California Wild Heritage Campaign, (415) 398-1111; Sierra Club, (951) 684-6172

Heart Rock Falls

The hike to Heart Rock Falls follows lovely Seeley Creek through wooded pine and cedar. An overlook provides the best views of the heart formation, and both the top and bottom of the falls can be visited. Several pools below the falls can be used for wading and swimming.

Start: At the end of FR 2N03

Distance: 2 miles out and back

Hiking time: About 2 hours

Difficulty: Easy

Trail surface: Singletrack dirt trail

Nearest town: Crestline

County: San Bernardino

Other trail users: None

Canine compatibility: Leashed dogs permitted

Trailhead facilities/amenities: None

Land status: National forest

Fees and permits: Adventure Pass required for parking

Schedule: Open year-round

Maps: Silverwood Lake, CA and Devore, CA

Trail contact: San Bernardino National Forest, 602 S. Tippecanoe Ave., San Bernardino, 92408; www .fs.fed.us/r5/sanbernardino/; (909) 382-2600 or (909) 382-2782

Finding the trailhead: From the intersection of I-5, US 101, and I-10, take I-10 east for 12.1 miles. Take exit 31B to merge onto I-605 north. Drive for 5.4 miles. Take exit 27A to merge onto I-210 east. Drive for 31.5 miles. Take exit 76 for CA 18/Waterman Avenue. Turn left and drive for 12.3 miles to the junction with CA 138. Turn north on CA 138 toward Crestline and drive for 1.8 miles to the left turn for Camp Seeley. Don't enter the camp, but take a left onto paved FR 2N03 as it crosses Seeley Creek, which can be forded by passenger vehicles. Look for the signed trail (4W07) and roadside parking on the right. GPS: N 34 15.25' / W 117 18.2'

A t the dirt parking area next to the swimming pool at the end of FR 2N03, head north along the road/trail marked 4W07. After a short distance the road narrows into a singletrack trail. At that point, the trail begins to descend, fairly steeply in spots, along the sides and narrows of the canyon carved out by Seeley Creek. The trees are tall and the route is nicely forested and shaded for the entire trip to the falls. It is easy to miss the overlook, so keep a watch out for an unmarked use trail leading off to the right at 0.7 mile. The main trail leads to the left, but an obvious path leads down to the right and over a large rocky outcropping. Scramble down and around the rock a bit to find the obvious viewpoint.

At the overlook, a less-obvious and more difficult scramble leads to the top of the falls, or hikers can return to the main trail and continue down below the 25-foot cascade. It is possible to hop across the creek and meander down among the pools below the falls, for those who are so inclined. The trail sits off to the west

Erosion has led to a perfectly formed heart-shaped basin. **Allen Riedel**

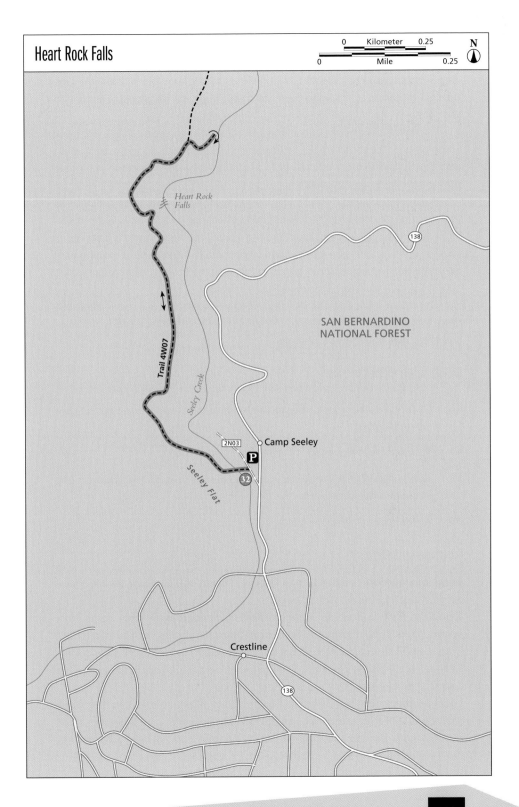

of the creek and is easy to pick back up from the bottom. Hiking down the trail, it is fairly simple to overlook the falls. The trail leads to two large pools below the falls, with gentle cascades dropping over into them. There are often people wading in the pools and many hikers like to bring children along on this trip.

Caution: If children do come along, it is important to keep an eye on them: Some parts of the route are very steep and there are roots along the trail, along with drop-offs. The rocky outcrop from which you view the falls could also prove problematic for very small children.

But anyone visiting is sure to love the wonderfully wooded surroundings and the peaceful atmosphere. The falls are quite enchanting and it goes without saying that the hiking is easy enough to bring a date. The heart shape is fascinating, caused by years of erosion into the perfect formation. If the water is running well, after rains and a good season of precipitation, with the flowing water pouring over and/or through the heart, the falls are quite magical.

The return route does climb rather steeply in spots, but it is such a short distance that anyone can make the trip. For those who need to take it slowly, just relax and enjoy the beautiful surroundings.

MILES AND DIRECTIONS

0.0   From the parking area, hike north along the trail/road marked by the pole labeled 4W07.

0.7   Turn right for an overlook of Heart Rock and the falls.

1.0   Take a fork to the creek and pools below the falls for an upward view. Return via the same route.

2.0   Arrive back at the parking area.

HIKE INFORMATION

Local information: San Bernardino National Forest, 602 South Tippecanoe Ave., San Bernardino, 92408, (909) 382-2600

Camping: San Bernardino National Forest campgrounds (first come, first served / 14-day stay maximum): Applewhite, Barton Flats, Big Pine Flats, Crab Flats, Dogwood, Fisherman's, Green Valley, Hanna Flat, Heart Bar, Holcomb Valley, Horse Springs, North Shore, Pineknot, San Gorgonio, Serrano, South Fork; www.fs.fed .us/r5/sanbernardino/

Local retailers: Big Bear Sporting Goods, 40544 Big Bear Blvd., Big Bear Lake, (909) 866-3222; Alpine Sports Center, 41530 Big Bear Blvd., Big Bear Lake, (909) 866-7541; REI Rancho Cucamonga, 12218 Foothill Blvd., Rancho Cucamonga, (909) 646-8360

Lodging/restaurants: Robin Hood Resort, 40797 Lakeview Dr., Big Bear Lake, (909) 866-4643; Nottinghams, 40797 Lakeview Dr., Big Bear Lake, (909) 866-4644; Old Country Inn, 41126 Big Bear Blvd., Big Bear Lake, (909) 866-5600; Paoli's Italian Country Kitchen, 40821 Penn Ave., Big Bear Lake, (909) 866-2020; La Montana, 42164 Moonridge Rd., Big Bear Lake, (909) 866-2606; Log Cabin Restaurant, 39976 Big Bear Blvd., Big Bear Lake, (909) 866-7300; Casual Elegance, 26848 CA 189, Rimforest, (909) 337-8932; Belgian Waffle Works, 28200 CA 189, #E150, Lake Arrowhead, (909) 337-5222

> *Hiking Tip: To increase safety, hike in groups. Join an outdoor club or find like-minded individuals online.*

Pools below Heart Rock falls offer a cool respite for those looking for a swim. Allen Riedel

Aspen Grove to Fish Creek

The Aspen Grove is one of the San Bernardino Mountains' sweetest gifts. The quaking trees display some of the finest fall color this side of the Rockies. Follow the trail through the arboreal splendor of the San Gorgonio Wilderness.

Start: At the Aspen Grove parking lot on FR 1N02

Distance: 4 miles out and back

Hiking time: About 2.5 hours

Difficulty: Easy

Trail surface: Singletrack dirt trail

Nearest town: Angelus Oaks

County: San Bernardino

Other trail users: None

Canine compatibility: Leashed dogs permitted

Trailhead facilities/amenities: None

Land status: National forest

Fees and permits: Wilderness permit required; Adventure Pass required for parking. Wilderness permits are available at the San Gorgonio Ranger Station, 34701 Mill Creek Rd., Mentone 92359; (909) 382-2882.

Schedule: Open year-round; road closes during inclement weather

Maps: USGS Moonridge, CA and San Gorgonio Mountain, CA; http://c0278592.cdn.cloudfiles.rackspacecloud.com/original/310397.jpg

Trail contact: San Bernardino National Forest, 602 S. Tippecanoe Ave., San Bernardino 92408; www.fs.fed.us/r5/sanbernardino/; (909) 382-2600 or (909) 382-2882

Finding the trailhead: From the intersection of I-5, US 101, and I-10, take I-10 east for 59.6 miles. Take exit 79 toward Orange Street/CA 38/Downtown Redlands. Turn left onto Pearl Avenue. Drive for 0.2 mile. Turn left onto Orange Street and drive for 0.6 mile. Turn right onto CA 38 east/Lugonia Avenue and drive for 13.9 miles. Turn right onto FR 1N02 signed for Heart Bar, Coon Creek, and Fish Creek. Drive for 1.45 miles on the dirt road. Turn right onto FR 1N05 and drive for 1.15 miles to the signed trailhead for Aspen Grove. GPS: N34 8.8666'/W 116 47.4'

THE HIKE

The San Gorgonio Wilderness is the premier wilderness area in all of Southern California. Aside from being the largest alpine acreage of wilderness south of the Sierra Nevada, its high slopes contain the tallest summits for hundreds of miles. Just below those peaks, in Fish Creek Canyon, lies a large grove of quaking aspen trees. The deciduous beauties are best viewed between spring and fall, but the true show happens in October when the shimmering leaves turn red and gold.

From the trailhead parking and kiosk, head southwest and down the trail into the canyon carved out of the surrounding mountainside by Fish Creek. The trail turns south and parallels the canyon before crossing the creek and entering the largest grove of aspens and the only set of groves in Southern California. A sign on the creek announces your arrival at the boundary of the San Gorgonio Wilderness. There are two more groves to the north, and a use trail branches off to head that way, but the trail on Fish Creek continues to the left (southward), following the lush

> *The aspen's flat leaves twist and bend in the wind, and may aid in photosynthesis or the intake of carbon. Aspens are part of clonal colonies rather than an individual tree; each tree is a clone from a single seedling.*

The aspens provide the color of fall in the San Gorgonio Wilderness. Sierra Riedel

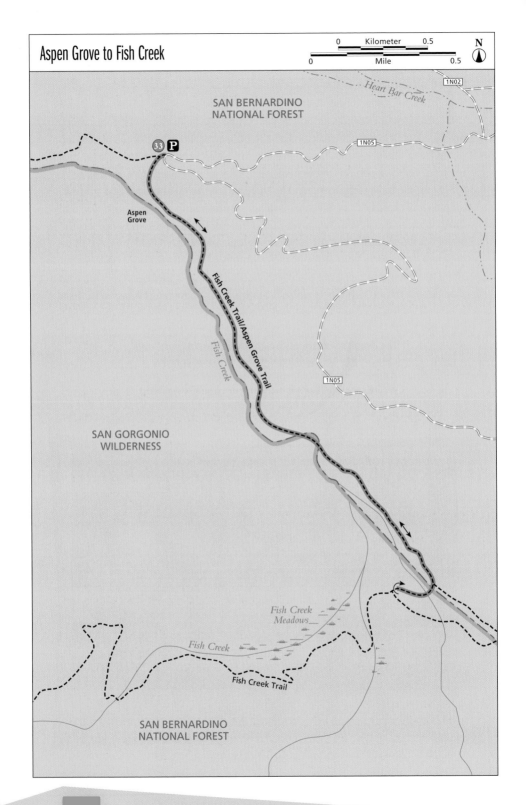

Aspen Grove to Fish Creek

0   Kilometer   0.5

0   Mile   0.5

N

SAN BERNARDINO
NATIONAL FOREST

Heart Bar Creek

1N02

1N05

33 P

Aspen
Grove

Fish Creek Trail/Aspen Grove Trail

Fish Creek

SAN GORGONIO
WILDERNESS

1N05

Fish Creek
Meadows

Fish Creek

Fish Creek Trail

SAN BERNARDINO
NATIONAL FOREST

San Bernardino National Forest

forest and the tall pines toward the higher elevations of the wilderness. Here, the Aspen Grove Trail is sort of a misnomer, because all of the aspens are to the north.

If timed right, the wind whipping through the trees makes a shimmering sound and from afar, in autumn, the trees look alive with a so-called golden fire. In winter the trees lose their leaves and the access road is most likely closed due to snow, but even in summer the trees and surrounding forest are quite impressive.

Spend some time at the grove and then continue southward along Fish Creek. Depending upon rainfall and time of year, the creek will probably be dry in spots. In the autumn it is especially intermittent, unless a really big snow year has left patches of snow on the mountains above. In the spring the creek should have a nice flow, perhaps even be torrential. The trail meanders alongside the creek for most of the trip, crossing only once more before a short climb leads to the connecting Fish Creek Trail. The elevation gain along the trail is gentle and makes for an exhilarating trip into the outdoors.

At the Fish Creek Trail junction, take a break, relax, and return via the same route.

MILES AND DIRECTIONS

0.0 Start by hiking down behind the kiosk at the Aspen Grove parking area.

0.3 Cross Fish Creek, then enter the San Gorgonio Wilderness and the aspen grove just southwest of the trail.

0.4 Head left and continue upstream, following Fish Creek.

1.5 Cross Fish Creek.

2.0 Reach the Fish Creek Trail. Return via the same route.

4.0 Arrive back at the trailhead and parking area.

HIKE INFORMATION

Local information: San Bernardino National Forest, 602 South Tippecanoe Ave., San Bernardino 92408; (909) 382-2600

Camping: San Bernardino National Forest campgrounds (first come, first served / 14-day stay maximum): Applewhite, Barton Flats, Big Pine Flats, Crab Flats, Dogwood, Fisherman's, Green Valley, Hanna Flat, Heart Bar, Holcomb Valley, Horse Springs, North Shore, Pineknot, San Gorgonio, Serrano, South Fork; www.fs.fed .us/r5/sanbernardino/

Local retailers: Big Bear Sporting Goods, 40544 Big Bear Blvd., Big Bear Lake, (909) 866-3222; Alpine Sports Center, 41530 Big Bear Blvd., Big Bear Lake, (909) 866-7541; REI Rancho Cucamonga, 12218 Foothill Blvd., Rancho Cucamonga, (909) 646-8360

Lodging/restaurants: Robin Hood Resort, 40797 Lakeview Dr., Big Bear Lake, (909) 866-4643; Nottinghams, 40797 Lakeview Dr., Big Bear Lake, (909) 866-4644; Old Country Inn, 41126 Big Bear Blvd., Big Bear Lake, (909) 866-5600; Paoli's Italian Country Kitchen, 40821 Penn Ave., Big Bear Lake, (909) 866-2020; La Montana, 42164 Moonridge Rd., Big Bear Lake, (909) 866-2606; Log Cabin Restaurant, 39976 Big Bear Blvd., Big Bear Lake, (909) 866-7300; Casual Elegance, 26848 CA 189, Rimforest, (909) 337-8932; Belgian Waffle Works, 28200 CA 189, #E150, Lake Arrowhead, (909) 337-5222

San Gorgonio Wilderness

The San Gorgonio Wilderness is the preeminent wilderness area in Southern California. With nearly 60,000 acres of wildland, much of it above 7,000 feet in elevation, the wilderness contains the six highest summits between the Sierra Nevada to the north and Picacho Del Diablo 300 miles to the south in Baja California. The San Bernardino Peak Divide Trail traverses the highest reaches of the wilderness, traveling 18 miles across the ridgeline of the wilderness to the summit of San Gorgonio Mountain, with over 10 miles of trail above 10,000 feet.

Home to lakes, waterfalls, meadows, streams, hundreds of miles of trails, historic cabins, plane crashes, and the baseline from which all of the Southern California basin was surveyed and mapped, the area is a beautiful forested paradise. By the 1920s, thousands of visitors attracted by the natural beauty of the area had begun to make their way into the San Bernardino Mountains and the San Gorgonio Wilderness. An outdoor group appealed to the Angeles National Forest to set aside the San Gorgonio region as a wilderness area, but developers and planners had decided upon using the region as the best place for skiing and winter recreation in Southern California.

A ski resort was planned for South Fork Meadows, and ski lifts were going to go straight up to the summit of Jepson Peak and San Gorgonio Mountain itself. Ski organizations and developers fought to have the area transformed, hoping to prevent it from being included in the Wilderness Act of 1964, but with the help of the Sierra Club, Defenders of Wilderness (now the San Gorgonio Wilderness Association), and conservationists, the region was preserved as a natural habitat for posterity—even though development interests attempted to develop the area again in 1971.

Jepson Peak

The hike to Jepson Peak is definitely a demanding one. Beginning in a dusty wash and ending on an alpine summit ridge, the trail leads to a short cross-country traverse up to the second-highest summit in Southern California. The views are stellar and wide.

Start: Parking lot at the end of Valley of the Falls Drive / Falls Road
Distance: 16 miles out and back
Hiking time: About 10 to 12 hours
Difficulty: Extremely strenuous
Trail surface: Singletrack dirt trail, use trail, and cross-country
Nearest town: Forest Falls
County: San Bernardino
Other trail users: None
Canine compatibility: Leashed dogs permitted
Trailhead facilities/amenities: All facilities available at trailhead
Land status: National forest

Fees and permits: Wilderness permit required; Adventure Pass required for parking. Wilderness permits are available at the San Gorgonio Ranger Station, 34701 Mill Creek Rd., Mentone 92359; (909) 382-2882.
Schedule: Open year-round
Maps: USGS Forest Falls, CA and San Gorgonio Mountain, CA
Trail contact: San Bernardino National Forest, 602 S. Tippecanoe Ave., San Bernardino 92408; www .fs.fed.us/r5/sanbernardino/; (909) 382-2600 or (909) 382-2882

Finding the trailhead: From the intersection of I-5, US 101, and I-10, take I-10 east for 59.6 miles. Take exit 79 toward Orange Street / CA 38 / Downtown Redlands. Turn left onto Pearl Avenue. Drive for 0.2 mile. Turn left onto Orange Street and drive for 0.6 mile. Turn right onto CA 38 east / Lugonia Avenue and drive for 13.9 miles. Make a slight right onto Valley of the Falls Drive and drive for 4 miles. Continue onto Falls Road and drive for 0.4 mile to the parking lot at the end. GPS: N 34 4.9' / W 116 53.4833'

THE HIKE

Most people who hike to the summit of Jepson Peak do so as a side trip to acquiring the very popular zenith of San Gorgonio Mountain. Sitting merely 1 mile apart, the 11,205-foot summit of Jepson Peak is barely a few hundred feet shy of claiming the mantle of tallest peak in Southern California. The views from on high are very similar—360 degrees in nature—but, on just about any given day of the week, the summit of Jepson will be quiet and full of calm serenity, whereas the summit of San Gorgonio will be anything but. Since San G (as it is colloquially called) is the highest summit, many people make the trek to its apex without a thought to its only slightly diminutive neighbor.

Even on a weekend, it is unlikely to find another visitor atop the summit of Jepson Peak. There is good reason for this. There isn't an established trail to the summits of San Gorgonio or Jepson that doesn't include at least 3,500 feet of elevation gain and between 16 and 25 miles of hiking. Simply put, most people who summit San Gorgonio are pooped, and they aren't looking to top out on another peak. There will always be those who are super gung ho (I will neither confirm nor deny if that means me), but it isn't that normal to run into them.

This route follows the very popular Vivian Creek Trail, which is the shortest maintained route to either summit. Be sure to get permits ahead of time, especially if traveling on a weekend or popular holiday. The route is all uphill, and steeper in

Take the trail to the left and head for the highest peak along the way. Allen Riedel

the first mile and in the last notch up to the saddle between the two summits than the rest of the trail, but hikers should expect a steady climb all the way to the top. It does not get easier around any corner. In fact, it is this author's opinion that the climb to San Gorgonio is tougher than the ascent to the summit of Mount Whitney, making this a fine training hike for that trip as well.

At the outset of the hike, follow the dirt road east beyond the gate for 0.5 mile, to where the trail drops down into the Mill Creek wash. Cross the rocky wash bottom and find the trail sign on the north side of the drainage. Here, the trail begins a brutal climb of almost 1,000 feet in just 0.5 mile. Ascending through oak and scattered desert brush, the trail seems dusty, rough, and not very scenic. Actually, the trail does ease up for a moment, just a little after the rise. The biggest change is in the flora of the area once Vivian Creek comes into view. A lovely verdant forested meadow of pine, cedar, and fern welcomes visitors to the San Gorgonio Wilderness. Shortly thereafter, the trail begins climbing sharply upward again, and follows Vivian Creek toward its source.

At 3 miles, the trail passes Halfway Camp—halfway to what nobody is sure, but that is the name of the lovely little forested campsite. The trail continues to climb and climb, but the forest is quite charming and the views of the Yucaipa Ridge to the south are vivid and stunning. The sawtooth crest is reminiscent of high Sierra summits, and it is almost hard to imagine that the ultimate destination of this hike will end up over 2,000 feet higher than the tallest peak along that ridge.

At 5 miles the trail reaches High Creek Camp, complete with resident waterfall. Sitting at 9,500 feet, the air is certainly thinner here, and nights can be a might chilly.

After the camp, the trail switchbacks up to a high knob just over 10,000 feet. It is from this point that hikers catch their first glimpse of the other monumental Southern California summit, Mount San Jacinto, to the south. From the viewpoint, it nearly seems possible to toss a stone and hit the other side. By this time the Yucaipa Ridge is well beneath you and not blocking any of the views. Looking to the north can be daunting for many, because the summits of Jepson and San Gorgonio loom overhead, nearly 1,500 vertical feet above.

At this point the trail begins to exit the forest and ascends a barren alpine slope until it climbs above tree line. What pines do exist are mostly little shrubs, battered by wind, storms, and snow. At around 11,000 feet though, even those disappear.

At 7.1 miles the trail junctions with the San Bernardino Peak Divide Trail. Turn left at the signed junction toward Dollar Lake Saddle. Follow the trail along the awesome ridgeline for 0.5 mile as it actually loses a couple of hundred feet before finding the use trail up the ridge to cone-shaped Jepson Peak.

The use trail ascends the slope for another 0.4 mile and reaches the summit of Jepson. Enjoy the views and the blissful emptiness, sign the register, and if you have enough energy, head to the summit of San Gorgonio Mountain, adding 1.2 miles to your hike, before returning via the same route to the trailhead.

Jepson Peak

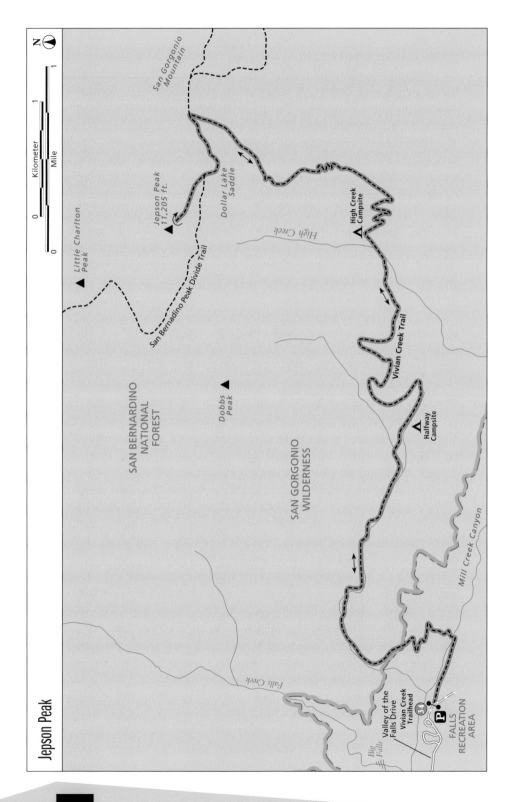

0.0 Begin by hiking east beyond the parking lot up the gated Valley of the Falls Boulevard.

0.5 Turn left and cross the Mill Creek wash to find the signed trailhead for Vivian Creek Trail.

1.1 Enter the San Gorgonio Wilderness.

1.3 Meet up with lush Vivian Creek.

3.0 Pass Halfway Camp.

5.0 Pass High Creek Camp.

7.1 Turn left at the junction onto the San Bernardino Peak Divide Trail.

7.6 Turn right onto the Jepson Peak use trail.

8.0 Arrive atop Jepson Peak. Return via the same route.

16.0 Arrive back at the Forest Falls parking area and the trailhead.

HIKE INFORMATION

Local information: San Bernardino National Forest, 602 South Tippecanoe Ave., San Bernardino 92408; (909) 382-2600

Camping: San Bernardino National Forest campgrounds (first come, first served / 14-day stay maximum): Applewhite, Barton Flats, Big Pine Flats, Crab Flats, Dogwood, Fisherman's, Green Valley, Hanna Flat, Heart Bar, Holcomb Valley, Horse Springs, North Shore, Pineknot, San Gorgonio, Serrano, South Fork; www.fs.fed .us/r5/sanbernardino/

Local retailers: Big Bear Sporting Goods, 40544 Big Bear Blvd., Big Bear Lake, (909) 866-3222; Alpine Sports Center, 41530 Big Bear Blvd., Big Bear Lake, (909) 866-7541; REI Rancho Cucamonga, 12218 Foothill Blvd., Rancho Cucamonga, (909) 646-8360

Lodging/restaurants: Robin Hood Resort, 40797 Lakeview Dr., Big Bear Lake, (909) 866-4643; Nottinghams, 40797 Lakeview Dr., Big Bear Lake, (909) 866-4644; Old Country Inn, 41126 Big Bear Blvd., Big Bear Lake, (909) 866-5600; Paoli's Italian Country Kitchen, 40821 Penn Ave., Big Bear Lake, (909) 866-2020; La Montana, 42164 Moonridge Rd., Big Bear Lake, (909) 866-2606; Log Cabin Restaurant, 39976 Big Bear Blvd., Big Bear Lake, (909) 866-7300; Casual Elegance, 26848 CA 189, Rimforest, (909) 337-8932; Belgian Waffle Works, 28200 CA 189, #E150, Lake Arrowhead, (909) 337-5222

San Jacinto Peak

San Jacinto is one of the most majestic peaks in Southern California. It is also one of the most heavily visited. The surrounding forest is supremely beautiful, and you'll get a great view of this forest as this hike gets its start by ascending via the magnificent Palm Springs Aerial Tramway. The summit block is one of the most picturesque in Southern California. John Muir once called the view from the top sublime.

Start: Palm Springs Aerial Tramway

Distance: 11.6 miles out and back

Hiking time: About 6 to 9 hours

Difficulty: Very strenuous

Trail surface: Singletrack dirt trail

Nearest town: Palm Springs

County: Riverside

Other trail users: None

Canine compatibility: No dogs allowed

Trailhead facilities/amenities: All facilities at tram debarkation

Land status: National forest, California state park

Fees and permits: You must purchase a Palm Springs Aerial Tramway ticket. Also, buy the required wilderness permit at the Long Valley Ranger Station; pick up your permit at the bottom of the hill in Long Valley after leaving the tram debarkation station.

Schedule: Open year-round; tram closes mid-Sept for 2 weeks for maintenance; Mon–Fri first tram up 10 a.m.; Sat, Sun, holidays first tram up 8 a.m.; last tram up 8 p.m. and last tram down 9:45 p.m.

Maps: USGS Palm Springs, CA and San Jacinto Peak, CA; www.parks .ca.gov/pages/636/files/Mt SanJacWebPDF2009.pdf

Trail contacts: Mount San Jacinto State Wilderness, P.O. Box 308/25905 CA 243, Idyllwild 92349; www.parks.ca.gov/?page_ id=636; (951) 659-2607. San Bernardino National Forest, 602 S. Tippecanoe Ave., San Bernardino 92408; San Jacinto Ranger District, P.O. Box 518/54270 Pine Crest Ave., Idyllwild 92349; www .fs.fed.us/r5/sanbernardino/; (909) 382-2600 or (909) 382-2921. Palm Springs Aerial Tramway, www .pstramway.com; (888) 515-TRAM

Finding the trailhead: From the intersection of I-5, US 101, I-10, and CA 60, take CA 60 east for 74.7 miles. Take the ramp onto I-10 east and continue for 18.3 miles. Take exit 112 to merge onto CA 111 south, heading toward Palm Springs, for 8.6 miles. Turn right onto Tram Way and drive for 3.9 miles to the parking lot. GPS: N 33 48.8'/W 116 38.3166'

THE HIKE

This adventure begins in the parking lot for the Palm Springs Aerial Tramway. Purchase tickets or get them ahead of time online (suggested for weekends), get in line, and ride the world's largest rotating tram from the desert elevation of 2,600 feet up to the cool alpine forest at 8,500 feet. At the top, the trail begins right outside the back doors. Start down the concrete path. There will be throngs of people at first, but follow the path to the ranger station at the bottom of the hill and get a wilderness permit. This is very important, because rangers will turn a party back even from very near the summit if they do not have one in their possession. Follow the Low Trail through blissful pine forest and meadows toward Round Valley. At 1.75 miles intersect with the High Trail, which turns eastward to the left; continue straight on the Low Trail toward the campground. At 2 miles, a trail on the right leads north to Tamarack Valley; continue straight.

In the next mile, the trail gains 800 feet to Wellman Divide. Turn right onto the San Jacinto Peak Trail. Here a nice window of viewpoints begins to open up of the lower peaks of the San Jacinto Mountains to the south. The high mountain air is crisp and invigorating. The trail circles beneath the contours of Jean Peak and winds through granite, prickly whitethorn, ceanothus, and manzanita. The outstanding views get better and better as the trail climbs fairly gently toward the summit. When the trail reaches a saddle between the summit of San Jacinto and

Marion and Jean Mountains were named for the two loves of topographer Edmund Taylor Perkins.

Allen Riedel

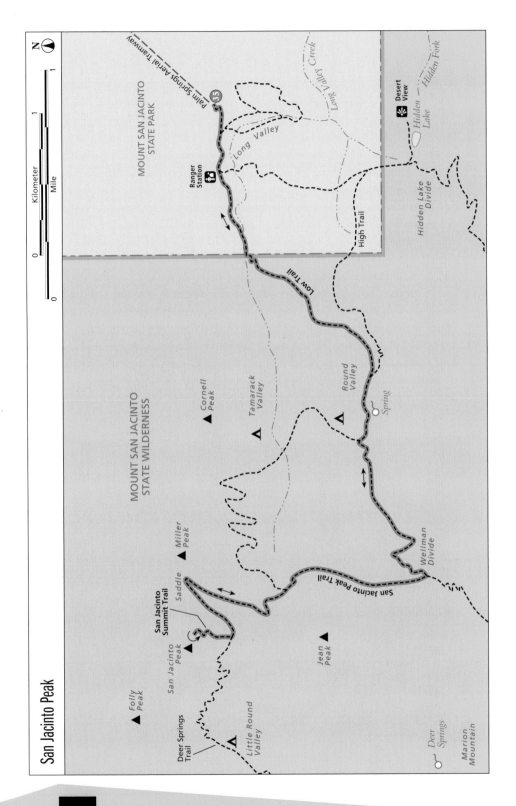

San Jacinto Peak

Miller Peaks, at just over 5.2 miles, it hairpins abruptly south and begins ascending sharply to the top of the mountain.

The San Jacinto Peak Trail junctions with the summit trail at 5.5 miles. Continue upward toward the right, and soon the stone summit hut, built by the California Conservation Corps in 1935, comes into view. Visitors can enter and write in some of the various summit registers. From there, continue 0.3 mile to the summit, which requires scrambling over large boulders to the rocky top of the peak.

The views are some of the best anywhere, due to the mountain's prominence and height. On a clear day, all of Southern California can be seen. It is reported that John Muir climbed to the summit in 1887 and said that the view at sunrise was the "most sublime spectacle on the earth." The quote does not come directly from Muir's writings, however, but from a text written in 1927 that credits the sentiment to him. Even if those words did not escape his lips, one can only imagine what the view must have been like at that time, without any smog or modernity. Most people will want to spend a good deal of time on the summit.

Return via the same route.

MILES AND DIRECTIONS

0.0 Start hiking from the southern exit of the Palm Springs Aerial Tramway's Upper Terminal.

0.3 Get a wilderness permit at the ranger station. Continue hiking on the Low Trail.

1.7 Stay to the right and continue straight ahead at the junction with the High Trail, toward Round Valley.

2.0 Continue straight and toward the left (west) at the campsite, heading toward Wellman Divide.

3.0 Turn right (north) onto the San Jacinto Peak Trail at Wellman Divide.

5.5 Turn right onto the summit trail.

5.8 Arrive atop San Jacinto Peak. Return via the same route.

11.6 Arrive back at the trailhead at the Upper Terminal.

> **Green Tip:**
> *Support environmental organizations and parks by donating time, energy, and money.*

HIKE INFORMATION

Local information: San Bernardino National Forest, 602 South Tippecanoe Ave., San Bernardino, (909) 382-2600

Camping: San Bernardino National Forest campgrounds (first come, first served / 14-day stay maximum): Boulder Basin, Dark Canyon, Fern Basin, Marion Mountain, Pinyon Flat, Santa Rosa Springs, Tool Box Springs, www.fs.fed.us/r5/sanbernardino/; Hurkey Creek, www.riversidecountyparks.org/locations/regional-parks/hurkey-creek/

Local retailers: Big Bear Sporting Goods, 40544 Big Bear Blvd., Big Bear Lake, (909) 866-3222; Alpine Sports Center, 41530 Big Bear Blvd., Big Bear Lake, (909) 866-7541; REI Rancho Cucamonga, 12218 Foothill Blvd., Rancho Cucamonga, (909) 646-8360

Lodging/restaurants: The Tahquitz Inn, 25840 CA 243, Idyllwild, (877) 659-4554; Knotty Pine Cabins, 54365 Pinecrest Ave., Idyllwild, (951) 659-2933; Idyllwild Inn, 54300 Village Center Dr., Idyllwild, (888) 659-2552; La Casita Restaurant, 54650 North Circle Dr., Idyllwild, (951) 659-6038; Cafe Aroma, 54750 North Circle Dr., Idyllwild, (951) 659-5212; Red Kettle, 54220 North Circle Dr., Idyllwild, (951) 659-4063; Oma's European Restaurant, 54241 Ridgeview, Idyllwild, (951) 659-2979

Clouds covering the Southern California basin sometimes have no effect on the higher elevations, but their effect can also be multiplied by factors of 10 on other occasions. Allen Riedel

Ernie Maxwell Scenic Trail

The Ernie Maxwell Scenic Trail is a great introduction to Idyllwild hiking and the San Jacinto Mountains. Children and hikers of all ages will enjoy the views, the shady forest, and the gentle trip to Humber Park and back.

Start: Trailhead on Tahquitz View Drive

Distance: 5 miles out and back

Hiking time: About 2.5 hours

Difficulty: Easy

Trail surface: Singletrack dirt trail

Nearest town: Idyllwild

County: Riverside Other trail users: Equestrians, bicyclists

Canine compatibility: Leashed dogs permitted

Trailhead facilities/amenities: Restroom and picnic facilities at Humber Park

Land status: National forest

Fees and permits: Adventure Pass required for parking

Schedule: Open year-round

Maps: USGS San Jacinto Peak, CA

Trail contacts: San Bernardino National Forest, 602 S. Tippecanoe Ave., San Bernardino 92408; San Jacinto Ranger District, P.O. Box 518/54270 Pine Crest Ave., Idyllwild 92349; www.fs.fed.us/r5/sanbernardino/; (909) 382-2600 or (909) 382-2921

Finding the trailhead: From the intersection of I-5, US 101, I-10, and CA 60, take CA 60 east for 52.3 miles to I-215. Continue on I-215 south for 19.1 miles. Take exit 15 for CA 74 east, heading toward Hemet. Follow CA 74 for 31.9 miles. Turn right onto CA 243 north and drive for 3.8 miles. Turn right onto Saunders Meadow Road and drive for 0.2 mile. Continue right to stay on Saunders Meadow Road and drive for 0.4 mile. Continue left to stay on Saunders Meadow Road and drive for 0.3 mile. Turn left onto Pine Avenue and drive for 0.1 mile. Turn right onto Tahquitz View Drive and drive for 0.6 mile. Park in the roadside turnout for the Ernie Maxwell Scenic Trail. GPS: N 33 44.4166'/W 116 42.15'

The Ernie Maxwell Scenic Trail is just that, scenic. It is a great place to bring children, though not very small ones, because the overall distance is a bit far to travel for really little ones. This easy trail works its way through a lovely forest canopy of pine on a fairly gentle incline, gaining about 300 feet or less per mile. The trail wraps just behind the town of Idyllwild and in reality is very close to houses, but they are unseen and the route feels very remote and secluded.

The trail was created way back in the late 1950s so that equestrian users of the wilderness could avoid confrontations with motorists on the way to Humber Park. The late Ernie Maxwell, founder of Idyllwild's *Town Crier* newspaper, led the charge in getting the trail established and was a frequent visitor on the trail up until his death in 1994.

The trail is a great hike for beginners and anyone looking to find a pretty spot in nature. And while there isn't a spectacular destination at the end of this hike, the

Corn Lilies grow along almost any wetland at higher elevations.

Makaila Riedel

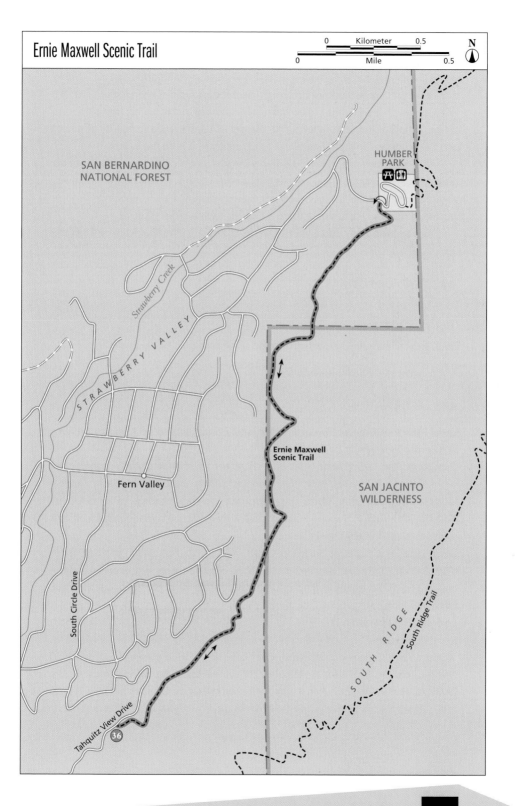

Ernie Maxwell Scenic Trail

| 0 | Kilometer | 0.5 |
| 0 | Mile | 0.5 |

N

SAN BERNARDINO
NATIONAL FOREST

Strawberry Creek

HUMBER
PARK

S T R A W B E R R Y   V A L L E Y

Ernie Maxwell
Scenic Trail

SAN JACINTO
WILDERNESS

Fern Valley

South Circle Drive

S O U T H   R I D G E

South Ridge Trail

Tahquitz View Drive

36

36

Ernie Maxwell Trail is one of those places where doing something for the sake of doing it is all that matters. The hike itself is the pleasure. It is gentle, but not so easy that there isn't some workout involved. There is mountain scenery galore, but the trail is wonderfully shaded, so the sun never becomes burdensome. Newcomers to hiking, children, and older adults alike can get out and enjoy the beauty of nature and the outdoors. The trail has a feel-good quality to it from the outset.

From the trailhead, hike north along the trail. For most of the route there are great views of Suicide Rock, and farther along, Lily Rock can be seen towering above. The trail parallels a nice creek for a short way just before reaching the turn-around at Humber Park, where there are picnic tables and restrooms.

Turn around and return via the same route, enjoying the scenery from the reverse perspective.

MILES AND DIRECTIONS

0.0   From the trailhead, hike north along the Ernie Maxwell Scenic Trail.

2.5   Reach Humber Park, return via the same route.

5.0   Arrive back at the trailhead.

HIKE INFORMATION

Local information: San Bernardino National Forest, 602 South Tippecanoe Ave., San Bernardino 92408, (909) 382-2600

Camping: San Bernardino National Forest campgrounds (first come, first served / 14-day stay maximum): Boulder Basin, Dark Canyon, Fern Basin, Marion Mountain, Pinyon Flat, Santa Rosa Springs, Tool Box Springs, www.fs.fed.us/r5/sanbernardino/; Hurkey Creek, www.riversidecountyparks.org/locations/regional-parks/hurkey-creek/

Local retailers: Big Bear Sporting Goods, 40544 Big Bear Blvd., Big Bear Lake (909) 866-3222, Alpine Sports Center, 41530 Big Bear Blvd., Big Bear Lake, (909) 866-7541; REI Rancho Cucamonga, 12218 Foothill Blvd., Rancho Cucamonga, (909) 646-8360

Lodging/restaurants: The Tahquitz Inn, 25840 CA 243, Idyllwild, (877) 659-4554; Knotty Pine Cabins, 54365 Pinecrest Ave., Idyllwild, (951) 659-2933; Idyllwild Inn, 54300 Village Center Dr., Idyllwild (888) 659-2552; La Casita Restaurant, 54650 North Circle Dr., Idyllwild, (951) 659-6038; Cafe Aroma, 54750 North Circle Dr., Idyllwild, (951) 659-5212; Red Kettle, 54220 North Circle Dr., Idyllwild, (951) 659-4063; Oma's European Restaurant, 54241 Ridgeview, Idyllwild, (951) 659-2979

Red Tahquitz

Travel up the invigorating South Ridge Trail, through tall pine forests, to the top of Tahquitz Peak, then drop into lush and lovely meadows and travel to the panoramic summit of a rarely visited peak in the lower San Jacinto Mountains.

Start: At the end of FR 5S11/South Ridge Road
Distance: 11.7 miles out and back
Hiking time: About 6 to 9 hours
Difficulty: Very strenuous
Trail surface: Singletrack dirt trail
Nearest town: Idyllwild
County: Riverside
Other trail users: Equestrians
Canine compatibility: Leashed dogs permitted
Trailhead facilities/amenities: None
Land status: National forest
Fees and permits: Adventure Pass required for parking; wilderness permit, also required, available at San Jacinto Ranger District, P.O. Box 518/54270 Pine Crest Ave., Idyllwild 92349; (909) 382-2921.
Schedule: Open year-round
Maps: USGS San Jacinto Peak, CA; www.parks.ca.gov/pages/636/files/MtSanJacintoSPmap.pdf
Trail contacts: San Bernardino National Forest, 602 S. Tippecanoe Ave., San Bernardino 92408; San Jacinto Ranger District, P.O. Box 518/54270 Pine Crest Ave., Idyllwild 92349; www.fs.fed.us/r5/sanbernardino/; (909) 382-2600 or (909) 382-2921

Finding the trailhead: From the intersection of I-5, US 101, I-10, and CA 60, take CA 60 east for 52.3 miles to I-215. Continue on I-215 south for 19.1 miles. Take exit 15 for CA 74, heading east toward Hemet. Take CA 74 for 31.9 miles. Turn right onto CA 243 north and drive for 3.8 miles. Turn right onto Saunders Meadow Road and drive for 0.2 mile. Continue right to stay on Saunders Meadow Road and drive for 0.4 mile. Continue left to stay on Saunders Meadow Road and drive for 0.3 mile. Turn left onto Pine Avenue and drive for 0.1 mile. Turn right onto Tahquitz View Drive and drive for 0.3 mile. Turn right onto FR 5S11/South Ridge Road and drive to its end. High-clearance vehicles are recommended. Park in the large dirt pullout lot by the trailhead sign. GPS: N 33 44.1166'/W 116 41.75'

THE HIKE

The hike up the South Ridge Trail begins in a mixed pine and oak forest. Fewer people take this route up to the popular lookout on top of Tahquitz Peak because of the dirt road driving required to get to the trailhead. The Devil's Slide Trail, which leads from Humber Park, is the more fashionable path, but it is also more heavily traveled. However, on weekends, it is still quite possible to see between thirty to sixty people along this route, so the trail does get a fair share of usage. Even so, it feels more remote.

It is tricky to get a solid and steady GPS reading along this trail, which makes measuring distances a little difficult, and there are many different estimates out there, even on published maps. Trip estimates vary in distance as much as 1 mile from the trailhead to the first summit. In my experience, it seems closer to the shorter distance than the longer one, but because of the elevation gained, it is easy to understand why others would rate this trip as longer. It can be a tough and long climb for some, especially in the sun.

From the trailhead, the trail starts climbing immediately and enters the wilderness in just under 0.5 mile. The 300 feet in elevation gain is fairly standard for 0.5-mile distances along this route, making it steep. It does get steeper in parts, sometimes gaining 500 feet per 0.5 mile. There are only a few places along the

Red Tahquitz Peak looks and feels like the most remote spot in the San Jacintos. Allen Riedel

way where it eases up until after summiting Tahquitz Peak. One of those places is a lovely open plateau at the halfway point, where the views open up and granite boulders line the trail through what is a lovely pine forest.

After the plateau, the trail begins climbing again among manzanita, whitethorn, and mountain chaparral. The route climbs along the western slope and is completely exposed in the midday sun. At the junction, turn right onto the short Tahquitz Peak Trail to Tahquitz Peak. Enjoy the lookout; it is a historic building and has been staffed exclusively by volunteers since 1998. On weekends and many summer days, friendly volunteers are available to talk and answer questions. The views are magnificent.

After spending some time at the lookout, head back to the junction and turn right at the sign marked for Saddle Junction.

The South Ridge Trail meets up with the Pacific Crest Trail (PCT) in 0.5 mile. Stay to the right and continue straight on the PCT, heading east as it skirts along the edge of lovely Tahquitz Meadow and Little Tahquitz Valley. Continue straight along the PCT for 1.4 miles, and watch for telltale signs on the right of the use trail leading to Red Tahquitz. Sometimes the trail is marked with a pile of rocks, known as a cairn, but people have been known to knock them down for various reasons. If there is no cairn, the trail looks like a little use path leading up to the south and eventually up to the summit of Red Tahquitz.

The summit of Red Tahquitz is wide open and rocky. There is a 360-degree view and the lookout atop Tahquitz seems near enough to touch. The summits of South Peak and some of the lower San Jacinto peaks drop away to the south. It is not likely that there will be anyone else on the top of Red Tahquitz, as this peak is quite remote and there isn't a designated signed trail leading to the top. However, those with a sense of adventure will love this destination.

Follow the same route back to the parking area.

MILES AND DIRECTIONS

0.0 Start north up the South Ridge Trail from the sign in the parking area.

0.5 Reach the San Jacinto Wilderness boundary.

1.7 Reach a level plateau about halfway to the top of Tahquitz Peak.

3.3 Reach the junction with the Tahquitz Peak Trail; turn right toward the summit.

3.4 Arrive at the summit of Tahquitz Peak. Return back to the junction.

3.5 Turn right (northeast) and take the trail toward the junction with the Pacific Crest Trail.

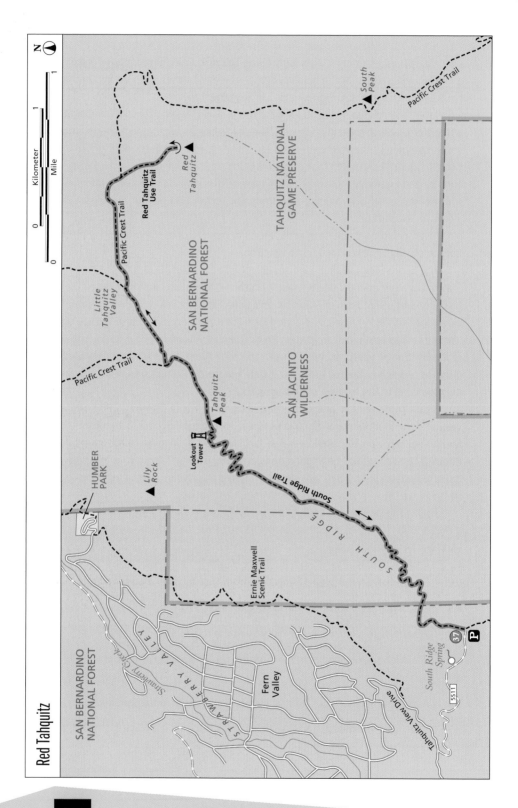

Red Tahquitz

4.0 At the Pacific Crest Trail intersection, stay straight and to the right on the PCT.

4.5 Stay straight on the PCT at the trail junction.

5.4 Look for the use trail on the right and follow it up to Red Tahquitz.

5.9 Arrive on top of Red Tahquitz. Return via the use trail to the PCT.

6.4 Turn left on the PCT to return via the same route.

7.8 Stay straight and left at the junction.

8.3 Take the South Ridge Trail toward Idyllwild.

11.7 Arrive back at the trailhead and parking area.

HIKE INFORMATION

Local information: San Bernardino National Forest, 602 South Tippecanoe Ave., San Bernardino 92408, (909) 382-2600

Camping: San Bernardino National Forest campgrounds (first come, first served / 14-day stay maximum); Boulder Basin, Dark Canyon, Fern Basin, Marion Mountain, Pinyon Flat, Santa Rosa Springs, Tool Box Springs, www.fs.fed.us/r5/sanbernardino/; Hurkey Creek, www.riversidecountyparks.org/locations/regional-parks/hurkey-creek/

Local retailers: Big Bear Sporting Goods, 40544 Big Bear Blvd., Big Bear Lake, (909) 866-3222, Alpine Sports Center, 41530 Big Bear Blvd., Big Bear Lake, (909) 866-7541; REI Rancho Cucamonga, 12218 Foothill Blvd., Rancho Cucamonga, (909) 646-8360

Lodging/restaurants: The Tahquitz Inn, 25840 CA 243, Idyllwild, (877) 659-4554; Knotty Pine Cabins, 54365 Pinecrest Ave., Idyllwild, (951) 659-2933; Idyllwild Inn, 54300 Village Center Dr., Idyllwild, (888) 659-2552; La Casita Restaurant, 54650 North Circle Dr., Idyllwild, (951) 659-6038; Cafe Aroma, 54750 North Circle Dr., Idyllwild, (951) 659-5212; Red Kettle, 54220 North Circle Dr., Idyllwild, (951) 659-4063; Oma's European Restaurant, 54241 Ridgeview, Idyllwild, (951) 659-2979

Tahquitz

The name Tahquitz was derived from the name of a Native American god/demon called Tachuish ot Dawkwish. Legend has it that the powerful spirit made his home high upon the mountain summits of the San Jacintos, where he resided in a cave and a canyon. His anger and wrath were felt through earthquakes, lightning, and thunder, the sound of which was considered to be his horrible howling as he prowled the landscape looking for humans to devour, especially young girls. In the tales, he would not only eat their flesh, but devour their souls as well.

The large piles of rocks spread across the valleys of the Inland Empire were said to have been hurled down from the mountains by mighty Tahquitz when he was enraged. He was feared to have the powers of the storm and the earthquake, and to this day, strange, unexplained "booming" noises sometimes creep from within the bowels of the San Jacinto Mountains. These are said to be the screams or the voices of the demon's victims as he devours them whole.

In some stories, Tahquitz is a Cahuilla chieftain who begins to capture young maidens and kill them; in others, he is a shaman that begins to play cruel tricks upon children, eventually culminating in murder; and in yet others he is the creation of Mukat and Temayawet, the Cahuilla creator and ruler of the dead, respectively. In all of the stories, however, Tahquitz shares a penchant for disguises and has the ability to morph into the physical features of other humans, beasts, and/or fantastical creatures.

A hero chief named Algoot is often connected with Tahquitz. It is said that a great battle occurred, with the giant boulders of Lily Rock and Suicide Rock being thrown by the chief and the demon and lodging in their present-day locations. Tahquitz was always killed in the legends, but not before his tail carved out what is now Lake Elsinore. As his body burned upon a funeral pyre, his spirit is said to have left his body in a puff of smoke and returned to the high mountaintops, wreaking havoc unto this day.

Spitler Peak

Take an excellent cardio hike up and through a transitional forest to the ridgeline, and then along a secluded section of the Pacific Crest Trail (PCT). Enjoy panoramic 360-degree views of all of Southern California from the summit block of Spitler Peak.

Start: At the trailhead parking area along Apple Canyon Road
Distance: 12 miles out and back
Hiking time: About 6 to 9 hours
Difficulty: Very strenuous
Trail surface: Singletrack dirt trail
Nearest town: Idyllwild
County: Riverside
Other trail users: Bicyclists (not allowed on the PCT), equestrians
Canine compatibility: Leashed dogs permitted
Trailhead facilities/amenities: None

Land status: National forest
Fees and permits: Adventure Pass required for parking
Schedule: Open year-round
Maps: USGS Idyllwild, CA and Palm View Peak, CA
Trail contacts: San Bernardino National Forest, 602 S. Tippecanoe Ave., San Bernardino 92408; San Jacinto Ranger District, P.O. Box 518 / 54270 Pine Crest Ave., Idyllwild 92349; www.fs.fed.us/r5/ sanbernardino/; (909) 382-2600 or (909) 382-2921

Finding the trailhead: From the intersection of I-5, US 101, I-10, and CA 60, take CA 60 east for 52.3 miles to I-215. Continue on I-215 south for 19.1 miles. Take exit 15 for CA 74, heading east toward Hemet. Follow CA 74 for 35.4 miles. Turn left onto Apple Canyon Road and drive for 2.6 miles. Park in the turnout parking area for the Spitler Peak Trail. GPS: N 33 41.85'/W 116 39.1333'

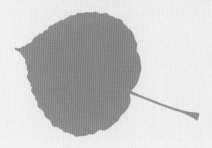

THE HIKE

ccording to thru-hikers, the first "real" chain of mountains the Pacific Crest Trail (PCT) runs through on its way north from Mexico to Canada is the San Jacinto range. The "Desert Divide" is the appellation given to the trail's passage through the lower section of the range. Along the way, the route skirts no less than ten named peaks, eight of which are higher than 7,000 feet, before entering Tahquitz Valley. Most of the summits provide spectacular clear-day views of the entire Southern California region. On clear days it is possible to see the Channel Islands, Mexico, and Arizona. The best thing about the Desert Divide is that it is much less frequented than the higher reaches of the San Jacinto Mountains and the state park that includes the namesake summit.

Hiking the Desert Divide is great in the late fall through early spring. Hot days are not pleasant, due to the lower elevations of the trailheads, the lack of pine trees and shade in certain areas, and the steep brutal climbs needed to ascend to the PCT. The Spitler Peak Trail is no exception. Starting at just under 5,000 feet, the trail gains 2,500 feet of elevation in just 6 miles, beginning its climb in a high desert ecosystem complete with yucca, chaparral, and cacti. The path quickly enters a mixed forest of maple and oak, interspersed with some varieties of pine. Due to the lack of heavy use, parts of the trail can be overgrown in areas, making this an ideal hiking spot for wearing pants, not shorts (and bare legs).

Apache Peak, Antsell Rock, Red Tahquitz, Tahquitz Peak, and Mount San Jacinto. Allen Riedel

The trail is easy to follow as it leads to the base of the mountain. In just under 1 mile the trail begins its climb, snaking its way up the contours of the mountain. Spitler Peak sits high overhead and its conical summit is unmistakable.

The trail gains elevation pretty steadily until the 3.5-mile mark. At that point a series of switchbacks take over for the next 1.5 miles, until you reach the ridge-line. The switchbacks gain elevation more rapidly than the previous section of trail, making this an excellent route for exercise and or trail running.

Once atop the crest, an old wooden sign illegibly marks the trail and gives mileage marks for several prominent trail features. Turn right (south) and head along the PCT toward Cedar Spring. Hike a short 0.3 mile south along the PCT to the obvious use trail up to the summit of Spitler Peak.

The route is surprisingly forested as it clambers up to the top. Once on top, the clear, boulder-marked summit block makes the perfect spot for a rest and an even better perch to take in all of the panoramic views. The best part about this hike is that most hikers hike in the summer, not the fall, spring, or winter when it's much more secluded. There is an excellent chance of being the only person on the summit and possibly even the trail, especially if hiking on a weekday.

Return via the same route.

MILES AND DIRECTIONS

0.0   Hike east through desert shrubs toward the mountains along the Spitler Peak Trail.

5.5   Reach the Pacific Crest Trail. Turn right onto the PCT.

5.8   Veer right up the use trail toward Spitler Peak.

6.0   Arrive at the summit of Spitler Peak. Return via the same route.

12.0   Arrive back at the trailhead.

HIKE INFORMATION

Local information: San Bernardino National Forest, 602 South Tippecanoe Ave., San Bernardino 92408, (909) 382-2600

Camping: San Bernardino National Forest campgrounds (first come, first served / 14-day stay maximum): Boulder Basin, Dark Canyon, Fern Basin, Marion Mountain, Pinyon Flat, Santa Rosa Springs, Tool Box Springs, www.fs.fed.us/r5/sanbernardino/; Hurkey Creek, www.riversidecountyparks.org/locations/regional-parks/hurkey-creek/

Local retailers: Big Bear Sporting Goods, 40544 Big Bear Blvd., Big Bear Lake, (909) 866-3222; Alpine Sports Center, 41530 Big Bear Blvd., Big Bear Lake, (909)

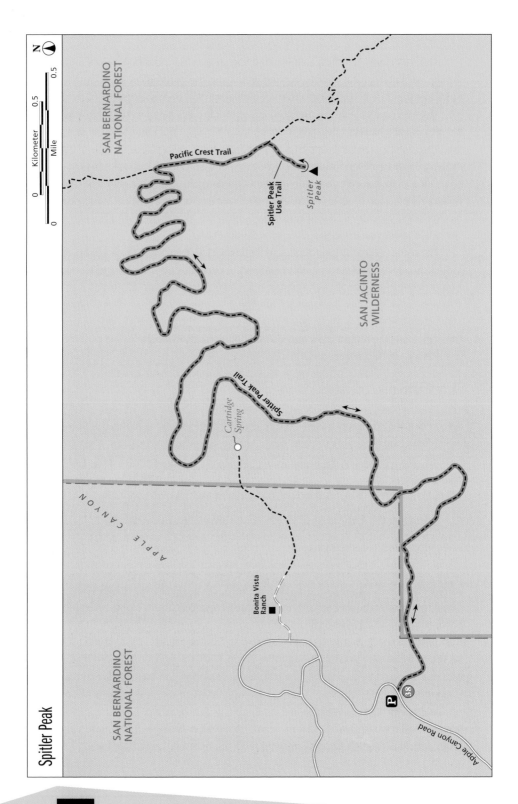

Spitler Peak

866-7541; REI Rancho Cucamonga, 12218 Foothill Blvd., Rancho Cucamonga, (909) 646-8360

Lodging/restaurants: The Tahquitz Inn, 25840 CA 243, Idyllwild, (877) 659-4554; Knotty Pine Cabins, 54365 Pinecrest Ave., Idyllwild, (951) 659-2933; Idyllwild Inn, 54300 Village Center Dr., Idyllwild, (888) 659-2552; La Casita Restaurant, 54650 North Circle Dr., Idyllwild, (951) 659-6038; Cafe Aroma, 54750 North Circle Dr., Idyllwild, (951) 659-5212; Red Kettle, 54220 North Circle Dr., Idyllwild, (951) 659-4063; Oma's European Restaurant, 54241 Ridgeview, Idyllwild, (951) 659-2979

Hiking Tip: Share your experience with others. Find special places and invite others to go along the next time.

Clouds can dazzle on cool wintry mornings, but so can the summits in the Lower San Jacinto Range.
Allen Riedel

Honorable Mentions

G. Grays Peak

Grays Peak is an enjoyable climb that travels around the back of the southern slopes of the mountains just north of Big Bear, surrounding the Fawnskin and Holcomb Valleys. The trail traverses up around the mountain, climbing very evenly for 3.5 miles before nearing the summit of Grays Peak. The views are more than worth it, but the outstanding vistas occur mostly to the north side of the trail, looking down into the valleys below. Giant boulders line the route, part of which travels up an old dirt road and some very rocky trail surfaces.

Looking out into the old northern valleys of the Big Bear region is like looking into history. Difficult-to-spot campgrounds sporadically line the valley now, where mining settlements once crowded the land and grizzly bear roamed, bestowing the region with its namesake. More than 10,000 people lived in the Holcomb Valley boomtown of Belleville, making it the largest town in San Bernardino County during its heyday. At the time, its population was even larger than the population of Los Angeles. It was a rough-and-tumble place; murder and lynching was commonplace. It's hard to believe such activities took place here a little more than one hundred years ago.

The mines are mostly gone now, though some of the remnants can still be seen from near the summit, and some prospectors still work claims in their spare time. The grizzlies are all gone now, the last one killed in the mountains in 1906, but the bald eagles have returned and they roost on Grays Peak. Due to this being sensitive habitat for them, the trail is closed from November 1 to April 1. The views of Big Bear Lake are fleeting, and unfortunately there are no sweeping viewpoints from the peak, but this is definitely a trail worth taking. The trail begins from Grout's Bay Picnic Area just east of the town of Fawnskin on CA 38. The round-trip to the summit is 7 miles.

H. Cougar Crest/Bertha Peak

The Cougar Crest Trail is one of the most popular in the Big Bear region. The large parking lot located near the Big Bear Discovery Center makes it an easy destination for Big Bear travelers and those looking for something to do. The wide trail, which used to be an old dirt road, is so broad that four people could easily walk hand-in-hand for at least the first mile, which is a very easy walk. After that, the trail actually becomes a trail, though it is still fairly wide for the remainder of the trip. The path climbs up to the ridgeline and the Pacific Crest Trail (PCT), which runs close to the Big Bear River for several miles along this section of the route.

What is truly spectacular about this trip are the expansive views of Big Bear Lake that open up shortly after the trail narrows. Jaw-dropping vistas of the San Gorgonio Wilderness sit behind the beautiful placid blue of the lake. The trail continues up to the PCT, which heads left (north) toward the Angeles National Forest and Canada, and right (south) toward the San Jacinto Wilderness and Mexico. Taking the right fork also leads to the summit of Bertha Peak. The views from Bertha Peak are well worth the effort, even though the service road leading to the top is rather steep. There are radio towers on top of the summit and they are gated off, so it is impossible to get a 360-degree view of the area, but it is still rather magnificent. There will be lots of other travelers along the route, some walking, some jogging, and maybe even some with strollers. Enjoy. The large parking lot for the trailhead is about 0.5 mile east of the Big Bear Discovery Center on CA 38. The round-trip to the summit is 5 miles.

I. Pine Knot Trail to Grand View Point

Grand View Point is a wonderful lookout spot close to FR 2N10, and hikers/drivers/mountain bikers can actually cheat, making the hike into a mere 0.2 mile to the top. But that would be a mistake, because all the fun is getting there. The trail leaves the Aspen Glen Picnic Area and heads up into the high mountains. The area is heavily wooded and carpeted with manzanita and whitethorn. During spring, the area is filled with wildflowers, and although it is popular with mountain bikers, it is a fantastic trail that gently climbs to nearly 7,800 feet above sea level, with incredible views of the San Gorgonio Wilderness and the Santa Ana River valley below. The trail passes directly through Deer Group Camp and intersects with several roads. Viewpoints of the lake begin to open up almost immediately on the trail, but you have to turn around to view them. Better to wait until you reach the turnaround point on the trip, then simply enjoy the opposing views on the way down. Clouds often float by right in front of the viewpoint, but the beauty lies in the simplicity of an open valley and a high mountain range that appears almost close enough to touch. The Aspen Glen Picnic Area is located near the junction of Mill Creek Road and Tulip Lane on the south side of Big Bear Lake. The trip to Grand View is 6 miles round-trip.

J. Fuller Ridge/Marion Mountain/Devil's Slide/Cactus to Clouds Trails to Mount San Jacinto

The Fuller Ridge, Marion Mountain, Devil's Slide, and Cactus to Clouds Trails are all alternate routes that lead to the top of Mount San Jacinto. For the most part, the standard trip to the top is via the Palm Springs Aerial Tramway—which is a fantastic way to travel—and then hiking through Round Valley as described in this guide. Most people do the hike this way; some people describe this route as the "easy" way. While the hike to the top of Mount San Jacinto from the tram is not really an easy hike, it certainly is easier than any of these four routes.

Fuller Ridge travels 7.3 miles, the first 5 of which follow the Pacific Crest Trail (PCT) from Black Mountain Road and Fuller Ridge Campground. Traveling along the awesome northeastern arm of the San Jacinto massif, loaded with trees and boulders, the 14.6-mile round-trip is quite an adventure. The route passes through Little Round Valley Campground and then heads up to the boulder-blocked summit. Take CA 243 from either Banning or Idyllwild; drive until you reach Black Mountain Road. Turn east onto the dirt road. It is rutted and rough, but you should be able to make it with even a low-clearance vehicle. Follow the road for 8 miles to the turnoff for the Fuller Ridge Trail road (signed). Drive to the parking area, and the posts for the PCT are easy to pick up.

The Marion Mountain Trail runs 5.3 miles from the trailhead to the summit, making this the shortest trip to the top, but the trail starts a full 2,000 feet below the upper terminal of the tramway, gaining nearly a mile of elevation in the process. The first 2.5 miles, which climb to the PCT, are a serious workout and are sure to stop some from making it to the summit; alternatively, the way down can be brutal on the knees and feet. It certainly qualifies as a toe-jammer. This trail works well for those ready to do some serious mountain training, or for the seriously masochistic. Its beauty cannot be understated though, and it is likely to have far fewer people on it than any of the other routes, with the exception of Cactus to Clouds. Drive north on CA 243 from Idyllwild a few miles to the Mount San Jacinto State Park entrance. Turn right and follow the signs for Marion Mountain Campground. Or drive south on CA 243 from Banning 19 miles to the turnout for Mount San Jacinto State Park. Turn left and follow the signs for Marion Mountain Campground.

The Devil's Slide Trail is a popular route up into the wilderness and to the Tahquitz Peak Fire Lookout on the southern side of Mount San Jacinto State Park. A few people use it to gain access to the higher areas by connecting with the Pacific Crest Trail at Saddle Junction and then taking the trip to Wellman Divide and on to the summit from there. The one-way distance is an 8-mile trek. This is a fairly tough route to take, starting at 6,500 feet at Humber Park, but again, the views are unmatched, and for those looking to explore all around the mountain, why not take all the different paths to the top? From Idyllwild, turn east on North Circle Drive. Proceed north for over a mile until you reach South Circle Drive. Turn right and then take your first left onto Fern Valley Road. Take Fern Valley Road to Humber Park.

Cactus to Clouds is an insane route for serious endurance hikers only. It begins on the desert floor near Palm Springs and gains 10,400 feet (nearly 2 miles) in elevation over 17.5 miles, the first 12 of which are spent hiking through dry, arid, and often brutally hot conditions. The trail starts out climbing and keeps climbing . . . and then climbs some more. After 1 mile of hiking, a sign warns hikers that there is no water on the trail for 8 miles and ten hours, and the sign actually errs on the side of the trail—the actual distance is 12 brutal miles to Round Valley and the Palm Springs Aerial Tramway's Upper Terminal. From there, the distance is a mere 5.5 miles to the top. Most people take the tram back down, making the whole adventure into a 23-mile round-trip, but for the ultraserious, taking the trail up and down is a 35-mile all-day epic. From I-10 take CA 111 into Palm Springs. Turn right in Ramon Road and park at the end of the street. The trail leads up the mountain to the right.

K. Suicide Rock

The route to Suicide Rock follows the Deer Springs Trail from CA 243 near Idyllwild for 2.3 miles to the Suicide Rock Trail, then travels for 1 mile to the site of Suicide Rock, the edge of which is a sheer precipice dropping some 1,500 feet to Strawberry Valley below. Some people say the rock received its name due to a Romeo-and-Juliet–like story, where two Indian lovers who were refused permission to marry leapt to their deaths from the rock, but it appears that there is no corroboration for such a story anywhere in the local Native American mythos. Apparently, the story has been told for quite some time and is interesting in that regard since it seems to be an urban legend about a proposed legend. The rock has been so named, at least colloquially, since the late 1800s, but it is unknown as to why it was given such a moniker, since there aren't any known occurrences of suicide at the rock. Perhaps due to its vertical drop-off from the face—it is impossible not to look up and imagine someone teetering dangerously close to the edge—it may have been the stuff of nightmares for old-timers in Idyllwild. Take CA 243 from Banning or Mountain Center. The parking area is marked with a sign that says DEER SPRINGS TRAIL PARKING. It is right across from Mount San Jacinto State Park. The parking is easy to find, and the myriad trails from the parking area lead to the actual trail, just keep going up.

Santa Rosa Plateau
Ecological Reserve

The adobes on the Santa Rosa Plateau are the oldest buildings in Riverside County. Allen Riedel

The Santa Rosa Plateau is the verdant gemstone of Riverside County. Loaded with history and beauty, the preserve is a haven for rare, endemic, and endangered species. Geologically speaking, the plateau is a rarity in that it contains most of the state's remaining vernal pools. A leftover volcanic remnant of hardened basalt lava, the region has been protected for posterity and presents a unique hiking experience in Southern California. Not only is the park strikingly beautiful, loaded with wildlife, and intriguing on many levels due to its historical, ecologic, and geologic considerations, it truly has something for everyone. Young and old can enjoy the trails of the Santa Rosa Plateau, and those wishing to make an epic transpreserve hike can string together a variety of trails for a lengthy all-day outing. There are spots in the preserve for equestrian users, mountain bikers, hikers, and runners. No pets are allowed due to the sensitive nature of the preserve, and due to the lack of dogs, other animals are abundant.

Located on the southeastern arm of the Santa Ana Mountains, the plateau is home to many different native plant communities, including Engelmann oak woodlands and bunchgrass prairie. The oldest surviving buildings in Riverside County are located within the preserve and can be reached via several different easy hiking routes. Docents lead guided tours on weekends through many regions of the park and can provide scads of information on the history and ecology of the preserve.

> **Visiting the Santa Rosa Plateau is like taking a walk through the past.**

The landscape of the preserve was actually highly indicative and common in the Southern California basin, but flat-topped regions were also ideal for housing subdivisions, which have ultimately replaced the natural settings with manufactured ones. Visiting the Santa Rosa Plateau is like taking a walk through the past. The flora, fauna, and geology are all highly reminiscent of that which used to be common throughout the southland. Best experienced in late winter through spring, the greens are vibrant after rains and the plateau is brimming with life. The preserve has an interactive visitor center, an informed and intellectual staff, and miles of well-marked, highly frequented trails. There are points of interest for almost every trail in the park.

Local organizations: Santa Rosa Plateau Foundation, (800) 369-4620; Santa Rosa Plateau Volunteer Opportunities, (951) 677-6951; California Wild Heritage Campaign, (415) 398-1111; Sierra Club, (951) 684-6172; The Nature Conservancy, (415) 777-0487

Santa Rosa Plateau Loop

Although any time of year would be rewarding for this serene and tranquil hike past vernal pools, oak forests, and historic adobes, springtime offers the greatest bounty for those seeking to catch a glimpse of the unique ecosystem that occurs once a year at the pools.

Start: At the roadside parking area along Via Volcano for the Vernal Pool Trail

Distance: 7.7-mile lollipop

Hiking time: About 4 hours

Difficulty: Easy

Trail surface: Singletrack dirt trail and dirt service road

Nearest town: Wildomar

County: Riverside

Other trail users: None

Canine compatibility: No dogs allowed

Trailhead facilities/amenities: Restrooms, picnic facilities

Land status: Riverside County reserve

Fees and permits: Day use fee

Schedule: Open year-round, sunrise to sunset

Maps: USGS Wildomar, CA; www .riversidecountyparks.org/loca tions/nature-historic-centers/ santa-rosa-plateau/plateau-map/

Trail contact: Santa Rosa Plateau Ecological Reserve, 39400 Clinton Keith Rd., Murrieta 92562; www. river sidecountyparks.org/loca tions/nature-historic-centers/ santa-rosa-plateau/; (951) 677-6951

Finding the trailhead: From the intersection of I-5, US 101, I-10, and CA 60, take CA 60 east for 28.4 miles. Take exit 29A onto CA 71 and head south toward Corona, driving for 13 miles. Merge onto CA 91 and drive for 4.2 miles. Take exit 51 onto I-15 south and drive 27.9 miles. Take exit 68 onto Clinton Keith Road and turn right. Drive toward the southeast for 5.1 miles. Turn right onto Tenaja Road and drive for 1.7 miles. Continue onto Via Volcan / Via Volcano for 0.9 mile to the roadside parking area on the left. GPS: N 33 30.55' / W 117 17.666'

THE HIKE

The Santa Rosa Plateau Loop trail is part of the Santa Rosa Plateau Ecological Reserve, which is comprised of 8,300 acres of land. This land was part of the original Rancho Santa Rosa, governed by the last Mexican official prior to California joining the union. The Santa Rosa Plateau is situated along the Santa Ana mountain range, sometimes referred to as the Ortega Mountains. The California Nature Conservancy currently administers the property. Docents can be seen year-round giving tours and guides to various points of interest along the trail.

Vernal pools, or ephemeral pools, are bodies of water that occur only once a year during springtime as a result of snowmelt and rainfall. Vernal, which means "of or pertaining to spring," signifies a unique ecosystem that has adapted over thousands of years to the conditions of this special biosphere.

During the dry season, the pools are empty of water but abound with wildlife and life-giving resources. Seasonal wildflowers that have been germinating under the verdant waters come into full bloom when the waters begin to dry. During spring, when the pools are full of water, a remarkable blend of creatures can be spotted in the teeming waters. One creature significantly absent from the pools is fish, because fish require a constant water supply.

One of the most interesting creatures found at the pools is the fairy shrimp. Fairy shrimp are a unique species because they exist in the form of a "cyst" that can survive many dry spells in the pool bed before finally "hatching" and growing to create a new cycle of life, endemic to the pools. Some of the other interesting creatures found at the pools are toads, snakes, and a variety of insects, all partaking in the life-giving waters of the vernal pools.

Also located along the trails of the Santa Rosa Plateau are what are considered to be the two oldest structures in Riverside County, the Moreno Adobe and the Machado Adobe. Other structures have been built on the land but were destroyed by fire; what still stands today are the original structures built by the Mexican land grantees in the late 1800s. They once served as a jail and bunkhouses for cowboys and ranch hands.

The Vernal Pool Trail begins at a parking area with a kiosk, restroom facilities, and informational brochures. The path from this area is easy to find and is well maintained. Continue past junctions with the Los Santos and Trans Preserve Trails straight toward the vernal pools to the right of the trail. If you are visiting during the springtime, you will be sure to see butterflies, dragonflies, and various insects. Watch your step because garter snakes are abundant on the trail, yet harmless. Once at the pools you will reach a boardwalk that makes a half-loop around the pools. The boardwalk offers an opportunity for an up-close and personal look at the myriad life forms that subsist in the waters. There are a few benches and informational placards along the boardwalk, which offers a perfect opportunity to explore before trekking on with the rest of the hike. (**Note:** The boardwalk has been closed since 2010 due to the sensitive ecosystem of the vernal pools.)

From the boardwalk, follow the Vernal Pool Trail toward the adobes; clearly posted signs will lead the way. The trail takes on a dramatically different appearance just past the vernal pools. The terrain becomes rockier and the trail becomes narrower at times. Depending on the time of year, there is often an overgrowth of coastal chaparral and various indigenous wildflowers canopying the trail toward the adobes.

Continue on the trail for 1.7 miles; turn right onto Ranch Road and walk for 0.3 mile until you reach the adobes. Here you will find a shady grove of trees and two old buildings. There are restrooms and tables and benches at the adobe area, along with a garden and informational plaques providing a perfect opportunity to soak in the history of the landscape. There are often friendly docents who are always ready to provide further information or instructions around the adobes.

From the adobes, follow the Lomas Trail between the adobes and the barn. The trail offers little or no shade for quite some time, and a view of the vast blue sky and prairie-like rolling hills of the plateau are visible for miles. Continue on the Lomas Trail, then turn right twice onto Monument Hill Road, and at 3.6 miles turn right onto Monument Hill Trail to the peak. Monument Hill is one of the highest points on the plateau and offers a panoramic view of the vast reserve.

After enjoying the breathtaking views of Monument Hill, follow the road back down (west) toward Lomas Trail and turn right back onto Lomas Trail, heading north. Follow Lomas Trail for 0.5 mile to Ranch Road. Take the unnamed junction right to the Trans Preserve Trail and then turn left. This part of the trail offers yet another glimpse into some of the unique ecosystems of the plateau. Here, you will encounter oak groves, riparian wetlands, and bunchgrass prairie.

At 5.9 miles the Trans Preserve Trail transforms into an almost jungle-like environment, with the trail narrowing and winding up over the hill through a dense forest of trees and coastal chaparral back toward Ranch Road. Cross over Ranch Road, staying on the Trans Preserve Trail to the Vernal Pool Trail. Turn right to get back to the trailhead and parking area.

MILES AND DIRECTIONS

0.0   Hike east along the Vernal Pool Trail.

0.25   Continue straight at the junction with the Los Santos Trail.

0.5   Continue straight at the junction with the Trans Preserve Trail.

0.7   Arrive at the vernal pool. Continue along the Vernal Pool Trail toward the adobes.

1.7   Turn right onto Ranch Road.

2.0   Arrive at the historic adobes. Take Lomas Trail north between the adobes and the barn.

2.1   Continue straight and to the left on the Lomas Trail.

2.7   Turn right onto Monument Hill Road.

2.9   Continue straight at the junction with the Lomas Trail.

3.6   Turn right onto Monument Hill Trail.

3.7   Arrive atop Monument Hill. Return to the road.

3.8   Turn left and return to the Lomas Trail.

4.5   Turn right onto Lomas Trail.

5.0   Turn left onto Ranch Road.

5.9   Turn left onto the connector to the Trans Preserve Trail.

6.0   Turn left onto the Trans Preserve Trail.

6.4   Cross Ranch Road and stay on the Trans Preserve Trail.

7.2   Arrive back on the Vernal Pool Trail, turn right.

7.7   Arrive back at the trailhead and parking area.

Trails wind and wander over the hills on the Santa Rosa Plateau. Allen Riedel

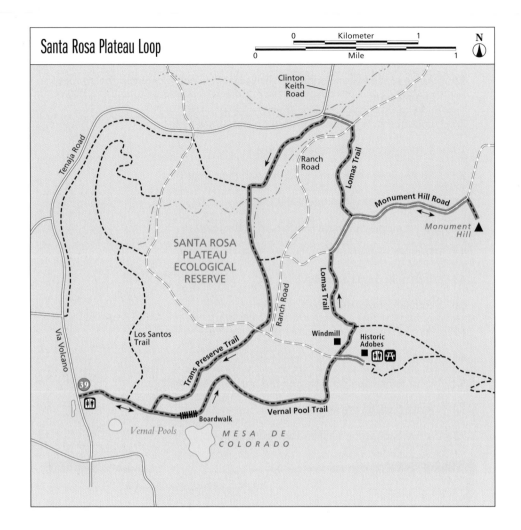

Santa Rosa Plateau Loop

Clinton Keith Road

Tenaja Road

Ranch Road

Lomas Trail

Monument Hill Road

Monument Hill

SANTA ROSA PLATEAU ECOLOGICAL RESERVE

Lomas Trail

Ranch Road

Los Santos Trail

Trans Preserve Trail

Windmill

Historic Adobes

Via Volcano

39

Boardwalk

Vernal Pool Trail

Vernal Pools

MESA DE COLORADO

HIKE INFORMATION

Local information: Santa Rosa Plateau Ecological Reserve, 39400 Clinton Keith Rd., Murrieta 92562, (951) 677-6951

Camping: Cleveland National Forest campgrounds (first come, first served/14-day stay maximum): Lower San Juan Campground, Upper San Juan Campground, Falcon Campground, Blue Jay Campground, El Cariso Campground, www.fs.fed.us/r5/cleveland/; Caspers Regional Park, www.ocparks.com/caspers/

Local retailers: Sports Authority, 24490 Village Walk Place, Murrieta; Dick's Sporting Goods, 40404 Murrieta Hot Springs Rd., Murrieta, (951) 894-5125

Restaurants: The Beer Hunter, 30080 Haun Rd., Menifee, (951) 301-4700; Crevello Ristorante Italiano, 32475 Clinton Keith Rd. #117, Wildomar, (951) 609-1266; Spelly's

Pub and Grill, 40675 Murrieta Hot Springs Rd., Suite B1, Murrieta, (951) 696-2211;
Los Jiliberto's Taco Shop, 23971 Clinton Keith Rd., Wildomar, (951) 677-3770
Special attraction: Glen Ivy Hot Springs, 25000 Glen Ivy Rd., Corona, (888) 453-
6489—A wonderful day spa that is great for a getaway

Vernal Pools and Fairy Shrimp

Vernal, of course, means spring, hence vernal pools are dry depressions that
fill with water after winter rains in the spring. The pools are intriguing because
of their life cycle. They dry up in the summer and then fill up in the winter,
creating an ecological niche with life forms that have adapted specifically to
this cycle. Vernal pools used to be fairly normal occurrences in California on
plateaus with many types of bedrock, where rounded-out depressions could
hold water without leakage. The water simply evaporates as temperatures
heat up, instead of connecting to another body of water.

However, flat plateaus also make excellent places to develop houses and
strip malls, so many of the pools have been covered over and bulldozed away.
The pools at the Santa Rosa Plateau, only one of which can be visited, are
basalt flow pools, which means they were once part of a volcanic lava flow.

Perhaps, the most wondrous thing about vernal pools is their inhabit-
ants. Fairy shrimp are tiny creatures, not much bigger than an inch in size
when fully grown, but they have a strange life cycle due to the inconsistent
nature of the pool. Sometimes rain will fill the pool and then dry up very
quickly, other times the pool will fill for most of the winter and spring, being
refreshed with new rains throughout the season. In order for the fairy shrimp
to survive, they have to have a reproductive strategy that accounts for all possible scenarios.

There are two types of eggs laid by the female fairy shrimp: One is
designed to hatch rapidly and repopulate the pool during the current season, and the other is encased in a hard cyst that can survive several seasons
without water. When the pool fills up, some of the eggs are designed to hatch
upon contact with water and immediately do so, whereas some of the eggs
do not hatch, in case the pool fills up and then immediately dries up, thus
ensuring the survival of the species in the next rainy season. It would seem
that this is nature's way of not putting all of its eggs into one basket.

Apparently, the cysts can survive boiling temperatures and being frozen,
and can live in what is called diapause (a sort of hibernation or suspended
animation) for hundreds—possibly even thousands—of years. One variety of
fairy shrimp at the Santa Rosa Plateau vernal pool is endemic to the main pool

only, meaning it exists nowhere else in the world. Since the tiny creatures are so small and the pool can be murky, they are very difficult to see. Easier to see are the garter snakes that swim across the pool and eat the tadpoles living there as well.

Please follow the guidelines posted around the pool, as this is a one-of-a-kind environment and very fragile.

The vernal pool in full glory. **Allen Riedel**

Cleveland National Forest

The trail follows a riparian canyon for part of the route. Allen Riedel

The northern portion of the Cleveland National Forest is primarily made up of the Santa Ana Mountains and surrounding foothills. The Santa Ana Mountains run roughly north from the Santa Ana River to the Santa Margarita and San Luis Rey Rivers in the south, dividing Orange and Riverside Counties; foothills ebb off into the Pacific Ocean in the west and taper into the Inland Valley in the east. Primarily a coastal range, the mountains are sparsely forested, vegetated mostly by coastal chaparral and sage scrub grasslands. Nonnative flora and grasses have changed the ecology of the region since the arrival of the Spanish, and fre-

Beautiful streams and canyons, sparkling riparian habitats, and clear views…

quent wildfires have altered the landscape, which little more than one hundred years ago was heavily forested.

Today, even the tops of the mountains are mostly without trees, and remaining stands of pine trees are few and far between. The hotter seasons and lower elevations, coupled with invasive species, have taken a toll on the native woodlands. Canyons and arroyos, along with many isolated pockets, still retain their arboreal splendor under the shade of cottonwood, laurel, sycamore, walnut, ash, willow, alder, and oak. The intermittent streams and canyons in the Santa Ana Mountains are some of the most beautiful in all of California; often magnificent, the riparian habitats sparkle, as do the clear views from on high.

Since the mountain chain is relatively low in elevation—all peaks sit below 6,000 feet—summer temperatures are often scorching. Ocean breezes do not make it very far inland, which makes the Santa Anas perfect for late fall, winter, and early spring exploration. Because most people hike solely in the summertime, there are miles upon miles of trails in the forest that go largely unvisited and are underexplored.

The mountain range is bordered by CA 91 in the north, CA 76 in the south, and divided by CA 74 almost directly through the heart of the range. National forest campgrounds and visitor centers are located in the most popular areas, and an Adventure Pass is required for parking in most spots throughout the region.

Local organizations: Sierra Club–Santa Ana Mountains Taskforce, (714) 968-4677; Fire Lookout Association, (661) 747-5517; Back to Natives, (949) 509-4787; SHARE Mountain Bike Club, (949) 636-0345; Warrior Society Mountain Bike Club, (714) 392-5395; Trails 4 All, (714) 734-8188; Sierra Club, (951) 684-6172; The Nature Conservancy, (415) 777-0487; San Mateo Wilderness Mounted Assistance Unit, (949) 661-7649

40

Tenaja Falls

Cascades of water plummet over four tiers, making this 150-foot waterfall one of the highest in Southern California. A short hike to the falls can be accomplished by almost anyone, and children will love the simple yet elegant fall.

Start: At the parking lot on Tenaja Truck Trail Road

Distance: 1.5 miles out and back

Hiking time: About 1 hour

Difficulty: Easy, with a knee-deep water crossing

Trail surface: Dirt road

Nearest town: Wildomar

County: Riverside

Other trail users: Equestrians, bicyclists

Canine compatibility: Leashed dogs permitted

Trailhead facilities/amenities: None

Land status: National forest

Fees and permits: Adventure Pass required for parking

Schedule: Open year-round

Maps: USGS Sitton Peak, CA; www.goodtime.net/mvi/lomvi091.htm

Trail contacts: Cleveland National Forest, 10845 Rancho Bernardo Rd., Suite 200, San Diego 92127; www.fs.fed.us/r5/cleveland; (858) 673-6180. Trabuco Ranger District, 1147 East Sixth St., Corona 92879; (951) 736-1811

Finding the trailhead: From the intersection of I-5, US 101, and CA 60, take CA 60 east for 28.4 miles. Take exit 29A to merge onto CA 71, heading south toward Corona. Drive for 13 miles. Merge onto CA 91 east for 4.2 miles. Take exit 51 to merge onto I-15 south, toward San Diego, and drive for 27.9 miles. Take exit 68 for Clinton Keith Road; turn right and drive for 5.1 miles. Make a slight right to veer onto Tenaja Road and drive for 1.7 miles. Turn right to stay on Tenaja Road and drive for 4.2 miles. Turn right onto FR 7501/Tenaja Truck Trail and drive for 5.2 miles. Park in the pullout parking area. GPS: N 33 32.9333' / W 117 23.666'

THE HIKE

The hike to Tenaja Falls is short and simple. From the parking area, the trail drops down into a surprisingly wet arroyo. Here, the tributary of San Mateo Creek that feeds the falls farther upstream crosses the pavement and pools, making the very first steps of the hike into a water crossing. If the falls are flowing, the water will be at least ankle deep, and in heavy flow nearly knee deep. It is possible to rockhop farther upstream and avoid the water, but it is also possible to walk through poison oak and brush heavy with ticks while doing so. In light of this there are a few possibilities: One, hike through the water, socks, boots, and all; two, remove socks and boots and ford the crossing barefoot, being aware that sharp rocks and slippery stones abound; and three, purchase some water shoes and walk across in those. If you do walk across, you will have wet feet, but it is a short hike, and isn't that just part of a nice adventure?

Tenaja Falls are the most dependable and spectacular waterfall in the Santa Ana Mountains. **Allen Riedel**

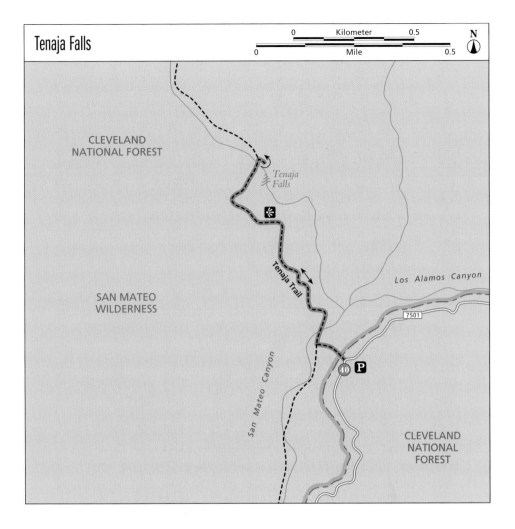

After the crossing the trail/road becomes rather pedestrian, climbing somewhat sharply for the next 0.4 mile to the top of the rise. Halfway along the upward path, the trees and brush diminish slightly, allowing the canyon to open up in spots. These clearings provide wonderful access to views of the falls. All four tiers can be clearly seen across the chasm. Water flowing down smooth time-worn rock stands in contrast to the blocky boulders and chunks of rocks near the falls.

Trees and shrubs block the view farther on and soon after, the trail nears the top of the falls. From the top the falls can be explored, but extreme caution should be taken. The rocks are worn and slippery near the falls. Years of erosion from the flowing creek have left the rocks smooth, and several drops can make climbing back upward difficult and dangerous without ropes and climbing gear. Hikers should descend to the pools at their own risk, and children are better off simply observing nature's beauty. A sign marks the route leading farther north along the Tenaja Trail into the San Mateo Wilderness toward the Morgan Trail.

If visiting after a heavy rain, the falls will be quite magnificent. Conversely, if there hasn't been much rain for quite some time, expect very little water at all. Return via the same route.

MILES AND DIRECTIONS

0.0   From the parking area along FR 7501, walk east down into the arroyo.

0.4   Look across the canyon for wide views of the entire falls.

0.75 Reach the top of the falls. Return via the same route.

1.5   Arrive back at the trailhead and parking area.

HIKE INFORMATION

Local information: Cleveland National Forest, 10845 Rancho Bernardo Rd., Suite 200, San Diego 92127, (858) 673-6180

Camping: Cleveland National Forest campgrounds (first come, first served / 14-day stay maximum): Lower San Juan Campground, Upper San Juan Campground, Falcon Campground, Blue Jay Campground, El Cariso Campground, www.fs.fed. us/r5/cleveland/; Caspers Regional Park, www.ocparks.com/caspers/

Local retailers: Sports Authority, 24490 Village Walk Place, Murrieta, (951) 894-4463; Dick's Sporting Goods, 40404 Murrieta Hot Springs Rd., Murrieta, (951) 894-5125

Restaurants: The Beer Hunter, 30080 Haun Rd., Menifee, (951) 301-4700; Crevello Ristorante Italiano, 32475 Clinton Keith Rd. #117, Wildomar, (951) 609-1266; Spelly's Pub and Grill, 40675 Murrieta Hot Springs Rd., Suite B1, Murrieta, (951) 696-2211; Los Jiliberto's Taco Shop, 23971 Clinton Keith Rd., Wildomar, (951) 677-3770

Special attraction: Glen Ivy Hot Springs, 25000 Glen Ivy Rd., Corona, (888) 453-6489—A wonderful day spa that is great for a getaway

Chiquito Trail

The Chiquito Trail is a secluded wonder known mostly to mountain bikers and those with the verve to explore out-of-the-way territory in one of California's more ignored mountain chains and national forests. The hike passes through a sylvan canyon, making parts of the trail well shaded, and traverses near a splendid seasonal waterfall. The downhill point-to-point nature of the hike makes it fairly easy for anyone wanting to attempt a longer hike.

Start: Parking area for Chiquito/San Juan Trail just before the turnoff for Blue Jay and Falcon Campgrounds

Distance: 8 miles point to point (shuttle)

Hiking time: About 4 hours

Difficulty: Moderate

Trail surface: Singletrack dirt trail

Nearest towns: San Juan Capistrano and Lake Elsinore

Counties: Orange and Riverside

Other trail users: Equestrians, bicyclists

Canine compatibility: Leashed dogs permitted

Trailhead facilities/amenities: All facilities available

Land status: National forest

Fees and permits: Adventure Pass required for parking

Schedule: Open year-round

Maps: Sitton Peak, CA and Alberhill, CA

Trail contacts: Cleveland National Forest, 10845 Rancho Bernardo Rd., Suite 200, San Diego 92127; www.fs.fed.us/r5/cleveland; (858) 673-6180. Trabuco Ranger District, 1147 E. Sixth St., Corona 92879; (951) 736-1811

Finding the trailhead: From the intersection of I-5, US 101, and I-10, take I-5 south for 53.1 miles. Take exit 82 for CA 74/Ortega Highway. Turn left onto CA 74/Ortega Highway and drive 19.4 miles east to the large parking area on the west side of the highway. Drop off one car at the parking area, turn left and head north on CA 74 for 2.4 miles to FR 6S05/Main Divide Truck Trail. Turn left and drive for 0.6 mile. Veer left onto Long Canyon Road and drive for 2.4 miles to the turnout on the left for the Chiquito Trail. GPS: N 33 39.1666'/W 117 26.9'

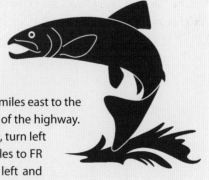

THE HIKE

The Chiquito Trail is not widely known in the hiking community. Most hikers take trips to the Angeles or San Bernardino National Forests to go for seemingly more glorious and esteem-worthy adventures. That is a shame, because there are some downright amazing places to hike that are not that far off the beaten path for those who live in Orange County and the southern sections of Riverside County. The region is better known to mountain bikers, and this is a premier destination for outdoorsy types looking for a little more adrenaline than that provided by just walking through the woods. There is a good possibility of running into mountain bikers on this route, so always be aware and on the lookout for those coming down the hill at a rapid pace.

The hike begins at the Blue Jay Campground along the San Juan Trail. Some of the route crossings are confusing, because newer trail work is not reflected on any map of the region, and some of the intersections are not that well marked. Just veer left at every trail junction, and the route will lead to the parking area for the San Juan Trail across from the Ortega Country Cottage Candy Store on CA 74/Ortega Highway. The lower elevations in the Santa Ana Mountains do not make for good summer hiking, and this trip is no exception: Take this one from late fall to early spring for maximum enjoyment and safety.

The trail winds through San Juan Canyon. Allen Riedel

The trail begins by wandering through the rather large Blue Jay Campground; it meanders for the first mile, losing and gaining only nominal elevation. The oak forest provides decent shade for most of this section, and at times views into the surrounding valley are quite exceptional.

Here, after the first mile, the trail begins to descend much more rapidly. The trail has been reworked in this area, so follow the signs pointing to the Chiquito Trail and stay left wherever there is a junction.

At 1.8 miles veer left at the fork to take the Chiquito Trail and leave the San Juan Trail. At 2 miles, turn left to avoid the Viejo Tie Loop, which connects again at 2.2 miles. Again, stay left and continue along the Chiquito Trail as it begins its descent through beautiful Lion Canyon. Water is generally present here, specifically during wetter months, but the creek dries up as the summer progresses. In early spring, the canyons are especially lovely, filled when blooming with wildflowers.

Oak trees and sycamores line the trail in most places, making this part of the trip particularly idyllic. Lovely Chiquito Falls/Lion Falls are rarely visited and sometimes not even noticed, because they are truly intermittent due to the lack of water generally found in the region. But when they are flowing heavily (mostly just after a rainfall), the 15-foot drop makes them one of the loveliest cascades around.

After the falls, the trail leaves the canyon behind and begins climbing around the contours of a higher unnamed summit to the east. The trail loses its shade here and winds around the southern edge of the summit block. At 5.2 miles a trail intersects on the left, heading up to the prominent unnamed peak. This is the only junction where you stay right; continue around the base of the summit and down toward a branch of San Juan Canyon.

The trail turns south into San Juan Canyon and connects with the San Juan Loop Trail at 7 miles. Turn left onto the San Juan Loop to take the shorter path to the parking area, where the shuttle awaits. At this point, noises from CA 74 will be apparent, making the ending feel all that much closer.

MILES AND DIRECTIONS

0.0 Start at the San Juan Trail just south of the entrance to Blue Jay Campground.

1.8 Turn left onto the Chiquito Trail.

2.0 Stay left at the junction with the Viejo Tie Loop.

2.2 Stay left again at the second junction with the Viejo Tie Loop.

4.2 Chiquito Falls/Lion Falls sits just off the edge of the trail before it begins climbing.

5.2 Continue straight and to the right avoiding the trail heading north, up the slope.

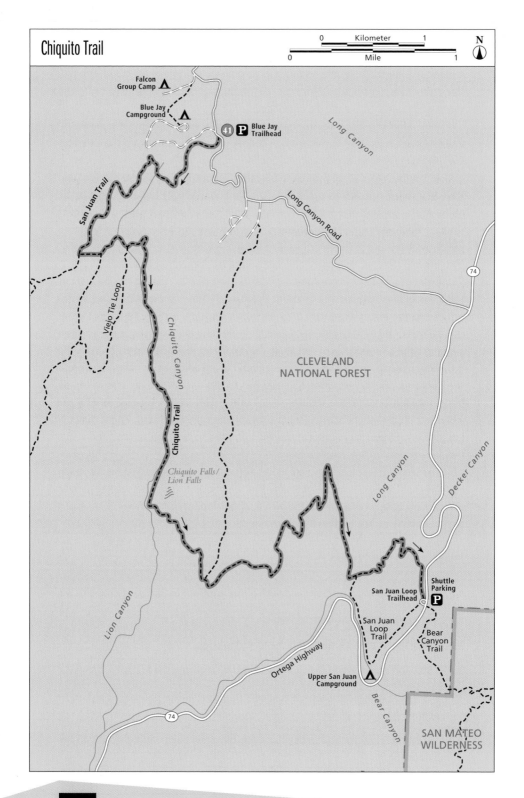

0   Kilometer   1

0   Mile   1

N

Falcon Group Camp

Blue Jay Campground

41 · P Blue Jay Trailhead

Long Canyon

Long Canyon Road

74

San Juan Trail

Viejo Tie Loop

Chiquito Canyon

Chiquito Trail

CLEVELAND NATIONAL FOREST

Chiquito Falls / Lion Falls

Long Canyon

Decker Canyon

Lion Canyon

San Juan Loop Trailhead

Shuttle Parking

P

San Juan Loop Trail

Bear Canyon Trail

Ortega Highway

Upper San Juan Campground

74

Bear Canyon

SAN MATEO WILDERNESS

7.0 Turn left at the junction of the San Juan Loop Trail.

8.0 Arrive at the shuttle parking area on the Ortega Highway.

HIKE INFORMATION

Local information: Cleveland National Forest, 10845 Rancho Bernardo Rd., Suite 200, San Diego 92127, (858) 673-6180

Camping: Cleveland National Forest campgrounds (first come, first served / 14-day stay maximum): Lower San Juan Campground, Upper San Juan Campground, Falcon Campground, Blue Jay Campground, El Cariso Campground, www.fs.fed. us/r5/cleveland/; Caspers Regional Park, www.ocparks.com/caspers/

Local retailers: Sports Authority, 24490 Village Walk Place, Murrieta, (951) 894-4463; Dick's Sporting Goods, 40404 Murrieta Hot Springs Rd., Murrieta, (951) 894-5125

Restaurants: Lookout Roadhouse, 32107 Ortega Hwy., Lake Elsinore, (951) 678-9010; Hell's Kitchen, 32685 Ortega Hwy., Lake Elsinore, (951) 609-3390; The Beer Hunter, 30080 Haun Rd., Menifee, (951) 301-4700; Crevello Ristorante Italiano, 32475 Clinton Keith Rd. #117, Wildomar, (951) 609-1266; Spelly's Pub and Grill, 40675 Murrieta Hot Springs Rd., Suite B1, Murrieta, (951) 696-2211; Los Jiliberto's Taco Shop, 23971 Clinton Keith Rd., Wildomar, (951) 677-3770

Special attractions: Glen Ivy Hot Springs, 25000 Glen Ivy Rd., Corona, (888) 453-6489—A wonderful day spa that is great for a getaway; Ortega Country Cottage Candy Store, 34950 Ortega Hwy., Lake Elsinore, (951) 678-2774

Holy Jim Falls graces the lovely little side canyon that bears the same name. Lined with fern and riparian splendor, the hike is a popular one, and the tranquil falls, while not overpowering, are quaint, contemplative, and pretty. In times of high water, the falls are more resplendent, but the creek crossings are also a bit trickier. This is a nice hike for all ages and it is one that won't disappoint.

Start: At the parking area along Trabuco Creek Road

Distance: 3.1 miles out and back

Hiking time: About 2 hours

Difficulty: Easy

Trail surface: Singletrack dirt trail and dirt road

Nearest town: Rancho Santa Margarita

County: Orange

Other trail users: Equestrians, bicyclists

Canine compatibility: Leashed dogs permitted

Trailhead facilities/amenities: None

Land status: National forest

Fees and permits: Wilderness permit required

Schedule: Open year-round

Maps: USGS Santiago Peak, CA

Trail contacts: Cleveland National Forest, 10845 Rancho Bernardo Rd., Suite 200, San Diego 92127; www.fs.fed.us/r5/cleveland; (858) 673-6180. Trabuco Ranger District; 1147 East Sixth St., Corona 92879; (951) 736-1811

Finding the trailhead: From the intersection of I-5, US 101, and I-10, take I-5 south for 38.6 miles. Take exit 96B to merge onto CA 133, heading north toward Rancho Santa Margarita (toll road). Drive for 3.2 miles. Take exit 14A to merge onto CA 241, heading south toward Santa Margarita (toll road). Drive for 9 miles. Take exit 19 for Santa Margarita Parkway (toll road). Drive for 1.8 miles. Turn left onto Plano Trabuco Drive and drive for 0.6 mile. Plano Trabuco Drive turns left and becomes Trabuco Canyon Road. Continue for 0.8 mile. Turn right onto Trabuco Creek Road and drive for 4.6 miles to the parking area on the left. Trabuco Creek Road is recommended for high-clearance vehicles only. GPS: N 33 40.6166' / W 117 31.0333'

THE HIKE

The hike to Holy Jim Falls is one that can be taken year-round, making it one of only a handful in the lower reaches of the Cleveland National Forest cool enough to do so. However, the best time to go is just after a rainfall, or after a winter where rain has been plentiful, because without a doubt the main attraction here is all the more dazzling when the waters are freely flowing. The canyon is lovely and shaded throughout the year, hence the capability of summer hiking. The riparian beauty is enough to attract visitors, but it is best to make the trip when the falls are in a downpour. It is a certainty that you will not be the only person in Southern California with the same idea; there will always be other hikers on this trail.

According to legend, James T. Smith, better known as "Cussin' Jim," planted figs and kept bees in the canyon and, according to one local author/historian, used such colorful language that his words could "peel the paint off a stove pipe." Government surveyors decided to use a more suitable name for the canyon, giving it the somewhat oxymoronic label of Holy Jim Canyon.

The road through Trabuco Canyon is an adventure unto itself—pocked with potholes, rough, rutted, and bumpy. It could also be described as swear word–inducing in honor of old Jim himself, especially if traveling in a passenger car. High-clearance trucks are recommended, though four-wheel drive is not necessary. People do drive to the trailhead in little sedans, but a will of iron and the patience of a saint are needed for such an unwise undertaking.

Foliage tunnel on the Holy Jim Trail. Bruno Lucidarme

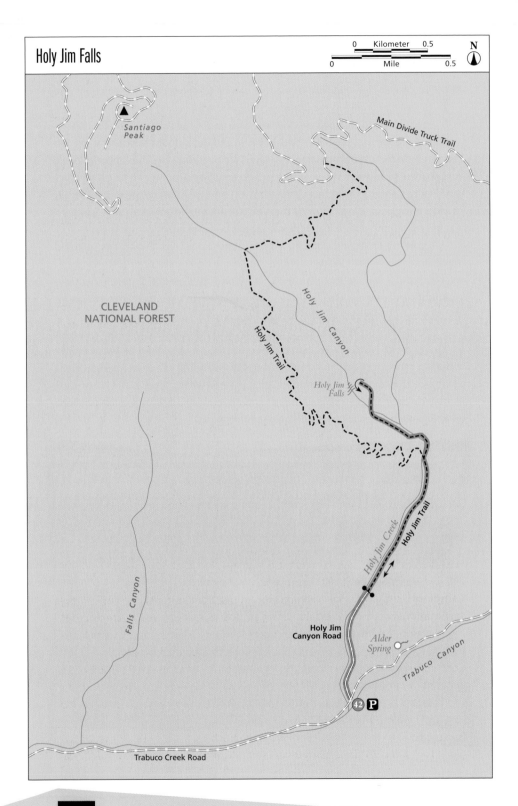

Holy Jim Falls

Once at the trailhead parking area, follow the signs and head up the small set of stairs for Holy Jim Trail. Several privately owned rustic cabins line the way for about the first 0.5 mile of hiking; there are a few intersections and creek crossings, but the route is quite popular and adequately signed, and it is nearly impossible to get lost.

At the 0.5-mile mark, the road becomes a trail proper, with a gate and a heavy-duty forest service sign. Go through the gate and follow the wide trail along the creek, making more than a half-dozen crossings. Depending upon the water level in the creek, these crossings can be more than a little difficult and time-consuming, especially if dry feet are the desired outcome. With wool socks and breathable boots, it is often a better idea to just go ahead and walk through the water, but rock-hopping can be a fun adventure in and of itself. There are four interpretative signs/stops along the route, placed for an Eagle Scout project.

After 1.1 miles of hiking, there is a fork where the Holy Jim Trail heads up toward Santiago Peak and the Main Divide Truck Trail. Turn right and follow the signs for the falls. In a short 0.4 mile, the trail ends at the lovely pool and tranquil falls, which cascade 20 feet over a small drop. Enjoy the beauty and return via the same route.

MILES AND DIRECTIONS

0.0 Hike north up the trail past the forest cabins.

1.1 Turn right onto the trail for Holy Jim Falls.

1.5 Arrive at the falls; return via the same route.

3.1 Arrive back at the trailhead and parking area.

HIKE INFORMATION

Local information: Cleveland National Forest, 10845 Rancho Bernardo Rd., Suite 200, San Diego 92127, (858) 673-6180

Camping: Cleveland National Forest campgrounds (first come, first served / 14-day stay maximum): Lower San Juan Campground, Upper San Juan Campground, Falcon Campground, Blue Jay Campground, El Cariso Campground, www.fs.fed. us/r5/cleveland/; Caspers Regional Park, www.ocparks.com/caspers/

Local retailers: A-16 (Adventure 16), 2930 Bristol St., Costa Mesa, (714) 966-6661; REI Santa Ana, 1411 Village Way, Santa Ana, (714) 543-4142; Sports Authority, 25462 El Paseo, Mission Viejo, (949) 448-8500; Dick's Sporting Goods, 24821 Alicia Parkway, Laguna Hills, (949) 472-8180

Restaurants: Trabuco Oaks Steak House, 20782 Trabuco Oaks Dr., Trabuco Canyon, (949) 586-0722; Rose Canyon Cantina & Grill, 20722 Rose Canyon Rd., Trabuco Canyon, (949) 766-6939; Carmelita's Restaurant, 31441 Santa Margarita Parkway, Rancho Santa Margarita, (949) 709-7600; Selma's Chicago Pizzeria, 30461 Avenida De Los Flores, Rancho Santa Margarita, (949) 709-8165; Tutto Fresco, 30642 Santa Margarita Parkway, Suite E104, Rancho Santa Margarita, (949) 858-3360; Wood Ranch BBQ and Grill, 22352 El Paseo, Rancho Santa Margarita, (949) 888-1100

Holy Jim / Cussin' Jim

Holy Jim is really a euphemism for the man known formally as James T. Smith. In his lifetime, James was known by several appellations, "Cussin' Jim" being but one of the few. Smith was a beekeeper who lived in Trabuco Canyon in the late 1800s; he occupied and improved upon a house built in the 1870s. It is said that he planted some of the fig trees that still grow in the canyon to this day.

According to the sign at the trailhead, Smith was not one to mince words—in fact, it seems that he could swear with some dexterity, being so adept that his words could "peel the paint off a stove pipe." It seems that everyone called him Cussin' Jim or some other nickname, and some of his friends gave him the pseudonym of "Salvation Smith," which was of great irritation to the man. It is entirely possible that this final moniker gave rise to the change from Cussin' Jim to Holy Jim, and that when mapmakers decided to name the area in honor of one of its settlers, they chose the more acceptable designation rather than the unseemly, blasphemous, and ungodly one that the man apparently deserved.

Along the trail, there are pictures of the namesake and his cabin, and there are wonderful cabins that dot the canyon to this day.

Honorable Mentions

L. Santiago Peak

Santiago Peak is the tallest mountain in Orange County and the highest in the Santa Ana Mountains. At 5,687 feet, the summit is tall enough to still have some remaining pine trees, though not very many. The peak was a sacred mountain to the Native Americans of the area.

The peak can be accessed via the Holy Jim Trail as a 16-mile round-trip journey with 4,000 feet of elevation gain. There is no 360-degree view from on top due to the massive installation of radio towers. But views of every corner of Southern California can be had from the summit, including the San Gabriel, San Bernardino, San Jacinto, Palomar, and Santa Monica Mountains, as well as the entire Los Angeles Basin, Catalina, and the Channel Islands. In order to see everything, a good fifteen-minute walk is needed to make the entire trip around the summit and its towers.

Several other routes to the summit are possible, combining driving and hiking. Taking a trip to the nearby, almost "twin" summit of Modjeska Peak is also a possibility. The trail to Santiago Peak starts at the Holy Jim Trail.

M. San Juan Loop Trail

The San Juan Loop is an enormously popular trail. It sits right off the Ortega Highway, across from the Ortega Country Cottage Candy Store at nearly the midpoint of the trip from Lake Elsinore to San Juan Capistrano. It is a nice little trip with some very worthwhile scenery, trickling brooks, and cascading waterfalls—not very large ones, but if rainfall has been heavy, there are some quite lovely spots. A very short hike, at 2.2 miles, it is a good one for families and people looking for a small breather to get out into nature. The oak canyons are lovely, and for being right off the beaten path, it is quaint, peaceful, and fairly secluded. There is definite car noise on parts of the route, but it is easy to ignore, especially when entranced by a wildflower display or an idling stream that floats by like a dream. Not for summer hiking, the lower elevations are positively desiccating in any sort of heat, but in winter and spring it is a near paradise. If traveling with small children, be mindful of poison oak and ticks. Take CA 74 east for 19.5 miles from the I-5 freeway in Orange County, or west from I-15 in Riverside County for 13 miles. Park in the large lot on the west side of the highway. The trailhead is directly across the road and next to the legendary Ortega Country Cottage Candy Store.

N. Sitton Peak

The trail to Sitton Peak is located just next to the Ortega Country Cottage Candy Store, across from the large parking lot for the San Juan Trail. This route up Bear Canyon is not as popular as the San Juan Loop across the street, and with good reason. There is not as much shade . . . no, there is not much shade at all. On hotter days, the trip is an accident waiting to happen, but hiking in the wintertime on a foggy or drizzly day can be a wonderful adventure. When the sun is out, it is best to get started early or on a cold day to avoid any kind of heat at all. The views from the summit are amazing. There is a nice 360-degree panorama, and since the mountain is the highest peak around for at least 5 miles in any direction, there isn't much in the way to block the view, especially looking down toward Orange County and the Pacific Ocean. The round-trip is 10 miles. Take CA 74 east for 19.5 miles from the I-5 freeway in Orange County, or west from I-15 in Riverside County for 13 miles. Park in the large lot on the west side of the highway. The trailhead is directly across the road and next to the legendary Ortega Country Cottage Candy Store.

The trail to Holy Jim Falls is nicely shaded, and early mornings are peaceful and quiet (hike 42) . **Bruno Lucidarme**

Palos Verdes Peninsula

Coastal views along the Palos Verdes Peninsula are spectacular. Monique Riedel

Palos Verdes means "green sticks" in Spanish and the name is probably derivative from the native palo verde tree common to the area. There are many open spaces left on the peninsula and access is relatively free to most of them.

Luxurious homes dominate much of the region, and equestrian trails abound. Tremendous views of the coast and coastal regions can be had at many different opportunities, and an escape to a seminatural setting is only minutes away almost anywhere in the area. Although the truly wild may be out of

> **Dedicated to restoring the land's original native ecosystems...**

grasp, most of these open spaces and parks will leave you satisfied with your ability to exercise and enjoy some time in the great outdoors.

The Palos Verdes Land Conservancy has purchased quite a bit of land over the past two and a half decades. These preserves are dedicated to restoring the land's original native ecosystems, those in place before the arrival of the Spanish. The conservancy has done a fantastic job of opening these lands to hiking and keeping them beautiful. Conservancy members have also been highly successful in restoring native habitat critical for the survival of certain endangered species. **Local organizations:** Sierra Club, (213) 387-4287; Los Serenos De Point Vicente, (310) 377-5370; California Native Plant Society, (916) 327-0714

Hiking Tip: Set a turnaround time and stick to it, no matter what.

Coastal views are the stock and currency of trails along the Palos Verdes Peninsula. Monique Riedel

White Point

Take a leisurely walk through a nature preserve that offers a glimpse of the native flora and fauna of the Palos Verdes Peninsula and a historical overview of this wondrous geologic structure. Conclude your stroll among the tide pools of historic Palm Beach, site of a grandiose hot spring resort of the Roaring Twenties.

Start: At the parking lot of White Point Nature Preserve
Distance: 2.6-mile lollipop
Hiking time: About 1.5 hours
Difficulty: Easy
Trail surface: Dirt road, single-track trail, and pavement
Nearest town: Rancho Palos Verdes
County: Los Angeles
Other trail users: None
Canine compatibility: Leashed dogs permitted; no dogs allowed on the beach
Trailhead facilities/amenities: All facilities available

Land status: Los Angeles city park
Fees and permits: None
Schedule: Open year-round, sunrise to sunset
Maps: USGS San Pedro, CA; www.pvplc.org/land/white_point/Whitepointsmall.pdf
Trail contacts: Palos Verdes Peninsula Land Conservancy, 916 Silver Spur Rd., Suite 207, Rolling Hills Estates 90274; (310) 541-7613; www.pvplc.org. Los Angeles Department of Recreation and Parks, 1200 W. 7th St., Los Angeles 90017; (888) LA-PARKS (527-2757); www.laparks.org

Finding the trailhead: From the intersection of I-10 and I-110, take I-110 south for 20.5 miles to its termination. Turn left onto North Gaffey Street and drive for 0.2 mile. Turn right onto West 1st Street and drive for 1 mile. Turn left onto South Western Avenue and drive for 2.3 miles. Veer left and continue onto West Paseo Del Mar for 0.4 mile. Turn left into the parking area for White Point Nature Preserve. The trail begins next to the visitor center. GPS: N 33 42.95'/W 118 18.8333'

THE HIKE

There has been some speculation as to how White Point received its name. One legend claims it was named for a sailor who jumped ship and landed in the cove at White Point. However, the Palos Verdes Historical Society confirms that White Point is named for the prominent white shale visible along the cliff walls.

White Point is located at the summit of the bluffs overlooking Palm Beach. A nature preserve provides a fabulous embarkation to this remunerative excursion. As you walk around the White Point Nature Preserve and Visitor Center, you'll see charming gardens brimming with native flora, as interpretive signs strategically placed throughout the gardens guide you through this enchanting little gem. Aside from information about indigenous plants, there are also interesting and fascinating postings featuring wildlife unique to the Palos Verdes Peninsula, such as the Allen's hummingbird, which is native only to the California coast and a diminutive part of the Oregon coast.

From the nature preserve cross Paseo Del Mar. It's is a busy roadway so use extreme caution when making this traverse. Once on the other side of Paseo Del Mar, you will find yourself at White Point Beach Park. There are bathroom facilities, park benches, picnic tables, and a web of small trails overlooking the bluffs down to Palms Beach Park. The park offers magnificent views of Santa Catalina Island and the Pacific Ocean.

The ocean puts on a spectacle at White Point. Monique Riedel

From White Point Beach Park, follow the road west down the canyon for 1 mile. The trail is a paved road that provides beach access to Palms Beach Park and the tide pools. Traffic can be heavy so make sure to exercise caution while making your descent to the beach area.

At the bottom of the road, turn left into the parking area for Palms Beach Park and follow the beach side to the rock formations just a few hundred feet up the beach. This is a popular destination for anglers, artists, sun seekers, historians, and explorers of the tide pools, so be prepared to share your experience with a variety of other travelers. This cove was once home to the majestic Royal Palm Beach resort, which boasted a natural hot spring, palm grove, and ambrosial gardens. All that remains today of the resort are fragments of the original concrete foundation and scattered palm groves. The hot spring was covered by an earthquake and is no longer accessible.

The tide pools are unbelievably easy to access. From the beach, large volcanic boulders have settled at the nape of the cove, creating the perfect environment for an intricate maze of tide pools. Be prepared to do some rock-hopping and traverse slippery rocks as waves crash tantalizingly close, dousing anyone seeking to explore the pools with a bit of sea foam. For optimal viewing of marine life in the pools, it is best to plan your trip at low tide.

From the tide pools, follow the main road up the incline of the cliffs to the parking area across Paseo Del Mar, returning to the trailhead in the nature preserve.

MILES AND DIRECTIONS

0.0 From the nature preserve parking area, hike east along the roadway that is now designated as the main trail through the preserve.

0.2 Turn left and hike north along the road. Next, turn left and hike west along the bluff.

0.5 Turn left and head south toward the ocean.

0.7 Cross Paseo Del Mar and enter White Point / Palms Beach Park. Turn right (west) and walk down the pavement to the beach.

1.0 Turn left (southeast) and walk toward the tide pools.

1.5 Reach White Point. Explore the tide pools, then turn around and walk back toward the parking area at White Point Nature Preserve.

The Palos Verdes Peninsula is home to many an open space park thanks to the Palos Verdes Land Conservancy Project.

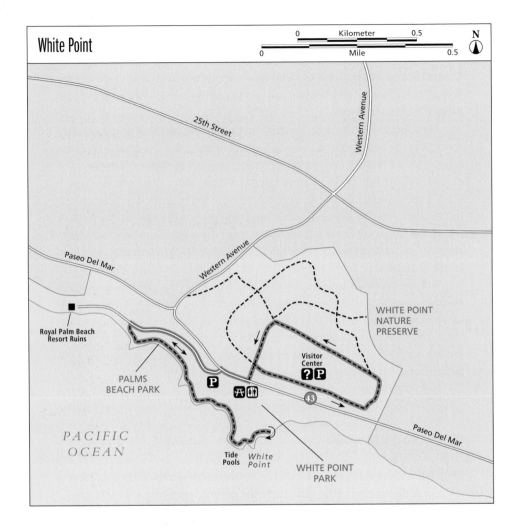

White Point

0 Kilometer 0.5

0 Mile 0.5

N

25th Street

Western Avenue

Paseo Del Mar

Western Avenue

Royal Palm Beach
Resort Ruins

WHITE POINT
NATURE
PRESERVE

Visitor
Center

PALMS
BEACH PARK

Paseo Del Mar

PACIFIC
OCEAN

Tide
Pools

*White
Point*

WHITE POINT
PARK

2.6 Arrive back at the trailhead and parking area.

HIKE INFORMATION

Local information: Palos Verdes Peninsula Land Conservancy, 916 Silver Spur Rd., Suite 207, Rolling Hills Estates 90274, (310) 541-7613

Local retailers: A-16 (Adventure 16) Torrance, 2533 Pacific Coast Hwy., Torrance, (310) 534-9683; REI Huntington Beach, 777 Edinger Ave., Huntington Beach, (714) 379-1938; Sports Authority, 6346-A East Pacific Coast Hwy., Long Beach, (562) 596-4607; Dick's Sporting Goods, 770 South Sepulveda, El Segundo, (310) 726-9123

Restaurants: Nelson's, 6610 Palos Verdes Dr. South, Rancho Palos Verdes, (310) 265-2800; Trio Mediterranean Grill, 46 Peninsula Center, Suite B, Rolling Hills Estates, (310) 265-5577; Think Bistro, 1420 West 25th St., San Pedro, (310) 548-4797; Chicago For Ribs, 1637 West 25th St., San Pedro, (310) 832-7774

Portuguese Bend

An easy stroll inland above the bluffs overlooking the Palos Verdes Peninsula, this trail presents the perfect opportunity to marvel at the lush landscape of one of several nature preserves on the peninsula while spotting wildlife uniquely endemic to this area.

Start: At the parking area at the end of Main Sail Drive
Distance: 1.9 miles out and back
Hiking time: About 1 hour
Difficulty: Easy
Trail surface: Dirt trail and dirt road
Nearest town: Rancho Palos Verdes
County: Los Angeles
Other trail users: Equestrians
Canine compatibility: Leashed dogs permitted
Trailhead facilities/amenities: None

Land status: Los Angeles city park
Fees and permits: None
Schedule: Open year-round, sunrise to sunset
Maps: USGS San Pedro, CA; www .pvplc.org/_lands/docs?Portu guese_Bend_Trail_Map.pdf
Trail contact: Palos Verdes Peninsula Land Conservancy, 916 Silver Spur Rd., Suite 207, Rolling Hills Estates 90274; (310) 541-7613; www.pvplc.org

Finding the trailhead: From the intersection of I-110 and I-10, take I-110 south for 20.5 miles to its termination. Turn left onto North Gaffey Street and drive for 0.2 mile. Turn right onto West 1st Street and drive for 1 mile. Turn left onto Western Avenue and drive for 1.7 miles. Turn right onto 25th Street/Palos Verdes Drive and drive for 2.2 miles. Turn right onto Forrestal Drive and drive for 0.7 mile. Turn left onto Main Sail Drive and drive to its end and park. GPS: N 33 44.5333'/W 118 21.2'

One of the lesser-used trails on the Palos Verdes Peninsula, Portuguese Bend provides a brisk hike through coastal chaparral, winding up to a summit that provides a dramatic view of the Pacific Ocean and, on clear days, Santa Catalina Island. Portuguese Bend is the largest area of undeveloped land on the Palos Verdes Peninsula, largely due to its geologic significance as one of the most unstable land areas in California. The land is considered to be perpetually in a state of landslide and has been determined to be so since the 1950s. Since the land is considered unstable for large developments, the nature preserve has flourished.

This trail is teeming not only with native flora, but is also home to several species of wildlife that are unique to this area. Several species of bird can only be found in this part of California and on the Channel Islands, such as the Allen's hummingbird, the orange-crowned warbler, and the Pacific slope flycatcher.

Some trails are marked better than others. **Monique Riedel**

Parking is free and easy, as there is plentiful space around the trailhead on surface streets to park. From the parking area, follow the wide dirt road called Klondike Canyon Trail, which takes a steep decline into a dry watershed and wraps up around a bend, beginning a moderate incline.

At 0.3 mile, turn right onto the Barn Owl Trail. The trail steadily makes an ascent up the bluffs of the nature preserve. At times the trail, while relatively wide, may become overgrown with verdant chaparral and wildflowers. Be prepared to navigate your way through dense foliage during springtime. At 0.6 mile, follow the Burma Road Trail to a summit overlooking the bluffs, affording you the opportunity to revel in captivating views of the Pacific Ocean and the coastline of the peninsula.

Although fauna is plentiful on the trail, there are little or no shade trees. For the majority of the hike you will be in wide-open space, akin to meadowlands on a hillside. This is advantageous for catching glimpses of the coastline and Catalina Island from different perspectives along the trail. The ocean breeze is a constant companion on your trek, and even on warm days offers a bit of respite from the sun.

From the top of Burma Road Trail, head back down the same way you came to Main Sail Drive at 1.6 miles. Turn left onto Main Sail Drive and follow this wide dirt path upward toward another small summit that provides yet a different and spectacular perspective of the coastline. From this summit, continue on Main Sail Drive to the parking area and arrive back at the trailhead at 1.9 miles.

MILES AND DIRECTIONS

0.0 Start hiking west down the dirt roadway near the end of the street, following the Klondike Canyon Trail.

0.3 Turn right onto the Barn Owl Trail.

0.6 Continue up on the Burma Road Trail.

0.8 Arrive at the top of the trail. Return via the same route.

1.6 Turn left onto Main Sail Drive.

1.7 Turn left onto a use trail to the top of the hill.

1.8 Arrive on top of an unmarked summit. Retrace your steps toward the parking area.

1.9 Arrive back at the trailhead and parking area.

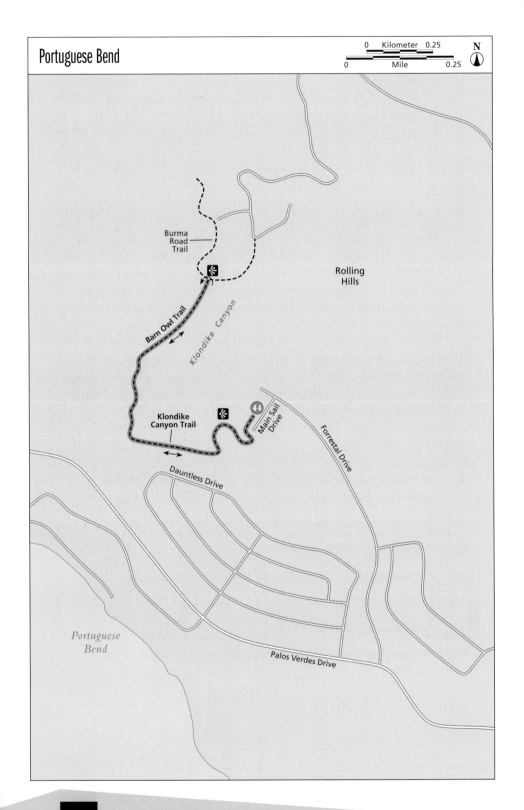

Portuguese Bend

0 Kilometer 0.25
0 Mile 0.25
N

Burma
Road
Trail

Rolling
Hills

Barn Owl Trail

Klondike Canyon

Klondike
Canyon Trail

44

Main Sail Drive

Forrestal Drive

Dauntless Drive

Portuguese
Bend

Palos Verdes Drive

Local information: Palos Verdes Peninsula Land Conservancy, 916 Silver Spur Rd., Suite 207, Rolling Hills Estates 90274, (310) 541-7613

Local retailers: A-16 (Adventure 16) Torrance, 2533 Pacific Coast Hwy., Torrance, (310) 534-9683; REI Huntington Beach, 777 Edinger Ave., Huntington Beach, (714) 379-1938; Sports Authority, 6346-A East Pacific Coast Hwy., Long Beach, (562) 596-4607; Dick's Sporting Goods, 770 South Sepulveda, El Segundo, (310) 726-9123

Restaurants: Nelson's, 6610 Palos Verdes Dr. South, Rancho Palos Verdes, (310) 265-2800; Trio Mediterranean Grill, 46 Peninsula Center, Suite B, Rolling Hills Estates, (310) 265-5577; Think Bistro, 1420 West 25th St., San Pedro, (310) 548-4797; Chicago For Ribs, 1637 West 25th St., San Pedro, (310) 832-7774

In spring the trail is loaded with wildflowers. Monique Riedel

Point Vicente

Walk leisurely atop dramatic bluffs overlooking the Pacific Ocean. Explore fascinating geologic formations and enjoy the scenery of Point Vicente Lighthouse on the site of historic Marineland of the Pacific, once the largest oceanarium in the world.

Start: At the parking lot along the west side of Calle Entradero

Distance: 2 miles out and back

Hiking time: About 1 to 2 hours

Difficulty: Easy

Trail surface: Dirt and pavement

Nearest town: Rancho Palos Verdes

County: Los Angeles

Other trail users: Bicyclists

Canine compatibility: Leashed dogs permitted

Trailhead facilities/amenities: All facilities available

Land status: Los Angeles city park

Fees and permits: None

Schedule: Open year-round, sunrise to sunset

Maps: USGS Redondo Beach, CA

Trail contact: Palos Verdes Peninsula Land Conservancy, 916 Silver Spur Rd., Suite 207, Rolling Hills Estates 90274; (310) 541-7613; www.pvplc.org

Finding the trailhead: From the intersection of I-110 and I-10, take I-110 south for 16.9 miles. Take exit 4 for CA 1/Pacific Coast Highway, turn right, and follow signs for Harbor City/Lomita. Merge onto CA 1/Pacific Coast Highway, heading west. Drive for 3 miles. Turn left onto Crenshaw Boulevard and drive for 3.4 miles. Turn right onto Crest Road and drive for 1.6 miles. Turn left onto Hawthorne Boulevard and drive for 2.1 miles. Continue on Via Vicente/Calle Entradero for 0.8 mile. Park in the lot on the ocean side of the road. GPS: N 33 45.2833'/W 118 24.8333'

THE HIKE

Some may consdier this trail to be a mild stroll rather than a traditional "hike." The dramatic ocean views and plummeting seaside bluffs provide an enchanting jaunt laden with opportunities to view ancient geologic formations and sea life. You can check out views of the Channel Islands and explore the historic sites of Marineland of the Pacific and Point Vicente Lighthouse, nestled on the bluffs of the Palos Verdes Peninsula.

Point Vicente Lighthouse is a fully operational lighthouse owned and operated by the U.S. Coast Guard and is registered on the National Register of Historic Places. The lighthouse has been operational since March 1926. There is also a Coast Guard museum on the premises. Visiting hours to the lighthouse are limited to the second Saturday of the month, and admission is free.

Be prepared to catch an ocean breeze on this well-maintained path. From the parking area, follow the paved walkway south toward the lighthouse. The first part

The lighthouse at Point Vicente can be toured on the second Saturday of every month. Monique Riedel

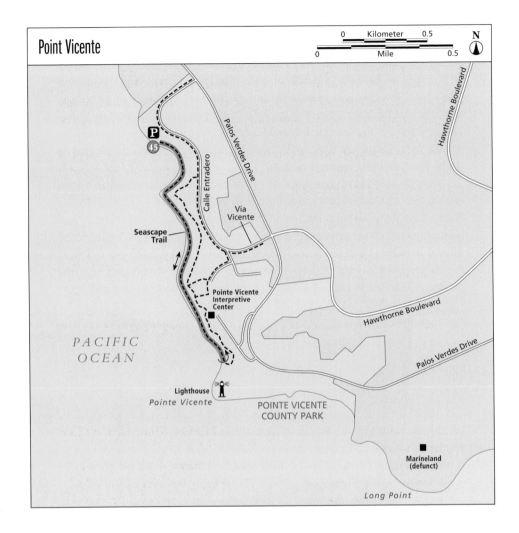

of the trail is in an upscale residential area and follows along steep ocean bluffs. There are a plethora of viewpoints at which to stop and soak in the panoramic ocean views. It is not uncommon to see a pod of dolphins chasing waves playfully along the shores of the coves. Farther up the trail, at the Point Vicente Interpretive Center, whale-watching is a popular pastime. Point Vicente Interpretive Center is located adjacent to the lighthouse. From December to May, the annual migration of the gray whale is a focal point of activity around the center. The interpretive center is also endowed with other attractive features, such as a native plant garden and museum. The interactive museum features a life-size model of a gray whale, historical information and memorabilia of Marineland of the Pacific, and displays of the native settlers of the Palos Verdes Peninsula.

The Palos Verdes Peninsula is a tectonic fault block that rose out of the sea floor over a million years ago. Palos Verdes, which in Spanish translates to "range of green trees," was inhabited by the Tongva/Gabrieleno natives for thousands of years before to the arrival of the Spanish and Mexican explorers, and eventually American developers. From the bluff trail, fascinating geologic formations can be spotted, giving a snapshot of the rich history of this colorful locale.

Whether exploring historic sites or reveling in natural splendor, once you have imbued your senses along this splendid trail, head back on the path north toward the parking area via the same route.

MILES AND DIRECTIONS

0.0 From the parking area on Calle Entradero, hike along the paved path toward the lighthouse.

0.9 Arrive at the interpretive center.

1.0 Arrive at the entrance to the Point Vicente Lighthouse. Access is restricted. Retrace your steps toward the trailhead.

2.0 Arrive back at the trailhead and parking area.

HIKE INFORMATION

Local information: Palos Verdes Peninsula Land Conservancy, 916 Silver Spur Rd., Suite 207, Rolling Hills Estates 90274, (310) 541-7613

Local retailers: A-16 (Adventure 16) Torrance, 2533 Pacific Coast Hwy., Torrance, (310) 534-9683; REI Huntington Beach, 777 Edinger Ave., Huntington Beach, (714) 379-1938; Sports Authority, 6346-A East Pacific Coast Hwy., Long Beach, (562) 596-4607; Dick's Sporting Goods, 770 South Sepulveda, El Segundo, (310) 726-9123

Restaurants: Nelson's, 6610 Palos Verdes Dr. South, Rancho Palos Verdes, (310) 265-2800; Trio Mediterranean Grill, 46 Peninsula Center, Suite B, Rolling Hills Estates, (310) 265-5577; Think Bistro, 1420 West 25th St., San Pedro, (310) 548-4797; Chicago For Ribs, 1637 West 25th St., San Pedro, (310) 832-7774

The lighthouse at Point Vicente is open for tours on the second Saturday of every month, except for March when it is open on the first Saturday.

Santa Catalina Island

The trail that heads toward East Peak gains awe-inspiring views along the ridgeline. **Allen Riedel**

Santa Catalina Island is one of the Channel Islands, located 26 miles off the coast of California, and is the only island populated with permanent residences and various attractions. On November 24, 1602, Spanish explorer Sebastian Viscaino visited the island and aptly named it Santa Catalina in honor of Saint Catherine's Day, the very day he happened upon this 22-mile-long, 8-mile-wide jewel of the Pacific coast.

Catalina, as the island is most often referred to, was a part of the original land grant awarded by Governor Pio Pico of Mexico. And as such, much like the rest of the California coast, it has changed ownership several times over the last century. In the late 1800s George Shatto, a real estate developer, purchased the land with the intention of creating a resort and getaway for the people of Los Angeles. His sister-in-law, Etta Whitney, is credited with coming up with the name Avalon after reading Tennyson's poem, "Idylls of the King," in honor of King Arthur. Despite changes of ownership over the years, the name Avalon endured. Modern-day Avalon is a hub of activity for the island and is the main launching point for all activities around the island.

Eventually, chewing gum tycoon William Wrigley obtained majority ownership of the island, with the ambition of improving upon the concept of transforming the island into a major resort attraction. He is credited with the development of the Catalina Casino, a unique art deco architectural structure on the shore north of Avalon. The casino is purported to be the "only building of its size erected in a full circular pattern."

Jewel of the Pacific coast

Today, Avalon is a bustling quaint town relatively free of traffic since there are only a limited number of vehicles permitted on the island. The most popular mode of transportation, aside from walking, is golf carts and bicycles.

Rudimentary signs lead the way on Catalina Island. Allen Riedel

Avalon Canyon/Wrigley Gardens

Explore spectacular botanic gardens and a majestic historic monument memorializing a world-renowned chewing gum tycoon and entertainment entrepreneur while hiking to one of the most breathtaking peaks on Santa Catalina Island. From a leisurely stroll to steep switchbacks, this trail offers something for everyone.

Start: Entrance to Wrigley Memorial & Botanical Gardens
Distance: 6.5 miles out and back
Hiking time: About 2.5 hours
Difficulty: Moderate
Trail surface: Dirt and pavement
Nearest town: Avalon
County: Los Angeles
Other trail users: Bicyclists
Canine compatibility: Leashed dogs permitted
Trailhead facilities/amenities: All available
Land status: Land conservancy
Fees and permits: Free permit from the Catalina Island Conser-
vancy is required (see below). Fee is charged to enter the botanic garden.
Schedule: Open year-round, 8 a.m. to 5 p.m. daily
Maps: USGS Santa Catalina East, CA
Trail contact: Catalina Island Conservancy, 125 Claressa Ave./P.O. Box 2739, Avalon 90704; (310) 510-1445 or 330 Golden Shore, Suite 170, Long Beach 90802; (310) 510-2595; www.catalina conservancy.org

Finding the trailhead: From Avalon, take a bus, drive a car, or walk north on Avalon Canyon Road for 1.2 miles to the entrance of the Wrigley Memorial & Botanical Gardens. Passage to Catalina Island must be arranged in Long Beach Harbor. GPS: N 33 19.6333'/W 118 20.3833'

THE HIKE

The Wrigley Memorial was constructed in 1933–1934 in honor of William Wrigley, whose devotion to the island is memorialized in the monument honoring his legacy. In 1935 Wrigley's widow, Ada, added the botanical garden to the premises with the help of horticulturist Albert Conrad.

The Wrigley Memorial is administered and governed by the Catalina Island Conservancy. Admission to the memorial and hiking trails requires a permit and a fee is charged at the entrance to the botanical garden. The botanical gardens offer an opportunity to stroll among rare and endangered plant species, most of which are endemic to Catalina Island. The facilities are beautifully manicured and offer restroom facilities, informational postings, and a kiosk. This is a perfect way to begin your expedition up the trail to the monument and the summit of East Peak.

From the botanic gardens, follow the road up toward the base of the monument and turn right. Pass through a gate onto a dirt road that follows the ridgeline of the

The Wrigley Memorial was originally intended for the interment of William J. Wrigley. Allen Riedel

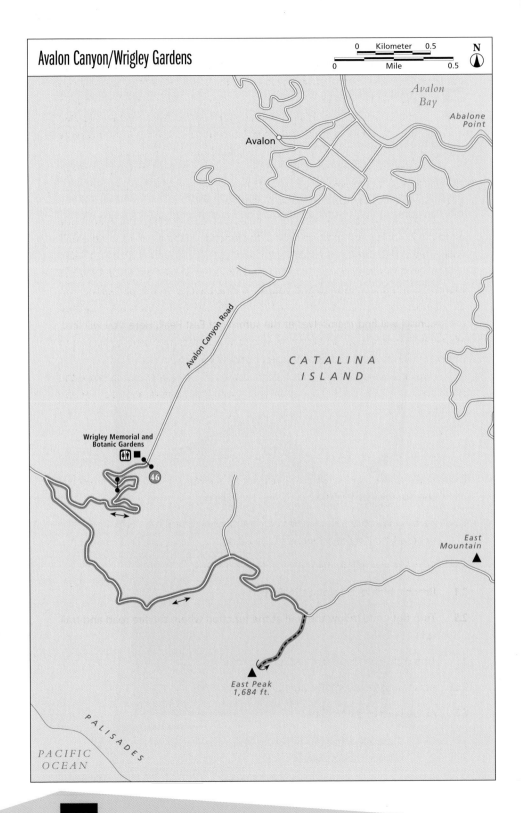

island. The trail is wide but begins a steady and sometimes steep incline up toward the imposing monument. You will easily spot the bright blue flagstone and clay embellishment to the ornate monument once you round the corner. At the monument, you can take time to explore the intricacy and detail of the craftsmanship used in its construction. From different vantage points on the monument, you can capture spectacular views of Avalon Bay—and the mainland coastline on clear days.

From the monument, prepare to begin a steady climb up toward East Peak. The trail is wide, but at times is rocky and uneven. There is little or no shade, so on a hot day make sure to have ample water for the ascent.

The trail follows the ridgeline to 2.1 miles and reaches a high point. Continue on to the 2.5-mile mark and turn right at the junction of the fire road and the trail. Follow the trail to the 2.9-mile mark and turn right, continuing on up to East Peak.

At 1,684 feet in elevation, East Peak bestows a breathtaking view of the entire island. It is not uncommon to find yourself a lone traveler on this part of the trail, as the most popular destination is the Wrigley Memorial. Only the most dedicated excursionists will find themselves at the summit of East Peak. Here, you will literally be able to view both sides of the island, and contrast the hustle and bustle of Avalon to the unpopulated pristine coast just over East Peak.

From East Peak, follow the road back to the trailhead, descending down the ridgeline toward the Wrigley Memorial and through the botanical gardens to the gate and trailhead.

MILES AND DIRECTIONS

0.0 Walk up the road toward the Wrigley Memorial. Enjoy the paths through the botanic gardens as well.

0.3 Turn right at the monument and pass through the gate. Continue on the fire road/trail to the ridgeline of the island.

1.4 Turn left and follow the trail along the ridgeline.

2.1 Reach a high point along the ridge.

2.5 Turn right and follow the trail at the junction where the fire road and trail split.

2.9 Turn right and follow the trail to East Peak.

3.25 Arrive atop East Peak. Return via the same route.

6.5 Arrive back at the trailhead.

William Wrigley Jr.

William Wrigley Jr. followed in the footsteps of his father and became a businessman. He had a penchant for sales and began his career selling his father's brand of soap. Wrigley was a master marketer and is known for creating some of the standards in advertising that are second nature to business owners today. He had the idea of selling his product and adding bonus incentive "premiums" to the sale. First, he tried adding baking powder bonuses to his soap sales, and the baking powder proved to be more popular than the soap itself. So Wrigley entered into the baking powder business. With the baking powder, he added chewing gum as the bonus, and again, the gum was the more popular item. Eventually, he rearranged his company to focus on chewing gum sales, and that is where he built his fortune and empire.

Wrigley advertised in every possible manner—in newspapers, magazines, and even on posters—nearly bankrupting himself and his company many times in the process. He believed in the products so much that he was willing to do whatever it took to get the name of the product into the minds of the consumers. It worked. By the late 1800s, his company had created its two most popular flavors, Juicy Fruit and Spearmint, adding Doublemint in 1914. By that time, he had already become the top-selling gum manufacturer in the world. He purchased the companies that had been making and distributing his gum, renaming the resulting corporation after himself. He eventually took his products to Australia, England, and New Zealand.

Wrigley had been a fan of baseball his whole life, and the Chicago Cubs were his favorite team. He began to buy stock in the Cubs in 1916, gaining control of the team by 1921. He purchased two other baseball teams as well, and redesigned the Cubs's stadium, which was eventually named after him.

In 1919, he bought Catalina Island. He built a resort and invited many Hollywood celebrities to come and visit. He lived there off and on with his family in a vacation home, and developed the island. He loved the island and brought many improvements, such as public utilities, to the residents. He set aside nearly 90 percent of the island to remain free and pure of development. His family donated the remaining land in 1975 to the Catalina Island Conservancy, which protects the island to this day. The memorial that bears his name is right next to a botanic garden and a hiking trail that leads to the crest of the island.

Hike Index

About the Authors

Allen Riedel MSE is a photographer, journalist, author, and teacher. He has authored multiple hiking guides, including *100 Classic Hikes in Southern California, Best Hikes with Dogs in Southern California,* and a number of Best Easy Day Hikes guides.

Monique Riedel JD is an author, businessperson, and outdoor enthusiast. She is also the author of *Best Easy Day Hikes Ventura.*

Monique and Allen live in the Inland Empire with their children, Michael, Sierra, and Makaila.

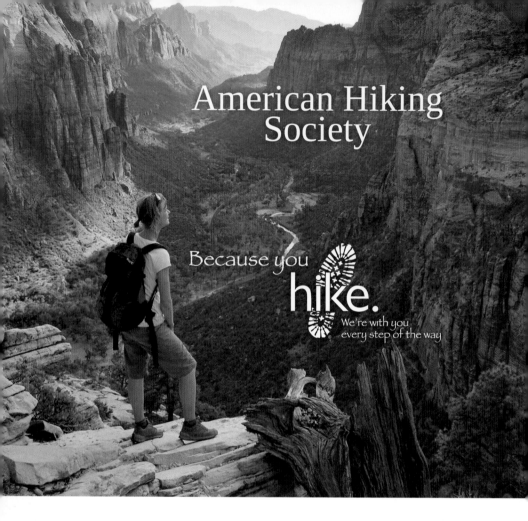

American Hiking Society

Because you
hike.
We're with you
every step of the way

As a national voice for hikers, **American Hiking Society** works every day:

- Building and maintaining hiking trails
- Educating and supporting hikers by providing information and resources
- Supporting hiking and trail organizations nationwide
- Speaking for hikers in the halls of Congress and with federal land managers

Whether you're a casual hiker or a seasoned backpacker, become a member of American Hiking Society and join the national hiking community! You'll enjoy great member benefits and help preserve the nation's hiking trails, so tomorrow's hike is even better than today's. We invite you to join us now!

American Hiking Society

liking.org